Voyage to Louisiana

by

C. C. ROBIN

1803 - 1805

—

an abridged translation
from the original French
by
STUART O. LANDRY, JR.

OUACHITA

D1474208

ATTAKAPAS

NEW ORLEANS

A
FIREBIRD
PRESS
BOOK
Gretna 2000

Manufactured in the United States of America

Published by Pelican Publishing Company, Inc.
1000 Burmaster Street, Gretna, Louisiana 70053

Voyages to the Interior of Louisiana, West Florida and to the Islands of Martinique and San Domingo During the Years 1802, 1803, 1805 and 1806.

Containing New Observations on the Natural History, Geography, Customs, Agriculture, Commerce, Industry and Diseases of These Countries (particularly on Yellow Fever) and the Means for Preventing them.

In addition, containing the most interesting aspects of what occurred relative to the coming of the Anglo-Americans to Louisiana

Followed by the Flora of Louisiana
with a New Map, engraved on Copper Plate
by C. C. Robin
Author of Several Works on Literature and Sciences

118-119 selling to pedlars
131 Natchez is American

Properly speaking, there is only one science;
the History of Nature.

— Condillac, "On the Art of Reasoning"

VOYAGES

DANS L'INTÉRIEUR

DE LA LOUISIANE,

DE LA FLORIDE OCCIDENTALE,

ET DANS LES ISLES

DE LA MARTINIQUE

ET DE SAINT-DOMINGUE,

PENDANT LES ANNÉES 1802, 1803, 1804, 1805 et 1806.

CONTENANT de Nouvelles Observations sur l'Histoire Naturelle, la Géographie, les Mœurs, l'Agriculture, le Commerce, l'Industrie et les Maladies de ces Contrées, particulièrement sur la Fièvre Jaune, et les Moyens de les prévenir.

En outre, contenant ce qui s'est passé de plus intéressant, relativement à l'Établissement des Anglo-Américains à la Louisiane.

SUIVIS

DE LA FLORE LOUISIANAISE.

Avec une Carte nouvelle, gravée en taille-douce.

PAR C. C. ROBIN,

Auteur de plusieurs Ouvrages sur la Littérature et les Sciences.

TOME II.

TRANSLATOR'S PREFACE

Curiously, we do not know the author of "Voyages dans l'Interieur de la Louisiane, etc.", for while this work is signed "C. C. Robin", it has not been established who "C. C. Robin" was. He has been almost universally confused with the abbé Robin who accompanied Rochambeau's army to Newport, Rhode Island and Yorktown. That such an identification is unlikely is evident to any reader of C. C. Robin's book. In the first place, C. C. Robin states in the introduction to his book (not included in this translation), that his only son died in his arms of yellow fever; hardly a priestly admission. In the second, no reader who examines C. C. Robin's prescription for converting the Indians will accuse our author of orthodox Catholicism; and lastly, the shrewd comments, the biting observations, and erudition of C. C. Robin do not at all square with the style of the abbé Robin of Rochambeau's army, who is generally acknowledged to have been a fool.

Frank Monyahan* states, "The error began, as I have been able to trace it, in a confusion of identity by J. M. Quérard in his *La France Litteraire* (1836), VIII, 83. It has been constantly repeated, with one very obscure exception.

It is not possible, after reading the *Nouveau voyage dans l'Amerique septentrionale* (1782) and the *Voyages dans l'Intérieur de la Louisiane* (1807) to believe that they could have been written by the same author. Beyond the difference in style, which is marked, is the approach to the materials. Claude C. Robin was a scholar, scientist, and a well-known naturalist. The abbé Robin was a credulous traveler whose most sober conclusions were termed 'ridiculous' by his contemporaries . . .

On the basis of internal evidence I had reached the conclusion that the Abbé Robin was not Claude C. Robin when I found a remark of A. L. Boimare supporting this view. Boimare settled in New Orleans in 1825, and probably had the opportunity of learning something about Claude C. Robin from people who had known him while he was there . . ."

Quérard states (J. M. Quérard, *La France Littéraire ou Dictionaire Bibliographique*, 1836 vol. 12 suppl., p. 536) : "Between 1760 and 1807 thirteen works appeared under the name 'Abbé Robin' without surname or other distinguishing mark.

"We believe our account of Claude Robin is correct, but we affirm less of the two following accounts". [My translation].

---

*French Travelers in the United States, 1765-1932. A bibliography, The New York Public Library, 1933. 114 pp.

The second of these "following accounts" is our C. C. Robin amalgamated with Rochambeau's abbé and, I think, at least one other person.

Many authorities, including the Library of Congress, further confound C. C. Robin with the above-mentioned Abbé Claude Robin, curé at St. Pierre of Angers and an antiquarian. This, at least, is a demonstrable error. In the *Catalogue Général des Livres imprimés de la Bibliothèque National,* edited by L. Delisle, 1938, we find this note on the Abbé Claude Robin in volume 153 on page 483: "The author had projected another volume, or perhaps two more, on this subject, but he died before he could carry out his project. He was drowned in the Loire at Nantes during the Revolution in 1794." [My translation]. The nomenclatoral combination "Claude C. Robin", which arises from the fusion of Claude Robin with C. C. Robin, has thus no basis for existence.

The best candidate for the identity of C. C. Robin would seem to be Charles César Robin. The *Catalogue Général* states of Charles César Robin: ". . . an ecclesiastic before the revolution, a correspondent of Marat, is almost certainly the same as the Abbé Robin, King's chaplain and member of the Lodge of Nine Sisters [Muses]. We have assembled his works following, L'Aimable, "A Masonic Lodge before 1789 . . . The Nine Sisters, Paris 1797, and following the indications of the texts themselves." [My translation].

Now, nowhere in the catalogue does there appear a work on whose title page is found the phrase "by the Abbé, Charles César Robin". It may be instructive, therefore, to list side by side, the works in the *Catalogue Général* under the entry Charles César Robin signed by that name, and those signed, "The Abbé Robin."

Abbé Robin

Histoire de la Constitution de l'empire Francais ou histoire des États-Généraux pour servir d'introduction à notre droit publique. (1789)

De l'influence du Christiqnisme sur le bonheur des peuples, pour servir de discours préliminaires aux vies des grands hommes du Christianisme. (1785)

Vie des grands hommes du Christianisme et de ceux qui se font fait connaitre relativement à cette réligion. (1787)

Charles César Robin

Les Billets de banque vont ruiner les assignats et feront pis. (No date).

Des intrigues et des actes arbitraires concernant les ventes des biens nationaux et notamment de Bourrault, dit Malherbe, principal Machinateur. (No date)

Observations sur le projet de loi de Dubois-Crancé proposé au Conseil des Cinq Cents. (No date)

Abbé Robin

Nouveau voyage dans l'Amérique septentrionale en Pannée 1781 et campagne de l'armée de M. le Comte de Rochambeau. (1782)

Recherches sur les initiations anciennes et modernes. (1779)

Du Traitement des insensés dans l'hopital de Bethléem de Londres. Traduit de l'Anglais. etc. (1787)

Charles César Robin

De la rareté de l'argent en France, et les moyens d'y suppléer, ou principes de l'économie de nos finances et de notre commerce. (No date)

De la réligion naturelle ou des rapports de l'homme avec la divinité. (No date)

Sauvons les Assignats, la République et Paris sont sauvé. (No date)

Societé d'assurances d'assignats. (No date)

Voyages dans l'intérieur de la Louisiane, de la Foride occidentale et des isles de la Martinque et de Saint Domingue pendant les années 1802, 1803, 1804, 1805 et 1806. (1807)

Almost all of the works under the name Charles César Robin are on subjects upon which Robin touches in this book; economics, the evil effect of scarce money; natural religion; indignant polemics against dishonest persons; almost all of them can be duplicated in tone and interest in the present volume. Not so the works listed under Abbé Robin. The only exception is the first. Of all the rest, except for the questionable 'Voyages' with Rochambeau, seem to me alien to C. C. Robin's tastes.

Indeed I suspect the list under Abbé Robin is heterogeneous. It contains at least one work, manifestly not written by either C. C. Robin or the abbé of Rochambeau's army, since it is a translation from English which neither man could speak.

Under the circumstances, I offer the tentative hypothesis that the author of our work was Charles César Robin, who was *not* the Abbé Robin, King's chaplain and member of the Lodge of the Muses; who may or may not have been Marat's correspondent (certainly this most intellectual of the Revolutionary leaders might have been expected to attract the scholarly C. C. Robin more than most of the others); and certainly was not the blockhead who accompanied Rochambeau's army, who may or may not have been the King's Chaplain, member of the Lodge of Muses, etc.

I do not wish to force the identification; indeed, there are some discordant notes. C. C. Robin professes a great interest in botany and natural history and claims on the title page of the *Voyages dan l'intérieur de la Louisiane*, etc. to be the author of works on literature and science. Somewhere, there should exist works on these subjects, but there are none on record attributed to any Robin, and certainly none attributed to Charles César Robin.

I cannot find any reference to a Robin in connection with botany and natural history in France. However, in his introduction Robin states that he had withdrawn from public life and may have turned to the study of natural history as a solace for personal tragedy. But this is speculation.

Be all this as it may, we can reconstruct a little of the life and personality of our author, C. C. Robin, from internal evidence, especially from the preface to his work. He was a widower, he came to the New World accompanied by his son, who subsequently died of yellow fever. He claims to be aloof from politics, but is rather obviously an enthusiastic bonapartist; indeed, he named one new plant *Napoléon* and another *Joséphine*. He was widely read; there are references to Plutarch, Buffon, Adam Smith, Thomas Jefferson, several works on Louisiana, including Du Pratz and Bossu and others on American civilization and history.

He refers to having resided during the very severe winter of 1793 or '94 in Lorraine, which may indicate either that he was a native of that district or that he spent the years of the height of the Terror away from Paris, or both, for the indication throughout his work is that he normally lived at Paris.

I should think that more information is available for those who will search it out. For instance, Robin was a landowner in the Atakapas district in 1805. The record at the court house at St. Martinville shows that he bought property there at a sheriff's sale in September 1804. He was a member of the first grand jury that sat in Atakapas county. Robin was especially friendly with the Marquis de Casa Calvo. Are any references to him to be found among Casa Calvo's papers?

There is a reference to a memorandum submitted by Robin dated 1808 urging Napoleon to occupy Florida as a base of action against both Britain and the United States in the *Archives des Affaires Étrangeres, Espagne* (Cox, Isaac John, *The West Florida Controversy, 1798-1815*. A Study in American Diplomacy. Johns Hopkins Press. xii + 699 pp. 1918, page 282). Is more available from that source?

Finally L'aimable's work and the Marat Correspondence should be gone over for any personal references to Robin that might be helpful. I do not think the last word has been said on the subject of the identity of C. C. Robin.

This translation of Robin is not complete. I have omitted the first volume entirely as it deals with the West Indian Islands. In addition, I have skipped several sections dealing with outdated speculation on natural history and geology. The skipped sections, with Robin's original pagination, are as follows:

Vol. I Entire Volume
Vol. II, Chapter 49, Pp. 268-279
Vol. II, Chapter 50, Pp. 280-297
Vol. II, Chapter 59, Pp. 450-483
Vol. II, Chapter 60, Pp. 484-498
Vol. III, Chapter 65, Pp. 117-161
Vol. III, Chapter 67, Pp. 185-191
Vol. III, Chapter 69, Pp. 237-243

I have omitted the Louisiana Flora entirely. It has been translated and commented upon by the French-American naturalist, C. S. Rafinesque, and to that volume the interested reader is referred.*

A translation must always steer between the Scylla of being over-literal, which produces barbaric English, and the Charybdis of too great departure from the original, which produces not only errors, but a style so English as to give no idea of the original flavor of the work. I hope this translation has sailed a reliable enough middle course. I have not hesitated, upon occasion, to tear up M. Robin's paragraphs and recast them entirely to give a rendering more in line with normal English usage. The French declamatory style, of long-winded periodic sentences, and rhetorical questions can become tedious, and I have sometimes chopped up these breathless perorations and recast them as independent declaratory sentences, in order to calm these utterances to a more English pace.

I do not flatter myself that I have weeded out all of the misrenderings of French words in this translation. There are some subjects (e.g. the lists of classes of textiles in use in France in the 1790's) about which I simply do not know enough to make good judgments. In addition, Robin's style in some places becomes highly ironic and elliptical, and positive statements come out a

---

*Florula Ludoviciana, or A Flora of the State of Louisiana. Translated, revised and improved from the French of C. C. Robin by C. S. Rafinesque, New York, Wiley & Co., 1817. 178 pp.

sort of negative-negative that is confusing. If anything I have wrongly interpreted has distorted Robin's intention, I can only apologize for it.

The value of Robin's narrative lies in the fact that it gives us a thorough and conscientious view of Louisiana at the beginning of its incorporation into the United States. The changes in the former colony were rapid and profound. New Orleans was catapulted from the status of the principal village of a backward colony in a declining empire, to that of the commercial center of an enormous region into which settlers were pouring and whose agricultural output correspondingly was rising spectacularly.

At a time when transportation by water was the only way to move cargoes of any size, New Orleans, located as it was at the mouth of the enormous navigable drainage basin of the Mississippi River system, was affected by the population growth and increase in productivity of the entire region. It was not merely a matter of more people arriving in New Orleans itself. Every settler who established himself west of the Appalachians increased the pressure for change in New Orleans; increased the necessity for English-speaking brokerage houses and commission merchants, American law, American money and familiarity with American ways of doing business.

It must be remembered that the Spanish never attempted to develop Louisiana. They held it merely as a buffer zone between the Anglo-Americans and their valuable colony of Mexico. Change had been held off for twenty years while the pressure for it had increased. When change came, it was sudden and dramatic. In a very short time indeed Louisiana was assimilated into the great, prosperous, bumptious, growing United States and the colonial French culture described here by Robin was largely submerged, although it did not disappear completely. Robin shows us what colonial Louisiana was like and describes the first stages of its metamorphosis into American Louisiana, and he is almost the only author to do so in any detail.

It is, of course, painful for us Louisianians to suffer the scorns of our critic for those aspects of life in Louisiana that displeased him. His detestation of the Creole ladies seems to be absolute. Not only does he explicitly expand upon their deficiencies, but he never praises a hostess without going out of his way to assure us that she, of course, was European. He admires the Canadians, the Acadians, the Catalonians, and the European French, but of the Creole his opinion is usually low. One would assume from Robin that almost the only recreation of the Creole man was gambling and of the Creole woman, beating slaves. Surely, things were not as bad as that. Slaves were expensive by Robin's own testimony, and it is a little hard to believe that the indulgence of sadistic excess would be common.

There is one opinion of Robin's that is startlingly modern. That is his view that the Negro is unintelligent because he is a slave and not that he is a slave because he is unintelligent. This opinion, even among abolitionists, was not very widespread in the 19th Century. It has the ring of the twentieth. Even his view that the slave owners, to protect themselves, should assimilate the half-breeds rather than driving them into the ranks of the Negroes, seems prophetic, for it has been by precisely this means that Portugal managed to exploit its colonies by a system very like that of slavery long after other colonial nations had abandoned the practice.

Robin's rather exotic views of economics are also more modern than they seem on first reading. His opinion that money should be abolished, is based upon the idea that fluctuations in the intrinsic value of a medium of exchange have a perjorative effect upon prices in that medium over and above the effects of demands for the goods themselves, an idea that reappeared in the "commodity dollar" proposed during the depression. Aside from that, Robin is generally an "easy money" man, decrying the strangling effect on commerce of the unavailability of money. He is in the lineage of the greenbackers, populists, and free silver men of later days and his ideas are not as archaic as they may seem, described in terms of 18th Century commerce.

It is a pleasure to acknowledge the assistance of Mr. Henry J. Dubester, Chief, General Reference and Bibliography Division of the Library of Congress, who drew my attention to Monyahan's remarks and Miss Carmen Kelley, who took time from her own studies to check certain bibliographic sources at the University of Paris. Also Miss Pearl Segura, librarian at Univ. of S.W., La., and Miss Hazel G. Sockrider, librarian of St. Martin Parish Library, helped with research of Attakapas records; and finally, my father, S. O. Landry, who helped with clues, and whose idea it was to translate C. C. Robin in the first place.

—STUART O. LANDRY, JR.

December, 1965

MONEY IN COLONIAL LOUISIANA

The basic unit was called the *piastre* by the colonists, although the actual coin was the Mexican *peso*, and it was so called by the Spanish officials. In some of the colonies this unit was called the *piastre gourde* or *gourde* (which is still the monetary unit of Haiti, as the *piastre* is still the unit of Viet Nam). The word *"piastre"* is Italian for "flat" and the coin originated in Venice, from which it spread to Turkey and from there through North Africa to Spain. The *piastre* was divided into 8 *escalins*, which were in turn divided into 12 *sous*. The *picayune* was ½ *escalin* or six *sous*. The French *franc* counted as 20 *sous*, or five to the *piastre*. The term *franc* was used interchangeably with *livre tournois*.

> 1 Piastre equals $1.00
> 1 Escalin equals .12½ (cents)
> 1 Sou equals .01 (1 cent)

TABLE OF EQUIVALENT VALUES OF MONEY USED IN SPANISH COLONIAL LOUISIANA

1 *piastre* = 1 dollar = 8 *escalins*   1 *escalin* = 12 *sous*

(*gourde*)   (*schellin*)

(*peso*)   (*real*)

1 *piastre* =   5 *francs*   1 *franc* = 20 *sous*

                       5 *livres tournois*   (approx.)

1 *piastre* = 1 2/3 *ecu*   1 *ecu* =   3 *francs* = 60 *sous*

                                             1 *sou* = 3 *maravedis*
                                                     = 1 cent
                                                     (approx.)
1 *ducat* = 1.38 *piastres* =   11 *escalins*

Neither five *francs*, nor five *livres tournois* equalled exactly one *piastre*, nor did they equal each other. One *piastre* did not exactly equal one dollar.

CHAPTER XXVIII

Description of Pensacola. What this colony was under the English; What it is under the Spanish. Agriculture, Soil, Industry, Inhabitants, Military Forces, Women, Commerce, Navigation, and the Methods of Improving it.

Pensacola, that region taken from the English by the Spanish toward the end of the American Revolutionary War, has declined considerably from what it was at that time. This town, situated on a pleasant and salubrious coast, at the end of a bay, facing its entrance, is spread out on a spacious and level plain, and is bordered on the right and the left by two streams called *bayous*. Behind this plain to the north, a little hillock dominates and protects it. The various streams which empty into this large bay, the long canal between the Island of Santa Rosa and the mainland, make this site a central point for the drainage of the region, a fact which will become of greater importance as the hinterland is settled. Already rye, corn and cotton are successfully cultivated here.

This propensity of English colonists for settling in the countryside, establishing economical agricultural activities which has contributed so much to their power, created numerous settlements along the harbor and along the banks of the streams. Masts, timber, naval stores, and furs, obtained from the Indians, became the most important items of commerce. The city grew proportionately. More and more neat and handsome houses, signs of increasing leisure, were built. A number of jetties or wharfs were built out into the harbor where 50 or so European ships were always anchored. Under the Spaniards, tradition alone has preserved a trace of the commerce in masts and naval stores. The rural settlements, the agriculturists, have disappeared. Corn is now only obtained from the settlements at Mobile, and even chickens are imported from there. Rice and flour are bought at New Orleans as well as all European provisions and wine. The costs of transport of these provisions almost doubles the price; bread, for instance, costs twelve sous a pound, whereas it is worth at most, half of that. At the same time, for lack of consumption there is no market. No one has anything to sell and could not recover the value of it if he did. I have seen fishermen, forced to jettison a part of their catch, after having sold the best of it at a miserable price. One unfortunate, located about a half-league from the city, grows watermelons (a natural crop for this country) and he has trouble getting rid of them. He is the only farmer in the colony. Oh, shameful! Fresh meat only costs three sous and this does not amount to even one sou in French money. But butter, whose production requires a little trouble, costs from 36 to 48 sous in summer and in winter goes to more than three francs. [*20 sous to the franc = 60 sous. — Tr. note.*]

Every settler has a herd of cows who stay at large in the woods, day and night, winter and summer and receive no attention except for being milked once a day. In order to do this the owners keep the calves to make the cows come in. Some have hundreds of these beasts. An English trading company, of which I will say more later, has a cowshed several miles from the city with more than two thousand animals. The cows wander at large mixed together. They are recognized by different marks which each proprietor places on them in the springtime when they are herded together. That is about the only care that they are given. A cow costs at most 30-36 francs. They are of an English strain and it has held up very well.

The soil of the town is only fine sand, so yielding that it is difficult to walk in the streets. However, it is productive of fruits and vegetables. Orange trees grow well there and the fig trees are splendid. Their fruit is delicious. Vines produce an abundance of excellent grapes. I have seen a vine or a bower loaded with fruit that was only two or three years old. The vines were as well developed as a planting eight or nine years old would be in France. Peach trees grow with astonishing rapidity, but they also die soon because they are allowed to bear too many fruits. There are plum trees of a type indigenous to the country, whose qualities are inferior to ours. Apple and pear trees grow only moderately well in this loose, hot soil. I do not know why the apricot and almond have not been introduced as the climate would be favorable for their cultivation. The common vegetables are the pumpkin, whose marrow is sweet, the sweet calabash, related to the cucumber, whose long runners grow in such profusion that they climb on the houses and produce an agreeable shade, and all types of melons which likewise grow without cultivation.

The Jamaica pepper, or pimento, is much used. The use of this powerful astringent is doubtless salutary in this country where excessive perspiration weakens the body. Lettuces, cabbages, and most of our French green vegetables also do marvelously well here; their flavor is of the best. Both the potato, as we have in France and the sweet potato of tropical regions, are grown. One individual has made a trial planting of sugar cane on this sandy terrain. I have seen this planting and it is as fine and well established as those in the islands. What would it be if only it were established several leagues in the interior where the soil is much better! Pensacola, situated like New Orleans, beneath the 30th degree of latitude, must have a climate still hotter and therefore still better suited to the culture of crops of this sort, because of the sandy soil.

All kinds of beans do well here. There are several kinds which we do not have, more productive and more delicate than ours among them, those called flat beans [lima beans.—Tr. note.] In winter the Indians bring in an abundance of game, ducks, deer (whose meat is so fat and wholesome), wild turkeys, also very fat, weighing up to 30 pounds costing only from two to five sous and that, not in money, but in kind.

Wood costs nothing, indeed, the country would benefit from consuming a great deal of it, but it does cost to transport it, and this cost may be considerable in a country where no one works, since one is not stimulated by pressing need. A cart load containing about two-thirds of a cord costs about twelve escalins (between six and seven francs). Those who own Negroes send them to cut wood at the edge of the harbor, and have it transported by water.

The streams and the sea swarm with fish. I have seen the fish schooling at the entrance to the harbor in such a great quantity that one would have thought that a light breeze was rippling the surface. Shellfish are just as abundant. In the coves, near the mouth of the river there are extensive banks of large and excellent oysters.

The air at Pensacola is so pure that invalids from Louisiana frequently come here to recuperate. The settlement is entirely military and the professions here are consequently only those serving the military. All of the commerce, therefore, turns upon the expenditures of the government. Agriculture and industry produce nothing except for a few ill-tended gardens. Only a small corner of this land is under cultivation. It follows, necessarily, that the maintenance of both houses and individuals will be proportional to the expenditures of the government. A great number of houses, therefore, that were occupied during the period of English suzerainty are today abandoned and in ruins. Of the several wharfs which originally were built extending out into the harbor, only one is left and it is dilapidated. One of the two handsome barracks built by the English has just burned down. What the government spends in this settlement, it does not recover from the produce of agriculture and commerce, in the form of a return on the money. A military population, accustomed to an indolent life for which it requires expensive pleasures, whose members do not regard the places at which they are stationed as more than temporary habitations, is hardly disposed, or indeed, is able to take up the fruitful enterprises of commerce and agriculture. A city consisting of soldiers will certainly never show an example of economy and labor.

A billiard room is the general meeting place of everyone from the Governor down to the laborer and the humblest clerk. Here the shoemaker considers himself as good as the highest military officer. Here, in short, equality reigns. Not that of the debased, coarseness of the lowest elements of the population, but that equality which raises people to the honest customs of sociability.

This billiard room takes up that part of the means of the inhabitants that is not required for subsistence. Here, one finds neither novelist nor scholar. Here people play billiards, drink punch or other refreshments, and talk, purely for the sake of talking. Here, the treatment of travellers could not be more considerate. They are deferred to by all.

The ladies have more regard for rank. Their company is pleasant; they are affable with strangers. The wife of the governor and her charming family provide an excellent example. I cannot refrain from singling out Madame d'Alva, a Frenchwoman originally from Louisiana, married to a Spaniard, who is director of the hospital. One could scarcely carry the virtues of nursing further. Her generous benevolence extends to everyone in the settlement who needs her.

These ladies follow all of the French fashions. Their dresses are slender-waisted and short sleeved. They show off the figure without embarrassment. In this respect they should be the fashion in all centuries and in all countries, but they are especially suitable in those regions where the summers are long and hot. All of the ladies nurse their children. They owe this custom to fashion. O Fortunate mistress! If only that were always her influence! The human species has noticeably gained from this circumstance. Children nursed by their mothers are larger and healthier.

Five or six small ships blown here by contrary winds, all of them not totalling more than six or seven hundred tons, are more than have been seen here in ten years, and they have not been able to sell enough to make expenses. Four or five schooners of from ten to twenty-five tons carry passengers and freight between here and New Orleans. That is all of the commerce of this colony, except for the fur trade of which I spoke earlier.

Conquered lands which, to ignorant people, are the source of rejoicing, are, to people of understanding, a subject of melancholy, when they fail to promote the multiplication of people (the first duty and the ultimate end of all institutions). The Spanish officials themselves contemplate with shame the record of the past prosperity of this colony.

The schooners mentioned above, being broad and flat-bottomed, follow a route to New Orleans much shorter and safer than by way of the mouth of the Mississippi. On leaving the harbor they follow the coast westward to the mouth of Mobile Bay. Here they enter the sound formed by the islands Dauphine, Horn, Ship and Cat. Other little islands pressed together form several narrow channels called the *Rigolets* which lead into Lake Ponchartrain. [*This description apparently ignores the existence of Lake Borgne, but is otherwise accurate. The land between the Chef, the Rigolets and Lake St. Catherine may easily be regarded as a series of islands.—Tr. note.*] From here the boats enter a short stream [*Bayou St. John—Tr. note.*] which communicates with New Orleans by an artificial canal [*the Old Basin or Carondelet Canal.— Tr. note.*] dug by the efforts of the Baron Carondelet, then Governor of Louisiana. This route is not more than 50 leagues [*125 mi. —Tr. note.*] in length and can be made in two days. Sheltered from storms, one can relax in all weather, and the route is sheltered from attack by any enemy. The route by the mouth of the Mississippi would be more than 80 leagues [*200 miles.—Tr. note.*], and it would be necessary to proceed along the Chandeleur Islands, whose storms are frequent, and fight the swift current of the river. Moreover, the land at the river's mouth is so low that it can be seen only when one is very near and hence is very dangerous to approach and even after getting into the river it sometimes takes twenty or thirty days to get up to New Orleans. [*When the wind was from the north, ascent was impossible, as a sailing ship could only move against it by tacking back and forth across the river whose current would cause the ship to lose as much, or more, distance as it gained by tacking. Ships would therefore have to anchor below English Turn and wait for a favorable wind.—Tr. note.*]

The present governor of Pensacola, M. Folke, [*Vincente Folch, Governor of Pensacola, was the nephew of Esteban Miro, a former governor of Louisiana.—Tr. note.*], a vigorous and worthy man, conceived the idea of shortening this route still further and making it even safer. One of the streams which empties into Pensacola Bay, as the Governor informs me, flows close to the Partridge River [RIVIÈRE AUX PERDRIX. *I suspect this means the* PERDIDO *River, which forms the present boundary between Alabama and Florida. A Frenchman speaking Spanish badly might easily confuse the sounds.—Tr. note*]. The land between these two streams is flat and soft and one could with little expense cut a canal between the two. With equal facility one could then make a connection between the Partridge River and Fish River (*Rivière aux Poissons*) which empties into the Mobile.

Thus the communication of Pensacola with New Orleans being almost entirely inland would not be endangered by high winds and in wartime would be immune from molestation by the enemy. The lands along these rivers would acquire ports for transshipment of produce and would thus be opened up for cultivation. Pensacola would then increase in importance as a port, both in traffic with Louisiana and in overseas trade.

These sagacious and practical proposals were turned down, it is believed, at the instigation of the governors of Louisiana, of which the government of Pensacola is a dependency. Almost all of the authorities of Louisiana regard any measures to increase the prosperity of West Florida (of which Pensacola is the capital) as harmful to the interests of Louisiana. What blind ignorance! Would not the riches of Pensacola, pouring into Louisiana enrich the commerce of the latter? And the more Pensacola prospered, would not the more Louisiana gain? It is by such errors of public policy that states ruin themselves. This almost self-evident observation should be repeated over and over to the Spanish Government.

CHAPTER XXIX

Harbor of Pensacola, Its importance, Its tides. Rationale of Government Expenditures in this Colony. Strange Abuses. A privileged English Commercial Establishment Still Remaining at Pensacola. Unwiseness of Maintaining This Establishment.

I learned at San Domingo the news of the cession of Louisiana to the United States and that Pensacola and West Florida would remain under Spanish dominion. This new order of things will have important consequences.

The harbor of Pensacola, because of its situation, its security, and because of the course of current events, will always be extremely important to the country which possesses it. It is the only harbor on the Gulf Coast capable of sheltering a number of large vessels against storms.*

Its bottom, a mixture of sand and mud, will hold an anchor very well. Surrounded on all sides by land and communicating with the sea only through a narrow channel, somewhat oblique, and by the very narrow Santa Rosa Channel, the water is never affected by the waves of the open Gulf. The channel is twenty-one feet deep at the shallowest and the harbor can thus receive vessels of sixty-guns. These advantages taken together assure control of the Gulf of Mexico to the power who knows how to take advantage of them. [*Ironically, control of Pensacola has never conferred any advantage whatsoever upon the nation possessing it. All of the time that the British held Pensacola the dominant power on the North Gulf Coast was either France or Spain, and from 1803 to 1819 while Florida belonged to Spain the dominant Gulf power was the United States.—Tr. note.*]

The hinterlands of the colony, moreover, can furnish almost all that is necessary for the refitting and construction of ships; pitch and rosin, pines and cypress for masts, hard green oak for the bows, and for planking between decks, oaks of many species, cedars, cypresses; also cordage, etc. If the active and ambitious Americans become mistress of such a place, they will soon have

---

*I must observe, however, that, in a hurricane which took place some twenty years ago, a frigate, which was anchored in the harbor, dragged its anchor and was blown ashore and was so completely lost that not the least trace of it was ever found. The ship had not been moored, however, at the most sheltered spot in the harbor.

a formidable navy. How would Spain maintain communication with Mexico if the Americans sought to cut them off? What expense in armaments it would cost them merely to escort convoys from Havana to Vera Cruz! Would not every stream from Louisiana to Mexico which emptied into the sea be a potential base for the Americans? This state of things would bring about the loss of Mexico and the other Spanish colonies, to say nothing of the French ones. There is, thus, no place that deserves more attention from Spain and her ally, France.

While the loss of Pensacola by Spain is to be greatly feared, keeping it will serve to keep the Americans in Louisiana in check. Spanish vessels of war can leave Pensacola on the spur of the moment to block at will the difficult passes of the River and those of the Attakapas [*Atchafalaya Bay.—Tr. note.*]. But how many cruel blows has Spain already allowed to fall on this property! The Americans have pushed their establishments in Georgia to less than 15 or 16 leagues from Pensacola. The upper reaches of the Mobile River from to about twenty leagues from the mouth are already in their hands. Under these conditions, it is already necessary to employ many more troops to guard Pensacola than formerly and, in addition, it is urgent that the hinterland be settled with farmers. Without this the Americans, sooner or later, will come in.

The tides at Pensacola are neither high nor very regular. Strong sea winds will raise them, while strong offshore winds will diminish them considerably. For this reason, it has been hardly possible to measure them exactly. In a twenty-four-hour period the tide will be falling in the bay from 18 to 19 hours, and will rise for only five to six hours. This enormous difference must be attributed to the effect of the numerous streams entering the bay, which must furnish two-thirds of the capacity of the water in the bay. Indeed, the water in the bay is much less salty than in the open sea and becomes less so as one approaches the shore. This is an important observation for vessels anchoring in the harbor. If they anchor close enough to the shore, they have nothing to fear from the ship worm, which cannot live in fresh water [TEREDO, *actually a mollusc.—Tr. note.*].

The tide seldom rises as high as three feet and sometimes does not rise at all. The currents likewise are variable, all of which as noted above must be attributed to the wind.

The streams which empty into the harbor, create currents which seriously derange the navigation of ships. What adds to the difficulties is the fact that close to the shore the water is so shallow in several places that ships must make considerable detours.

The Fort at Pensacola, raised on a mound of sand, is extremely important, as large ships must pass within half a cannon shot of it in order to enter the harbor.

This colony, although it has deteriorated under Spanish rule, is still a costly burden on the Spanish government. A garrison of 500 men is maintained, out of which only 200 are ready for duty. There is a Governor, who holds the military rank of Colonel, whose salary is three thousand piastres; a military commander of the same rank, supply and finance officers, and a host of junior officers, whose sole duty is to collect their salaries. The government pays customs inspectors who have no inspections to make or duties to collect. It employs carpenters, joiners, caulkers, blacksmiths; all of the artisans necessary for the maintenance of a fleet which consists of one small sloop.

The minor officials receive from twenty-five to forty or fifty *gourdes* [*A monetary unit identical with* PIASTRE. *The gourde is still the official monetary unit of the Republic of Haiti. The original form is* PIASTRE GOURDE, *"thick piastre", from Spanish* GORDA, *fat.—Tr. note.*] per month, in addition to their lodging, rations, and other benefits. There are storehouses from which these functionaries draw items ostensibly for the replacement of damaged goods. A certain quantity of powder is used up in firing practice, but not a single cap is fired. [*I.e., the powder is diverted to other purposes, presumably being sold off.—Tr. note.*] These prerogatives of position are ordinarily worth more than the salaries themselves. These abuses are so commonplace that no one even bothers to hide them. They extend throughout the administration of the various colonies and even an administration of the strictest probity would, by this time, find them extremely hard to suppress. There are countries where these abuses are even more glaring. How would such a government not be poor, even with such riches, or feeble with so many expenses. The miracle is that it has endured this long.

Several years ago more than 1,500,000 francs were spent upon putting the fortifications in condition, and today they are in a state of dilapidation with the exception of the fort built of brick at the entrance to the harbor, and even it is cracked everywhere because of being built on shifting sands, on pilings, no doubt, poorly sunk. Most of the buildings are already in ruins. I noted above that one redoubt on the island of Santa Rosa on the opposite side of the channel was built of wood so rotten that the least spark, such as the firing of a cap, would burn it to the ground. Artillery here would do more damage to the fortification than to the enemy.

On the hill to the north which dominates the city the English built three sturdy forts surrounded by a deep ditch. The city itself was, moreover, surrounded by a wide ditch, whose parapet was provided with a palisade of tree trunks about twelve feet high. At the center of the city another fort formed a citadel where all of the citizens could seek shelter in time of need. Several blockhouses constructed of wood contained cannons firing over the palisade which could sweep the principal streets. Of all this defense, only a few of the wooden blockhouses remain, which, being isolated, would not be a very formidable obstacle.

When Pensacola was taken from the English, there was one commercial firm which had a monopoly of the fur trade. This monopoly has continued under the Spanish Government. One may judge how unwise was this continuation. This firm, first known as the Planthon Company [*The Scottish firm of Panton and Leslie. —Tr. note.*], from the name of one of its directors, has offices in London and in the Island of Providence [*New Providence in the Bahamas, containing Nassau.—Tr. note.*] The company trades with the Indians for a distance of 80 to 100 leagues inland. Its agents are all English and trade only in English goods; rum, powder, lead, guns, blankets, blue cloth, woolen ribbons, colored cloth, axes, knives and other knickknacks of apparel.

These savages, however fickle they may be, have certain habits, as, for instance, blankets with certain stripes, cloth of blue, woolen ribbons of blue or yellow, silver plaques of a certain shape, glass beads of milk white. They prefer guns of a certain shape, ordinarily carbines, and the powder must be fine. Accustomed to trading with the English, they have become thoroughly accustomed to their goods, even to the saddles of those among them who have horses. Thus all of the advantages of the fur trade, which is the sole resource which the Spaniards could exploit, there being no agriculture, accrues to their enemies and damages the Spanish Government. At the same time, under the pretext of bringing in trade goods for the Indians, the same company actually imports merchandise for the colonists. Thus the entire colony, for which the King of Spain pays all the expenses, is run for the profit of England. The English sell in the colony and buy furs which are sent to London, from where they are reshipped to other countries. The company sells to the inhabitants on credit and is thus able to raise prices and oblige the inhabitants to trade with them by preference. The company has all of the fur trade and almost all of the hard cash in the colony. But already recent events have exposed the colony to great dangers on account of this unwise policy.

CHAPTER XXX

History of an Englishman named Bawles. High Chief of the Indians. War of the Indians with the Spaniards. Dangers to the Colony of the rights of Man applied to the Indians. Observations on the Courses of this War.

An Englishman named Bawles [*William Bowles.—Tr. note.*], who in England was a lieutenant in a company of Grenadiers, went to Providence Island, the English colony [*i.e., Nassau in the Bahamas.—Tr. note.*]. After a lengthy stay in this colony he learned a great deal about the fur trade, which the privileged company mentioned above conducted in West Florida. Bawles wished to judge for himself the extent of this trade and to take part in it. Whether this idea was suggested to him in England by the Government, or whether he conceived it for himself in New Providence, the fact is that he left the island for Florida with a quantity of trade goods. He soon made contact with the Indians and ingratiated himself with them. Bawles, a large and well-built man, combined in his person a martial appearance with an open and agreeable face. He had both genius and a cultivated mind, he was enterprising and audacious, sociable and easy-going, and he knew how to accommodate himself without difficulty to whatever conditions circumstances dictated. He was generous, vain, ostentatious when it was necessary, and he was easily able to accommodate himself to the simple and austere savage life.

Bawles, at first trading with the Indians, soon became their friend and companion; conforming to their customs, speaking their language, directing their hunts, and joining in their celebrations. Like them, he went naked, except for a breech cloth, shod in *mitasses* [*moccasins.—Tr. note.*]. He slept on the ground and lived on corn boiled in water, or game and stripped dried meat [VIANDES RACORNIES À BOUCAN. *The French renegade inhabitants of the West Indian Islands who prepared this delicacy were called* "BOUCANIERS", *hence our buccaneer.—Tr. note.*].

Living this type of life, although having been accustomed to the benefits of European civilization, Bawles prepared a general insurrection among the Indian nations against the Spanish. He sold the merchandise he had brought for prices much under those the Indians would have paid at Pensacola, promising them a greater abundance of these goods in the future. Most of all, he offered credit, always an attractive lure for the Indians. Thus he alienated them more and more from the Spaniards. "These despotic misers," he told them incessantly, "are getting all the fruits of your hunting. They are leaving you to poverty which makes you almost slaves. The storehouses that they have established in your villages are only well stocked because of the pelts that they have extracted from you for a pittance, and they will overcharge you with impunity for the goods you need, because you cannot obtain them elsewhere." The Indians, inflamed by these words, wanted to loot the storehouses, but Bawles, too crafty to permit such a dangerous occurrence, played the part of a moderate. He fixed the price of the Spanish goods at the same level as those that he had sold. By this apparent act of justice, he put the Pensacola Company out of business, by making it impossible for the Company to continue to pay subsidies to the Spanish Government. Thus, he managed to break off all relations between the Spaniards and the Indians, and to foment the hatred of the Indians for the Spaniards, to gather more and more of the trade of the area for England, and organize a general insurrection, which, combined with the war between England and France, facilitated the English conquet of all of Florida. [*Pensacola was founded by the Spaniards in 1696 under whose suzerainty it remained until 1763 (except for a brief period of French occupation, 1719-23). Great Britain acquired Pensacola along with the rest of Florida in 1763. Pensacola was retaken from the English by the Spaniards under Galvez from New Orleans in 1781 and remained in Spanish hands until the cession of Florida to the United States in 1819.—Tr. note.*]

In these circumstances, every tribe of Indians sought Bawles' friendship with the greatest alacrity and all vied with each other in electing him chief. Bawles, without in any way changing his frugal personal life, as their leader displayed the pomp of a high ranking general; he decked himself in gaudy plumes, flashing weapons, and he distributed these to his warriors according to the ranks that he assigned them, and he had already installed in them that fundamental obedience which prepared them for the rules of military discipline. When hostilities began, Bawles had enough authority from the beginning to repress the Indians' avidity for blood and pillage, which typified their own fighting. He forbade them to slaughter the enemy who asked for quarter. He returned in safety all non-combatants, and whatever he did he treated everyone with the greatest consideration. The wounded were well cared for. These ministrations consisted only of washing the wounds with cool water and sucking them [*to re-*

move pus.—Tr. note.], and of flushing deep wounds with the aid of a reed and finally applying herb medicines. These operations were done by Indian doctors to the accompaniment of invocations, the tracing of mysterious figures on the ground, and trances. Nevertheless, these suctions and applications of plants and their accompanying incantations promptly cured the patient. I have seen individuals at Pensacola wounded and treated thus returned to Pensacola completely cured, while others wounded at the same time who were treated in the European manner were not cured until long afterward.

These hostilities spread consternation throughout Florida. The Government was thoroughly frightened. No one dared to travel in the interior. The enemy's incursions came as far as Pensacola itself, and the Indians carried off everything they found. How could one march against them through these forests where they dispersed so rapidly, only to be reported again in another place? How could troops be removed from the city, where whole families had gathered and where munitions were stored? Besides, the city no longer had defensive works and was vulnerable from all sides. No doubt the governor of Louisiana then realized the deplorable effects of that jealousy and those narrow politics, which kept Pensacola in abasement before New Orleans, which failed to populate its fields with farmers, who could have come to her defense in time of need.

The Governor of Louisiana had recourse to a means of combatting the uprising, far from the honest dealing which, down through the centuries has characterized the Spanish nation, a means of which, no doubt, the Spanish Court would not have approved; that is, treachery. He opened a correspondence with Bawles, offering concessions. He flattered Bawles and praised him and, little by little, persuaded him to come to New Orleans for a parley. The officer, who brought a safe conduct for Bawles, assured him that his person would be inviolable and gave him as a pledge the Governor's word of honor. Bawles, a noble and ingenuous person, presented himself at New Orleans. On his arrival he was clapped in irons. "What", he cried in the Governor's presence, "officers of a great king, laden with emoluments and honors, would play thus with their sacred word of honor? You have taken my baggage, stolen my money and confiscated my papers and placed me in fetters!" "Ah", he cried, wildly shaking his chains, "this ignoble violation of faith will find avengers."

I give the words exactly, because they leave no doubt that Bawles was the agent of the English government. He was taken to Havana, the residence of the Captain General to whom the Governor of Louisiana was subordinate, and from there he was embarked for Spain. This was during the last war, and the vessel was captured by the English and taken to their ports. Bawles, accompanied by his Indians, created great excitement in London. The Duke of York visited him, and one presumes that this visit was not out of idle curiosity. Some time later this Indian chieftain sailed for Jamaica. It should be noted that this was aboard a frigate and that upon his arrival he appeared to be very well off. He was noted for his honorable generosities. Among other things, having learned that a young man of a well-known New Orleans family who had run away from home was in need, he had him provided with all the necessities of life without revealing who the young man's benefactor was and finally persuaded him to return home and gave him the means to do so. One day this young man found doubloons in some oranges that he had at home, and he realized who it was that had put them there. He went immediately to thank his benefactor, but Bawles refused to admit that he was the author of this generosity.

A few months later Bawles took ship for Florida with his Indians. Note again that this was in a pretty little sloop of war with a double copper bottom. He was liberally provisioned with objects of trade. Several other shiploads were sent at a later time. Almost no one could approach these coasts, which are difficult of access on account of sand banks, currents and sudden storms. [*Robin exaggerates. The ease with which Cuban rebels slip in and out of the coastal waters of Florida shows that it is not so difficult of access.—Tr. note.*]

Thus Bawles, back among the Indians, now had the means to execute the several plans of attack he was contemplating upon the Spanish settlements, and also the means of retaining and increasing the confidence of the Indians, who, always enthusiastic, but always fickle, are ever ready to sacrifice the most important future interests to the interests of the moment.

In these circumstances, Bawles appeared with a troop of Indians before the fort of Apalache [St. Marks], situated about 50 leagues to the east of Pensacola at the head of a bay formed by the confluence of the Talauatchina and Touskachie rivers. [*Robin's spelling.—Tr. note.*] His men had no balls for their guns, only powder, but he declared that he was going to besiege the town and ravage the surrounding countryside and that he could not control the excesses of his large army. The horrified garrison forced the commander to surrender the fort. This event spread the alarm again at Pensacola, and if Bawles had marched immediately he could have taken it, for Pensacola had really a weaker defensive system than Apalache, since it was open from all directions. Pensacola could have been destroyed, and its harbor would have had to have been abandoned. The Governor, M. Folke, hastened to have a palisade erected around the city. I have seen it, and I am bound to say that if this were the sole means of defense it would have been a feeble defensive work in case of attack.

The Governor of Louisiana [*Baron de Carondelet, Governor of Louisiana from 1791-1797.—Tr. note*], no longer able to entrap Bawles, attempted next to corrupt the Indians themselves. He placed a price on the head of the great chief. Four to five thousand gourdes in a helmet was the reward offered with a flourish to the Indians who had, in the meantime, come to New Orleans.

These savages, dazzled by the heap of money, which was more than they had even seen, and discontented anyway because they had not received the articles that Bawles had so often promised them, particularly those things necessary for hunting, found accomplices by whose help they surprised Bawles and delivered him to the Spanish. Taken for the second time, Bawles was immediately shipped again to Havana. What has become of him is unknown, but he is presumed to be still in prison. During the war the Spanish were afraid to send him to sea again. He was not taken again by the English. After peace is signed, he will doubtless be returned to the English.

[*William Augustus Bowles, a soldier in the loyalist Maryland militia during the American Revolution, was sent to the British garrison at Pensacola in 1779. While there he was dismissed from the service for some misconduct and went into the woods, where he joined the Indians and learned their language and customs. However, he returned to the British after the surrender of Pensacola to the Spanish under Galvez in 1781 and returned with the British garrison to New Providence Island in the Bahamas. Here he fell in with the agents of the trading firm of Miller and Bonamy, who wanted to break the trading monopoly in Florida held by the Scottish firm of Panton and Leslie. (This is the monopoly referred to by Robin.) Bowles went to Florida in 1788. He succeeded in raising a large band of Indians and in 1791 captured the principal store of Panton and Leslie at St. Marks. Bowles' idea was to set*

*up an independent Indian state with himself as head, and to nego-
tiate trade treaties with the Spaniards; treaties, of course, that
would replace Panton and Leslie with Miller and Bonamy as principal suppliers of trade goods. The Spanish governor of Louisiana,
Carondelet, lured Bowles to New Orleans on the pretext of nego-
tiating a treaty, but when he arrived, promptly clapped him in
irons and shipped him off to Havana. The Spanish sent him from
here to a prison in Manila, where he stayed for several years, but
eventually they decided to return him to Spain. Bowles jumped
ship at Sierra Leone in Africa and succeeded in reaching the British authorities. He traveled to London and obtained backing for a
new venture in Florida. Bowles landed for the second time in 1799,
and, as before, succeeded in raising a powerful Indian force. By
1800 he had seized the Spanish fort at St. Marks, and the Spaniards
were offering 4,000 pesos reward for his capture. Bowles set up
the independent Indian state of Muskogee and proclaimed himself
its head. Governor Folch of Pensacola blockaded the coast and prevented Bowles' trade goods from getting through, a circumstance
that did loosen his hold on the loyalty of the Indians, but it was
the enmity of the Americans that eventually brought him to grief.
The Americans had no wish to see a powerful Indian state under
British auspices in the southeast, and it was the American Indian
agent, Benjamin Hawkins, who engineered Bowles' capture, again
by treachery. Bowles was handed over to the Spanish authorities
in 1803 and was said to have died in the Moro Castle in Havana
three years later. See an excellent account of Bowles by McAlister,
Fla. His. Quarterly, 40: 317-328.—Tr. note.]*

Bawles' conduct, examined from the legal point of view, raises
some embarrassing new difficulties. Should Bawles be considered
an individual, who in defiance of the laws of a country had violated its territory? Or should he be considered a free man who
went to the territory of a free people and, naturalizing himself,
partook of their prerogatives?

Florida is recognized as being under the dominion of Spain
by all civilized nations, including England, of which Bawles was
a subject. Spain has the right to make whatever laws or regulations it sees fit and to permit entry of, or deny admission to,
whomever it pleases. If this is the case, then Bawles entered a
country recognized by all nations, including his own, as being
under Spanish dominion, he became liable to the punishments pre-
scribed by Spanish law against those who entered the country
without authority. But Bawles went further. He committed hos-

tilities, he extorted, pillaged, ravaged and killed, and he did this without announcing that he was engaged on any official mission, without displaying any authority or title from his government. Bawles was, then, just a vagabond, a freebooter or brigand who should be treated as such. The protestations of his government in his favor could not save him from the legal penalties which he incurred, because, if Bawles was recognized as having acted as a private person and not as an agent, his actions were criminal and nothing that his government did would make legal an action that was criminal when committed.

A government can no more give a retroactive effect to its actions than a legislature can to its laws. Thus, in order for Bawles to be aided by his government, it would have to show that Bawles had acted, not on his own volition and according to his own plans, but on the orders and with the backing of his government, and it would be necessary that this authority and these orders be exhibited with such proofs that would leave no doubt of their existence at the time of Bawles' invasion. Failing this, the interested party, that is, the Spanish Government, is within its rights in refusing to recognize any documents given to it.

On the other hand, could not Bawles say: I left my country with the leave of its laws, and if I had broken them I would not be accountable to the Spaniards, but only to my own government. It is true, that the regions I went to are recognized as being under your dominion, but you are not the exclusive sovereign there because the title of the natives is better than yours. Yours is founded upon the law of *primo occupanti*, but that of the Indians far antedates yours. You don't even know at what time they arrived there. Therefore, recognizing that several sovereigns had dominion there, I penetrated to the region and incorporated myself into the nation that pleased me most. I adopted their customs, their laws and received their titles. It is because of these titles that I acted as I did, not as a European or an individual. Do you yourselves, might have added Bawles, not accord to the Indians all the prerogatives of independent people? You do not extend your laws to their territories. You do not impose taxes, and in their own lands you give them the power of life or death over their own subjects, to make war or peace. You expressly forbid your magistrates and your officers to interfere in their affairs. Are these not the characteristics of sovereignty? In your wars with them you do not treat these people as rebels. They send you ambassadors and you send them ambassadors. You make treaties of peace, alliance and commerce with them and you accord to their envoys distinctions that you would not give to individuals. Their chiefs you treat with especial distinction.

If the Indians enjoy by prior right and continuing usage, as well as by the effect of your own conduct towards them, the right of sovereignty, they can then adopt as members of their nations those over whom you have no authority, without your being able to do anything about it. In this manner, I was invested with all of the rights of an Indian and in the fighting that followed you could only regard me as an Indian and when I was raised to the position of a chief I became, even for you, an Indian official, and when so many confederated nations then raised me to the higher position of high chief I acquired new rights and prerogatives which you as a civilized nation were bound to respect even as a captive. Did I not make use of my authority in your behalf to suppress pillage and the letting of blood? Did I not care for your wounded? These prisons where I am locked up, these fetters with which I am loaded, are, therefore, violations of international law. This right, the fortunate benefit of civilization which reminds nations that even their enemies should be regarded as human beings. Can this law be violated with impunity when applied to Indians because they are weak? Ah, if you intend to admit any such proposition, what will be the consequences!

These different perplexing reflections show the defects of international law and, consequently, of the bases upon which it is erected. This doubt will become more favorable to the accused as the weaker party.

The story of Bawles' and the dangers that threatened the colony and Pensacola proves that the Spanish Court has not appreciated the dangers of having in its colonies a foreign company of privileged traders who are foreign to the customs and language of the colony, opposed to its interests and often enemies of the colonials. Bawles would never have learned at London or Nassau of the lucrative trade of West Florida if the English company had not existed at Pensacola. Bawles would never have dared to have penetrated into the interior of the country to prepare an insurrection if he had not known that the Indians were accustomed to trading with the English and to using English goods. And if Bawles' ships, loaded with goods, had reached Florida, he would have ruined the colony, and she would have fallen to the English.

CHAPTER XXXI

Natural History. Observation on the Origin of Ore Deposits. Ochre. The Disposition of the Creoles Toward the Arts. Great Variety of Oaks. Useful Land. Other Plants. Extraordinary Plant Destroying Insects.

The terrain behind the city is more elevated and forms a spacious plateau covered with woods. It is sandy, but the sand is variously colored, brown, yellow, or red, indicating that it contains metallic compounds. The sand of the seashore, as at Santa Rosa Island, is a very pure white. I think we may conclude from this that the sea water, loaded with salt, dissolves the metals disseminated in the earth by vegetation and redeposits them according to their specific gravities in separate beds. It is thus that we may explain the formation of ore deposits, several of which may be fused together by the action of volcanic fire, forming thus in the cracks of the earth the long veins that we know. [*This explanation is quite wrong.—Tr. note.*] To the east of Pensacola are to be found deposits of ochraceous earth showing beautiful different colors of saffron, orange, deep red, blue, brown, and white. Already a considerable amount is exported to Louisiana to be used as house paint.

An elderly surgeon spent, while I was there, all of the fees collected from his patients to make bricks, which, however, he could not sell, although they were of very good quality; much superior to those of Louisiana. Another individual manufactured a heavy and sturdy pottery, but had no better market for it than the surgeon. That is the story with all manufactures in this colony.

These Spanish-Americans, however, do have great abilities; what they require is some way to make use of their talents. I was shown drawings by a young man who had studied only six months. They were comparable to those of a European student who had been studying for 18 months or two years. Someone had brought to the colony two silver candlesticks, exquisitely made in the form of corinthian columns. He desired to have two others made. Two young Spanish creoles, who had never been out of the colony, blacksmiths by trade, succeeded in imitating them so perfectly that when they were shown to me I could not tell them from the originals.

These sandy soils produce a magnificent growth of pine trees of several species. The navies of Europe could be supplied with masts and tar from here. The different species of oak are so numerous that nature seems to have provided every conceivable shape of leaf. Some, shaped like those of a peach tree, are long and narrow and show no indication of any indentation on their edges. Others are slightly wider, as though they are striving to form angles. Still others show wavy borders, other display stiffened tips, their shape approaching that of the holly leaf; others are sculptured and etched even more and in a different manner: one of them takes the shape of a pear. Finally, there are some indented so deeply that they are reduced almost to naked midveins, as though caterpillars had eaten them, while others are of a wide oval shape and show only the very slightest indentations. [*The non-botanical reader should be warned that oak leaves are rather variable in shape and that not all of these are from different species.—Tr. note.*]

The acorns, also, vary as to shape, size, color, and flavor. Some are no bigger than large peas and are almost entirely covered by their cups with serrated edges; while others, as large as a medium-sized nut, rise gracefully from their widely opened cups. There are acorns which are elongate like an olive, while others are almost, or entirely, globular. The color of some is light, others are darker, a brownish purple, and others, a dirty white. The flesh may be white, greyish, chocolate colored, or yellow. The taste of some is very bitter, others less so, some still less, and finally, some are edible raw or cooked or can be rendered so with lye by the Indians.

The form of the tree among these oaks also varies greatly. Some are small with crowded branches forking and crossing with small leaves so numerous that these trees would make a nice hedge. Others with sparse foliage raise their crowns majestically to the height of the forest top, spreading their bare branches as if to give air to the humble shrubs which grow in clumps beneath them and as if to adorn themselves with those leafy vines which climb tortuously on their trunks in rounded columns which grow up to their branches, from which they hang down in green curtains. Others, whose trunks are straight and clothed in a smoother bark, show a widespreading, bushy crown, whose branches bend down to the ground. These plants spread mysterious shadows which seem to say to a man, "Come here to enjoy coolness and peace."

The same diversities are to be noted in the color of the wood, in its hardness, or porosity, and in the uses to which man can put it. Some woods are white, some greyish, others are tinted as though by the dregs of wine. Some are light and flexible, others are heavier, stiff and brittle. Several can be easily split into long rails, while others, because of their compressed and interlacing fibers, resist the wedge better than the hardest woods of Europe and will withstand for a long time the destructive action of the humid heat of these countries. Some can be used to make shingles or poles or for fence posts. Others can be bent into hoops, sawed into small boards for cabinet work. Still others are more suitable, for larger boards for the construction of ships, and these last for the hubs of wheels and for the shaft and the screw of presses and for all demands of the wheelwright for the hard and durable woods of America. One can find in the single family of the oaks all of the woods that are needed for these diverse uses.

At some distance from the city one finds growing in humid places the cypress, a large tree and one of the most desirable timber trees in the country on account of the diversity of its uses. A little further away grows the cedar, the tree justly renowned since Biblical times. The English had already begun a lucrative trade in these trees, cutting them into logs 10 or 12 feet long which they shipped out as ballast in their ships. I will not describe here a large number of plants which I will have occasion to mention elsewhere. I shall note only that among the forest trees are to be found many species of walnut trees, including the pecan, which is of the same family, mulberries, olive trees, plane trees [*sycamores.—Tr. note.*], magnolias, ashes, linden trees, elms, and holly, for holly is a large and handsome tree in this country. Near the sea, along both running and stagnant waters, are found numerous shrubs grouped in clumps. Among these are laurels of several species, sassafras, wax laurels from whose berries can be obtained a green aromatic wax and whose foliage, being bushy and elongated, is extremely pleasant. Another species of laurel is much like that which we employ in cooking. It bears black berries all year round. Still another, with green foliage, diminutive and graceful, gives an almond taste to dairy foods, but is different from the species we use for the same purpose. The horse chestnut with its yellow flowers is often found in the uplands. *Callicarpus* is especially noticeable there with its red berries compressed into rings along its dun-colored branches.

Near the city, clear streams, which would rival in transparency the purest crystal, run over a fine sand as white as silver. Often the streams disappear under thick groves formed by the little magnolia with its large, white flowers with golden stamens, these shrubs interlaced with vines whose leaves are almost smooth, and with morning glory vines with reddish flowers, and suddenly the waters reappear, scouring out a charming little pool around which hang clusters of vines with supple stems. There, beneath these shady vaults, the African maid displays her ebony charms and disports herself among the transparent waves.

The surface of the still waters are covered with double flowered water lilies, white as snow, exhaling a fragrance like that of orange flowers. Along the edge of the water and in damp spots grow a number of mints, especially the one that we cultivate in the garden under the name peppermint.

I have found near marshy areas on sites where the land begins to rise a plant of a truly remarkable form. Its leaves, all basal, are grooved. From the center arises a stalk, rounded and smooth, to a height of about two feet which broadens slightly at its tip, which is hollowed out into the form of an elongated, conical vase, somewhat resembling a goblet, but narrow and long. Its entrance is about an inch and a half in width and the color of the stalk grades imperceptibly into white from bottom to top. The edge is wavy; it is capped by a wide strap-like structure with a ruffled surface which covers the opening without, however, closing it tightly. Rain water, however, cannot get in. This umbrella is thus of the same form as the crest on a helmet as seen on coats of arms. This flower and its umbrella, colored white with veins of red, shows no vestige of any reproductive parts, stamens, pistils or ovaries.

It is odoriferous, its fragrance resembling that of honey. When one pushes a finger inside the side is soft to the touch, but in pulling it back one feels the projections which point backward and are sawtoothed. These resist the withdrawal. Insects, attracted by the bright colors of this flower, alight upon this stalk and then, attracted by the sweet odor, push their way down into the vase to reach the honey as in other flowers. Death awaits them. These points, arranged to point downward, prevent the insects from climbing out. Others are attracted to perish in their turn. The corpses are packed in a heap of prodigious numbers. When the vase is so full that it can no longer retain the insects that it attracts, it withers and dies in its turn. This plant is not found in the swamps themselves where the insects swarm in the air and waters and which is their true home, but on the edges of the swamps in drier places where nature has produced other creatures whom she would defend against their voracity. She, therefore, contrives these traps in order to destroy the insects. Would it be true that an order so admirable, which functions to preserve each species and to limit it to its proper place, could be the result of blind chance? If it is true, I want nothing to do with this odious truth. You would stop up the source of my dearest pleasure, that of observing nature.

CHAPTER XXXII

Departure from Pensacola. The Trip through the lakes. Dauphin Island, the first settlement of the French. Motives for choosing this Island. Its present condition. Observations on the lakes and the surrounding terrain. Manufactures. Description of the production of pitch and tar.

The continuing contrariness of the winds had prolonged our stay at Pensacola for more than a month. The many dangers that we would encounter by attempting the Mississippi had decided us to go to New Orleans by way of the lakes, a more direct and safer route, but to send our effects on by ship by the river route. But the winds, which were blowing from the northwest, prevented the sea from entering the lakes and left the water too shallow for navigation so that the Pensacola schooners were stuck in New Orleans and could not return until about the middle of September. We left at the earliest opportunity. The fare is ordinarily five or six piastres, but one must pay for his food in addition.

We ran along the coast after having left Pensacola harbor until we reached Mobile Bay which we entered and then turned through the channel which separates Dauphin Island from the mainland. Dauphin Island is six or seven leagues in length, but at its widest point only about one league in width. It is sandy, but more wooded than Santa Rosa Islands. There is a good growth of pines there. This island should be celebrated in the annals of the colony as the place of first settlement by the French. Its port at that time was a port of call for merchant ships and ships of war, and a town of considerable size began to grow on the island. However, a hurricane piled so much sand in the harbor that it was afterwards unable to hold any except the smallest ships so that this settlement was abandoned and the colony was transported to the fertile banks of the Mississippi. Raynal has asked why this miserable little island shuold have been preferred by the French to so many other sites in this immense colony, so much more productive and spacious. Those who founded the colony were Canadians, simple individuals who had neither the vision nor the means of a wise and vigilant government to foresee the needs of a distant future. Those Canadians, accustomed to wandering in the woods, to living principally by hunting and fishing, and to following bands of nomadic savages in order to obtain furs by trading, paid little attention to the advantages of agriculture. The court of France, occupied with intrigues, religious quarrels and fashion, surrounded by public misery and the center of vain pomp in its splendid palaces, had neither the insight nor the will nor the power to found a colony which would stimulate the growth of its population, its agriculture, its commerce, or its shipping. The Canadians, therefore, abandoned to themselves, concerned themselves solely with a place most favorable to the fur trade and easiest to defend and least expensive to establish. They found these *desiderata* in Dauphin Island. Small, but with an adequate harbor, it did not require a great deal of fortification, or large numbers of troops to hold it against the Indians. Surrounded entirely by the sea it was not watered by sizeable rivers, as would be comparable site on the mainland, and hence would not be subject to floods. There was thus no necessity for building and maintaining a system of dikes and embankments. The land being flat, sandy, and thinly wooded, did not require a great deal of labor in clearing it for settlement. The neighboring seas, lakes, and rivers are incredibly productive of fish and shellfish.

The Mobile River, at the head of the bay, can be ascended to the north up to the Appalachian Mountains establishing communication with the Indians, spread out between these mountains and West Florida, itself watered by rivers paralleling the Mobile. Across this great region were found numerous Indian nations, the Chocktaws, Alabamas, Chickasaws, Pascagoulas, Biloxis, Talabughas, and Mobile. These nations bordering the Mobile River drainage, must have become famous and powerful many centuries ago for each of them spoke its own language, very different from the others. They had adopted as a common language, Mobilian, which, much after the manner of Latin in Europe, had become their public and political language.

Since Dauphin Island is adjacent to Lakes Pontchartrain and Maurepas, communication with the Mississippi River is easy and therefore communication with many other Indian nations from Mexico and Canada and up to the unknown regions of the northwest was possible. This area embraced many different climates and offered opportunity for trade in furs, both abundant and various. One other consideration rendered the establishment of the colony at Dauphin Island important to the French; that is, its strategic position. Dominating as it does Mobile Bay and its river, it could be a base for spreading colonies along the river to form a barrier against penetration from the English colonies, the Carolinas and Georgia, which have. in fact, in succeeding periods, proved so harmful to the interests of France and Spain. [*The real reason for the earliest settlement being at Dauphin Island is probably more prosaic. The difficulty in former times of making a given landfall on an uncharted and featureless coast like that of the north Gulf, is difficult for the modern traveler to appreciate. We have only to recall that LaSalle, for instance, could not find the mouth of the Mississippi from the Gulf even when he knew what he was looking for. Until the coast was explored it was absolutely necessary that the settlements be as close to the coast as possible or there was a very real danger that they might not be found again.—Tr. note.*]

The French, therefore, in the light of their purposes and means, had good reason for the establishment of the colony at Dauphin Island. Little by little, their colonies dispersed along the Mobile and Pascagoula Rivers, near the lakes and finally, the Mississippi. Left to themselves, the colonists required nothing to cause the expansion of agriculture and commerce, but protection from the Indians and other enemies. But an exclusive company became the manager of this naissant colony and changed everything. The company sent out, not only officers and soldiers, but large numbers of clerks, tax collectors and very few workers. The small settlement at Dauphin Island could not even find room for so many people, still less feed them all, for as usual the useless mouths consumed the most. It was, therefore, necessary to move the headquarters to the mainland. The site chosen was not far away, almost directly across from Dauphin Island at the place called Old Biloxi, and soon after another move was made to "New Biloxi" which was, however, equally disadvantageous as it was too far from the anchorage of the ships. The necessities of the colony had to be shipped all the way from France since there were so many consumers and so few producers. Famine soon removed a portion of these settlers.

What remains of the settlement of Dauphine Island founded less than a century ago? These remains are sought in vain on the island as one searches for the ruins of Babylon on the Euphrates. A few bricks, a few pieces of iron corroded by rust lead us to conjecture where the settlements must have been, and the present inhabitants know almost as little about the former settlements as do the present inhabitants of ancient Chaldea. They have even more quickly forgotten where their fathers, the founders of the colony, landed. On the island once lived families. Around their village were gardens and orchards, while their cattle wandered over the island. Today, a single person is the sole inhabitant. One man—and he is so poor that he must be a pilot on the lakes in order to live and that would not suffice if the King of Spain did not give him thirty to forty piastres a month. You who meditate upon the inconstancy of human affairs and on the fall of empires, go to Dauphin Island.

From Dauphin Island, where we had stopped for almost half a day, we ran along the north coast of Horn Island and Ship Island, which has quite a good anchorage [*Good enough that it was used as a base by Admiral Faragut's fleet attacking New Orleans in 1862.—Tr. note*], and then along the coast of Cat Island and Pea Island [*Pea Island was the name given to the land between the two Pearl Rivers now known as Honey Island—Tr. note*]. The soil of all of these islands is sand. Finally, we entered the Rigolets, the multiple channel whose passage requires an experienced pilot. Among these channels are many flat, drowned islands, composed of trembling soil and covered by high marsh grasses. The soil upon which the vegetation stands is composed of sea sands and lake deposits. The air is filled with swarms of insects. Woe to those travellers who are becalmed in these tortuous channels! They would be devoured without the help of a mosquito net.

The navigation of the lakes requires the highest skill on account of the very low water to be found at various points. I was assured that these lakes are filling up little by little and I can well believe it. They are traversed by an arm of the Mississippi, called the Iberville River. [*This name refers to the lower course of the Amite River which empties into Lake Maurepas, together with Bayou Manchac which approaches the Mississippi just south of Baton Rouge.—Tr. note*]. When the river is in flood its muddy waters deposit a sediment in these lakes which must appreciably raise their bottoms. While at the same time, the sea, pushed in the opposite direction by wind and tide, deposits sand which mingles with the mud to hasten the filling process. [*This mechanism is a physical impossibility. The periodic floods would scour out the channels. The velocity of water determines its capacity to carry sediment.—Tr. note*]. Everywhere the bottoms of the lakes tends to fill up, to form swamps and finally, dry land, if man (out of shortsightedness) does not disturb the work of nature. The water of torrents, streams, and brooks rushing swiftly in flood time, slow down upon entering the widened basins of lakes and leaves them flowing quietly, purified of foreign matter.

Thus, while Lake Pontchartrain receives, with the arms of the Mississippi noted above, several streams, its waters are passably clear, but as soon as we had left there to enter Bayou St. John we found the water brownish and thick with sediment. [*Lake Pontchartrain, being shallow, the water contains a good deal of sediment when the water is rough. Bayou St. John, on the other hand, being protected from the wind and having little current is, in reality, quite clear. Its brownish color, of course, is due to decaying vegetation.—Tr. note*].

We noted at long intervals along the lakeshore, houses, which seemed to be well built. The soil is almost entirely sand, but in spite of that, some individuals have become rich from the raising of cattle and lumber which they sell in New Orleans. The lime that is made here of the shells picked up on the shores is of superior quality and whiter than that of France. The most lucrative industry of the region, however, is the manufacture of pitch, which requires fewer men than would agriculture. Four men are sufficient to produce an annual revenue of three or four thousand *gourdes.*

The pines from which it is extracted should be cut down a long time before use and in this area, the driftwood brought in by the floods and current is eminently suitable. The older the log, the better. The logs are sawed into lengths of about two feet which are split into small pieces. A square basin is dug in the ground from four to six feet long and about five or six inches deep. Nearby are dug several pits several feet deep, each communicating with the basin by a drain. Across the basin are placed four or five bars of iron and on these are placed, crosswise, the sticks of wood, leaving intervals between them. The wood is piled up into a pyramid. Finally, the top of the pyramid is set on fire. As the wood burns down the pitch liquefies and runs into the basin and from there into the pits.

To make the raw pitch into tar, iron balls are heated red hot and thrown into the collected pitch, which bursts into flames with a loud explosion and throws off a thick smoke. When the pitch is judged to be concentrated enough, the pits are covered with a screen which is then covered with turf. The fire is smothered, the tar then cools and hardens. It is then cut out with an ax.

CHAPTER XXXIII

Arrival at New Orleans. Description of the City. The Causes of its unhealthfulness.

The entrance of Bayou St. John is guarded by a fort. The defense is not difficult, for the bayou is narrow and the bar at its mouth is so high that there is hardly three feet of water over it. The bayou has no current beyond that given it by the lake, that is, when the lake rises because of winds or tides, the bayou fills to point of overflowing and it lowers when the lake does. The land through which it passes in its multiple windings is everywhere flooded by the water of the stream and lake; stagnant, or at best showing a current so slow as to be barely perceptible. Only here and there are places that are not flooded. These stagnant waters swarm with reptiles, especially alligators and are divided into so many channels that it is easy to lose one's way in them. They are shaded by tall trees which are, however, crowded and deformed and covered from their tops to the ends of their branches with a lugubrious covering of a plant parasite, a kind of greyish moss which hangs down in festoons up to seven feet long, which causes the branches to bend under their weight. This covering conceals most of the foliage and gives to these wild places a strange air of sadness. As one proceeds, however, the land gradually rises and soon is high enough to be inhabited. Here the land is cleared and one sees here and there the handsome houses of the country-side. They are of the most varied form. Some built of wood, surrounded by galleries in the Chinese fashion, others built of brick are surmounted by a gallery in the Italian manner. Several have colonades and there are among them some that would do credit to the suburbs of Paris. All of them have a garden in front. Avenues of magnificent orange trees can be seen, especially those which bear a sour fruit which rejuvenates itself.*

Bayou St. John can only be navigated to within a league of New Orleans, where the bayou loses itself in a cypress swamp. It is true that a canal has been dug from this point to the city, but it is already so choked with mud that it can only be used by small pirogues [*It was eight years old at this writing.—Tr. Note.*] This

---

*These sour oranges have this peculiarity; the fruit is retained on the tree all winter, during which they become flabby, losing some of their juice and acidity. When spring comes they fill out again, regaining their shape and acid juice.

canal also serves to drain the streets of New Orleans into Bayou St. John. Here at New Orleans and for a distance extending 100 leagues along the river, the drainage is in the opposite direction from what we see in Europe. Our streams receive from their tributaries the water running off of the land, whereas here the water runs from the river, whose banks are higher than the surrounding land, back into the swamps. I will explain this reversal of the usual order of things later.

We arrived at New Orleans on the fourth day. During our stay at Pensacola drought was continuous except for two or three brief showers, but we found the streets of New Orleans soaked. It had rained every day for three months. The inhabitants complained they had had two of the wettest moons that they had ever seen, whereas I had seen people at Pensacola anxiously awaiting each new phase of the moon in the hopes that it would bring rain. Those who know so much about the influences of the moon should really explain to us how it is that the moon can emit rays which cause clouds to gather and torrents of rain to occur, while not far away the clouds are dispersed and drought prevails.

The streets of New Orleans were, in some places, impassable even to carriages. There were chasms where carriages would be broken to pieces if they attempted it. The pedestrians could take refuge on the sidewalks or *banquettes*, built along the houses. These sidewalks presented difficulties themselves. They end at each block in large planks which stretch across to the street. In many places they are broken and covered with mud, so that one must be an expert in the art of equilibrium in order to follow these pieces of wood without slipping, inclining as they are to one side or the other, depending upon how the soil under them has sunk.

Along the sidewalks ditches have been dug to carry the water from the river to Bayou St. John, but the ditches themselves being caved in or filled in and their common entrance into the bayou being in equally poor repair, several of the streets were converted into swamps, which necessitated long detours in order to reach one's destination. This is no small matter for the stranger, because if he asks after an address in such and such a street, no one, or almost no one can tell him where it is, not even those who live there. The townspeople designate streets, like neighborhoods, by the name of some prominent person who lives there. No one has thought of writing the names of the streets on each corner. They are only written in the archives of the town, but it must be admitted that even if there were signs only a very few could read them.

I expressed astonishment at finding so many difficulties in getting about in a city so populous and so visited. I was told that funds for alleviating the situation were in hand, but that the prospective change of government had caused the actual expenditure to be delayed. On the contrary, this situation should have stimulated the officials to do their duty. By ending their service with these acts of public usefulness, they would have left honorable memories, not only for the citizens, but for themselves. Everyone thus suffered from the uncertainty of what would be the effects of the new order, and hardly dared to make the simplest assumptions. However, the city every day acquired new population, European Frenchmen, fugitives from San Domingo and Anglo-Americans. Housing was becoming scarcer and scarcer. A small cottage in an isolated neighborhood, rented for ten to twenty piastres a month and a shop or store, advantageously placed rented for from 25 to 80 piastres.

The enormous income from houses has encouraged the building of new ones, but it will take a great deal of building to get rid of the miserable hovels that make up most of the city which mar the effect produced by the quite beautiful houses that are being erected here and there. Those along the river, which fetch a very high rent, already make an attractive sight. They are of brick, in the Italian style, coated with that excellent lime made from shells, whiter than plaster and binding almost as well. Most of the houses are raised on blocks, since it would not be possible to dig foundations as water is encountered less than a foot below the surface and is often on the surface. When the river is high, which it is especially from March to the middle of August, the water is actually above the level of the soil itself. It is contained by a dike, otherwise the city would be flooded and might be washed away. This dike prevents flooding, but it does not prevent the water from filtering through the ground and rendering the soil so soft that it cannot support buildings of any size without pilings and it is necessary to dig ditches to drain the soil in gardens and courtyards.

Already houses several stories high are to be seen in the city and when all the streets are lined with these, one must expect that maladies like yellow fever will take a great toll. This low soil is bordered on the river side by the embankment, and on the opposite side, by the swamp, the nearby portion of which is cleared, but further away a curtain of tall cypress trees blocks the horizon. Thus, from two sides the circulation of air is restricted and a stay in this city must become more and more dangerous by the day. One should not be surprised at the diversity of the accounts of travellers on the healthfulness of colonial towns and particularly of New Orleans; accounts that ignorant persons have not been slow to call lies. This is apparently easier for them than to reflect that the difference may be due to differences in the time that the observations were made. When New Orleans was first laid out its little wooden houses were well spaced and did not confine the air or reflect the sun's rays as the present large, closely-built edifices coated with lime must do. The swamps, in the midst of which the young town was built, shaded the city with its trees and spread a coolness over it which purified the air. Thus, the present-day ravages of fever were unknown and one could boast of the healthfulness of the climate. [*Neither yellow fever nor malaria were native to Louisiana and they must have been imported at some time during the colonial period. If, among those accounts boasting of the salubrity of the Louisiana climate, one includes the propaganda of John Law's Mississippi Company, we must align ourselves with the opinions of the "ignorant persons" cited above. —Tr. note.*]

The river opposite New Orleans was about sixty to seventy fathoms deep. [*This is the French fathom, about 5 feet, instead of six, but even that would make a depth of 300-350 feet. The exaggeration is not really remarkable, if one recalls that a lead lowered in a deep, swift-running river like the Mississippi would be carried a considerable distance downstream before touching the bottom.—Tr. note.*] The bed of the river is such that boats may anchor so near shore that a wharf reaching out into the stream is unnecessary. Two longitudinally-built ones are sufficient. The great width of the river, about five hundred *toises* [*an old length measure of about six feet, i.e., 3,000 feet.—Tr. note.*] permits a great number of boats to anchor here. The mouth of the river is only about 30 leagues distant and is thus easy to reach. However, those 30 leagues that the river traverses to reach its mouth constitute really only a tongue of sand. Thrust out into the sea like a jetty, where the city is located at the heart of this tongue, the land is constricted so that it is only four leagues wide including the river. To the east, only two leagues away is Lake Pontchartrain which opens to the sea and communicates with Biloxi, Mobile, and Florida. On the other side of the river, equally close is Lake Barataria which communicates with the sea by the Bay of Ascension. [*Or as we would say today, Lake Salvador communicating with Barataria Bay. Actually closer to New Orleans would be Lake Cataouatche.—Tr. note.*] Thus, in crossing this narrow neck of land one can go from Lake Pontchartrain to Lake Barataria in four or five hours ,whereas by sea the distance from one of these lakes to the other would be 80 leagues because one would have to go around the jetty formed by the river. This unique situation of having available several different routes to the sea heightens the advantage of the site of the city and the city thus profits by its commanding all of the far-off ramifications of the river.

The site of the city is only a narrow ridge along the river about a quarter of a league wide [*six-tenths of a mile.—Tr. note.*] Behind the city to the east lie swamps which merge into Lake Pontchartrain. To the west lies higher ground along the river, which here makes a bend.

The city was laid out in the month of August, 1718 by one, de Latour, Chief Engineer, on the orders of the Commandant General, M. de Bienville. Several Canadian families, who had come down from Illinois, had already established themselves there and had made some clearings. No doubt we owe to these families, who had familiarized themselves with the nearby lakes and forests, the knowledge of the advantages of the site. [*This account is almost entirely inaccurate. The suggestion that a post be established at this site was made at least as early as 1702. The city was not laid out until 1722 and then by Adrien de Pauger, not de Latour.—Tr. note*].

The site, flooded in its rear, would not admit of a plan that extended very far back from the river. The engineer limited the depth to 300 *toisses* [*1800 feet*], while he gave it a frontage along the river of 600. He divided this space into ten streets as straight as a string, ending at the river and five others running parallel to the river, cutting the first ten at right angles. This cut the city into 66 equal block or islands, eleven along the river and six deep, each containing fifty square toises [*1800 square feet*], to be occupied by 12 families. The streets were approximately sixty feet wide from which should be deducted eight or nine feet for sidewalks. That would be enough for pedestrians and carriages, but not for the circulation of air or for avenues of trees, so necessary for health. This plan has been followed from that day to this, and will probably be continued. A suburb along the river, above the city has been established and is growing on the same pattern. A levee was constructed along the river which still protects the city against floods and at the same time, ditches were dug around each block which run into larger common ditches, to carry off into the swamps the rain water and the water that filters through the soil from the river.

The inhabitants were then offered the opportunity of taking a lot, that is to say, one twelfth of a block with an obligation to erect a cabin, or at least to surround the lot with a palisade. One entire block was reserved for the Place-d'Armes, that one which is the center block of the eleven facing the river. This space of 50 toises squared [*300 feet squared, or 90,000 square feet*] today is lined on the site away from the river by the facade of the cathedral, flanked on either side by two other buildings. On its right is the Town Hall, built in quite good taste. The building on the other side is not yet finished. It is to house the Capuchins who will serve as *curés*. On either side of the *Place,* like two wings, are two long, straight buildings containing a large number of shops. The whole view of this place with the bustle of commerce forms an attractive scene, but it would be more so if trees were planted, all the more necessary since in this country the swamp enclosing the city from the rear means that there are no shady spots in which to walk except along the river and on the road along Bayou St. John. A remarkable fact is, that the cathedral, the two buildings beside it, and the two other buildings along the square were all built at the expense of one man, a Spaniard named Don Andreas Almonaster, recently deceased, who came to Louisiana a poor man. In addition to these, he had built the church of the hospital of the Ursuline nuns. These buildings cost a total of about two million francs. All of these titles to sainthood, however, did not indicate a reputation of sanctity. His legacy, even after this, was still the largest fortune in the colony.

When the center of the colony was at Dauphin Island and Biloxi, two boatloads of prostitutes arrived there who were married off so rapidly that the last one, like another Helen, almost caused a serious quarrel. It was necessary to draw lots to see who would be privileged to possess her. A third cargo of the same sort arrived to fertilize the infant city of New Orleans. It must have been as well received as the first two, for the girls were snapped up just as promptly. These girls, in fact, became good mothers who gave rise to numerous honest descendants. It is true then, that the human species does not nurture in its breast a tendency to evil. It is what surrounds man that corrupts his inclinations and leads him to evil. The way to correct men, then, is not to punish them severely, but to remove from them the necessity for crime.

The population of the city must be about ten or twelve thousand souls. It is composed of Frenchmen most of all, but also Spaniards, Anglo-Americans, several Bohemian families, Negroes, and mulattoes, some free, but most of them slaves. Almost everyone has a trade. In the New World there are as yet very few of those useless families that permit themselves the crime of doing nothing. The universal desire to acquire wealth insures that no profession is despised as long as it makes money. The baker, the tailor, the shoemaker, are prominent people. They are rich and are the equal of the most important people. But woe to the worthy man who is poor. In Louisiana one needs more courage than elsewhere to brave misfortune, but there also, hard work and good conduct are more likely to lead to success.

The highest profession is that of merchant, that is to say, one who buys cargoes of ships to sell wholesale or who receives them to sell on commission. Few of them are actually ship-owners or speculators in their own right. Rather, they are simply commission merchants or wholesalers, selling to retailers or distant farmers who buy their provision in bulk once a year, who pay with their cotton or other produce. The retail merchants of the city are given credit for three or four months, and mark up their goods about twenty-five percent. That is not excessive, considering the expenses of renting, the maintenance of their establishments, food and servants, and the fact that stock that does not sell for any reason is sold at public auction at a great loss. There are many who fail through not being able to sell. Peddlers who carry goods to the far-off localities in the interior of Louisiana make up a considerable proportion of the retail merchants. They take almost all payment in furs or agricultural produce and ordinarily get a year's credit in order to facilitate their business. Among the retailers, the wine shop keepers and food merchants make up a numerous group who, with proper conduct of their business, get rich very promptly. Those who particularly embrace these trades are Catalans, active, industrious, and frugal people, who may be compared to our Savoyards. So accustomed are the New Orleanians to seeing them in these professions that the wine shop keeper and grocer are grouped together under the generic name *marchand catalan*. Catalans arriving from their country in poverty will always receive help from their established compatriots and the aid will be repeated, provided that their difficulties are not the result of their own mismanagement. How desirable it would be for Spain to fill all of her colonies with these useful people! However, by an incredible injustice, they are very little regarded. They seem to be held to be on a level with Negroes.

The profession of baker is one of the most lucrative. Several people have made a considerable fortune out of it in a few years. This is not surprising. Kentucky and the other regions of the United States, which are drained by the Mississippi, send their flour to New Orleans. This flour is of diverse quality and therefore fetches various prices. Flour sells for from three piastres for a barrel weighing about 190 pounds up to ten or twelve piastres. Sometimes flour is so abundant in the city that it sells for a lower price than in its country of origin. A great deal of damaged or fermented flour is to be found. Navigation permits it to be transported only between the months of March and September. The bakers who have ready cash can thus provision themselves at a good price at certain times of the year. They can increase their profits by mixing poor quality flour with good. It is true that the Spanish government fixes the price of bread at one picayune (six sous) per one pound loaf, but when the price of flour rises, the weight of the loaf drops proportionately. The bakers know how to get around the government in this matter.

Many individuals practice themselves (or have practiced by their slaves) the trade of butcher. In no other country in the world do the inhabitants eat so much meat. The Louisianian deserves the title of "carnivore". Everywhere on the table one finds small pieces of bread and large pieces of meat. The children eat so much of it that a European would fear for their health, but they grow tall and vigorous and appear perfectly healthy. In France both the doctors and the servants agree that meat is deadly to children. The reason for this prodigality with meat is quite simple. It is the cheapest thing in the country, cheaper even than vegetables. It sells for only six sous a pound and in hard cash, only two or three. At the market one pays six sous, or a picayune, for three or four onions or turnips, about the size of an *écu*. It would cost three or four times as much for a plate of spinach and proportionately more for other greens. Vegetables are found only on the tables of the rich. Meat is the food of everyone.

Thus, there are many butchers all doing a good business. Business is so brisk at their stalls in the market that they are sold out by eight or nine o'clock in the morning. They hardly kill anything but cows here because their flesh is said to be tenderer than that of steers. They are fat in the summer and thin in the winter. Ordinarily the animals weigh from four to five hundred pounds and they sell in the city for about fifteen piastres. The seller grosses at least twice this on the meat. In addition, the tallow sells for twelve to fifteen sous a pound and the hide for a piastre and a half. The meat of pigs and calves sell for eight sous per pound. This calf is a young animal of two or three years. [*A two- or three-year-old cow would be full grown. The story that the butchers slaughtered only cows is absurd on the face of it. It would be uneconomical to do such a thing. The citizens of New Orleans may have thought they were eating cow's meat, but that is another story.—Tr. note.*]

CHAPTER XXXIV

More details on the commerce and industry of the City of New Orleans. Customs.

A French tailor is paid up to ten piastres for making a simple suit, and usually the customer furnishes the material which in itself adds to profit. I saw some of these who had made five or six thousand piastres in two or three years The competition of colored men practicing this trade does not noticeably cut down the profit of Europeans, who are assumed to be better acquainted with the fashions.

So many shoes and boots of poor quality have been imported from France and the United States that the citizens prefer to have them made locally, although the leather is bad from being insufficiently tanned. A pair of shoes cost two or three piastres and boots, twelve to fourteen. Good shoemakers who would acquire leather from Europe that had been well prepared, would make their fortunes in short order, and the trade is already a lucrative one. I have found one or two upholsterers here, but they can do nothing. The climate is not compatible with this type of furniture.

The carpentry of the colored people is always defective; in order to have a good job done, one must employ either European or American workers and the excessive price of labor has soon made the fortune of those who practice this trade. A fugitive from San Domingo who arrived in New Orleans without a sou has, in three or four years, already built a house worth thirty to forty thousand francs, without counting the capital of his establishment.

Cabinet work is only done here by the Anglo-Americans, whose work is inferior to that of France, especially Paris. However, the diversity of the hardwoods available in Louisiana could make this art extremely productive. A cherry wood *armoire* of old-fashioned design sells for from forty to 100 piastres (that is from 200 to 500 francs). People here are so ignorant of the goods they acquire, to say nothing of the luxury of fine arts, that a beautiful piece of marble is hardly held any more valuable than a common stone. They don't trouble themselves to make the distinction. The trade of carpenter in a country, where building is going on constantly, where the floors, sides, and roofs of buildings are all of wood, sometimes so held together with timbers that they can be moved forward or backward all in one piece; in such a place the trade of carpenter would have to be one of the best and it is, particularly for those who in addition have some knowledge of the mechanics of cotton mills, saw mills, or rice mills.

Iron work is limited to large-scale structures for houses, factories, and agricultural instruments which are excessively expensive. But no one is interested in locksmithing, cutlery, or hardware. So many cheap objects are obtained from Europe that a broken lock is cheaper to replace than to repair. It is thrown out. A European who has some ideas of economy and respect for artisanship observes with surprise, articles on the scrap heap that could be easily repaired and put back into service and the colonist must not only spend money, but must be continually without the service of some object for the lack of repair men. The European who despises the industrious hands employed in these minor repairs scarcely reflects on the very great economies he owes to them. A broken watch can cost more in a year in repairs than its original price. The repair of a clock costs more than the value of the clock, so that many people do without a watch; almost no one has a clock and the few watchmakers see their business stagnate.

Blacksmithing does not exist here. Horses are not shod, since there are no stones, neither pebbles nor hard sand, but only a soft and yielding soil. The wheels of ordinary carriages are not provided with iron tires. For the most part, transportation both of persons and goods is by water. However, the wheelwright's trade is still a necessary and lucrative one in the interior of the country where wheeled travel is difficult.

Bricklaying here consists of nothing more than throwing up walls of brick held together with mud and covered with chalk. Pharmacy could not fail to be a necessary enterprise in a country of *gourmands*, where people drink to excess, where the greatest fatigues are passed in the greatest idleness, where the women are active enough only to insure the obedience of their slaves, where the temperature is subject to sudden changes, and where ignorance prevents the citizens from finding in change of habits, in the choice of foods, and in the plants of the countryside, the easy means of maintaining and restoring health. When we Europeans must employ drugs from three or four thousands miles away for our cures, or salts and spirits from chemical laboratories, let us not blame the simple Louisianians for making quick fortunes for their apothecaries. The fortunes of the doctors are assured as a consequence. One does not occur without the other.

The Aesculapiuses of the New World have one great advantage over those of the Old. They are able to dispense with studies, degrees, or anything that smacks of science. Relieved of this paraphenalia, they are able to enter practice much sooner and to begin caring for the sick earlier in their careers. Leafing through books, studying, reflection, observing nature; all of this takes a good deal of time. A doctor from Paris, brought up in Paris and educated at the University of Paris and a scholar, had so neglected his practice that he almost starved and had to leave the city, while his unlearned colleagues, whom he would scarcely have wanted as assistants, filled their pockets everyday, made merry, and splahed mud [*This may be a reference to Dr. Paul Aillot, a French physician, who was arrested in March of 1803 and deported, for practicing medicine without a license, at the instigation of the influential physician, Montaigu. See his letters in "Louisiana Under Spain, France, and the United States." James A. Robertson, Arthur H. Clark Co., Cleveland, Ohio, 1911. Volume I.—Tr. note.*] on him as they passed in their carriages, making fun of him. These doctors are so convinced of the uselessness of books that all of their books together would not make a good enough one for an apprentice. M. Lebeau, a doctor of great merit, to whom the Cabinet of Natural History in Paris is indebted for some interesting animal and bird specimens, acquired such a great reputation in Louisiana, that now, fifteen or twenty years after his death, he is still spoken of. I do not know what could have caused this strange celebrity.

What was happening at the time I arrived shows the type of great speculation Paris offers for the colonies in the mysterious manipulations of the manufacturers of secret remedies, people whose zeal for the public welfare is such that they need no encouragement from the government. An immense shipment of one of those secret remedies called the "Universal Regenerator" arrived with four large pages of printed matter explaining all of its regenerative virtues on the blood, the humors, the nerves, against all viruses, removing all blockages, soothing, stimulating, making fat people thin, and thin people fat, etc., etc. The name *Regenerator* in a country where so many kinds of regenerations are needed, no doubt, insured its success. People no sooner had tasted it than they proclaimed a miracle. Everyone wanted to be regenerated by this mixture of sublimate and muriatic acid. What even the most unabashed libertine would not have done in Paris, here was done by the ladies, who queued up openly in the streets to buy the Regenerator. [*The sublimate referred to is mercuric chloride, and indicates that the "regenerator" was basically a remedy for syphilis. Hence the reference to libertines.—Tr. note.*]

The large shipment was soon exhausted, and it would have been a long wait for the next shipment from France. The apothecaries then, also zealous for the public good, made up a batch locally that no one could tell from the original. But one of their number, who was not sharing in the profits, denounced the counterfeiters publicly. The customers found suddenly that the taste was not the same and recalled accidents which had been occurring frequently, all of which they laid to the account of the false elixir.

The vogue for this remedy, although it has diminished greatly, has lasted for three or four years and will continue until some new nostrum with a title equally as pompous and promises equally as dazzling, arrives to push it entirely into oblivion.

The Louisianians hold the "Generator" in such esteem that they concluded that he must be a personage of consequence in France, loaded with honors and rewards and venerated by the public. They did not believe me when I told them I never heard of him, although I would not guarantee that his name was not often in my pocket among the many handbills that the advertisers hand out *gratis* on every bridge, quay, and sidewalk with such a celerity to every passerby who doesn't look too poor . The first test I ever saw of the Regenerator was during the passage from Martinique. A passenger named Mermet used it for seasickness, according to the label. As a consequence he was sicker than anyone else on the ship and sicker than he had ever been before.

CHAPTER XXXV

Nature of the goods imported into Louisiana. Observations on that subject.

In describing the different branches of commerce in the city I will take up first the import of commestibles and first, wine. Wines of different types are brought in, principally those of Madeira, Malaga and especially those of Bordeaux and the coasts.

The English drink the Madeira and the Spaniards the Malaga, but the French, being the most numerous, insure that the greatest consumption is of French wines. Besides, the Spaniards have adopted our ways and also taken up drinking them and their greater abundance is more conducive to habitual use. It is hardly possible to ascertain the wholesale price of wine because it is so variable, but the consumption of French wines is so great that their abundance never lowers the price for long. One can always make a reasonable profit out of wine. Brandy sells only fairly well, for tafia [*low grade rum.—Tr. note.*] and rum replace it. If the price of brandy were lower, the people would become accustomed to it and would prefer it, but as it is, brandy is too expensive. I believe this observation to be of great importance to the interests of France. [*It is difficult to see why the tastes in strong drink of a backward colonial community should be of especial importance to France, but perhaps Robin was thinking of the popularization of brandy in the New World generally. Doubtless he would be gratified by the flossy advertisements of today for the various cognacs in the* NEW YORKER MAGAZINE.*—Tr. note.*]

Olive oil is also consumed in large quantity in the colony. The English-speaking peoples do not use it, even for salad, but in compensation the French and Spanish greatly prize it. Olive oil is imported from France, ordinarily in baskets containing twelve bottles. These bottles are small, containing only two-thirds as much as the bottles in Paris. The baskets sell presently for seven to ten piastres and the bottles retail for a piastre or a piastre and a half. One can see how enormous is the profit on this item.

Already one can see that Frenchmen, transplanted even to colonies not under the French government, by their own customs and by introducing their customs to others, favor the exports of

---

*In the colonies all wines not from Bordeaux, but from other coastal districts, are lumped as "wines of the coasts."

France. I have repeatedly observed this to be so, but this fact is little noticed by traders and economic statisticians.

After oil come other luxury items of which there is a prodigious consumption. Vinegar, liqueurs, sausages, anchovies, pickles, fruit preserved in brandy (peaches, apricots, plums), and dried fruits, figs, almonds, raisins, and especially prunes. Cheeses are also imported, but the heat usually spoils them, and this fact prevents any great increase in this trade. Vermicelli and the other pastas also enjoy a large sale. The consumption of this type of goods is not limited to the city. They are sent to the most distant settlements, crossing hundreds of leagues and vast wildernesses, to gratify sensuality.

The Louisianians, whose palates are continually coated with the grease of the meat which so abundantly fills their stomachs and who never, as we do, finish their meals with desserts of tart fruits to clean the mouth and restore to the nerve endings of taste their tone and sensitivity, require more than we do, restoratives of a hot, spirituous, or stimulating nature. I have often heard Europeans say that they did not find the meats of the country as tasty as those of Europe. This may be true in part, but the principal reason for thinking so is the monotony of the continual serving of meat which, even in Europe, would dull the nerves of the palate which we restore by the use of fruits.

Our fine porcelains do not sell well here; first, because the populace is so unknowledgeable that they are not distinguished from ordinary china, and, second, because the care of the tableware is given over to the Negroes, who are so clumsy and destructive that it does not last long and must be highly expendable. The tableware is a nice English earthenware, so cheap that the French product cannot compete with it. With lowered prices and increased quantity the chinaware industry could become one of our most important branches of trade. The consumption of china throughout Louisiana is enormous. No one, not even the poorest, uses simple pottery, not even our sturdy and solid Rouen ware.

Cooking utensils in Louisiana consist entirely of cauldrons of small or large size among rich and poor alike, and from my observation it is a waste of money to equip them with handles, since Negroes do all the cooking and they never use them.

The preference in clothing and household items is no longer for French manufacture, and I must admit that this is less the fault of the Louisianians than the European French, for the Louisianians retain their loyalty to the mother country; I have seen proof of this everywhere. The women dress in calico, muslin or, occasionally, silk. Our calicoes, especially the beautiful product of Jouy, are superior to the English product in beauty of design and the quality of the weaving, but in spite of this they cannot compete with the English calicoes here. They are too expensive. A defect of all of our manufactured goods. The English calicoes are thin and light, which gives them a decisive advantage in this climate. These light cloths, which are woven by machine, do not last. The colors are not fast, often fading with the first washing, but the cloth only costs from 36 sous to 5 francs an ell at retail, in widths of from two-thirds to one ell. They are thus so cheap that the Louisiana ladies can wear them until they are worn out without washing them at all and without mending them. With little trouble or expense the ladies can have the pleasure of always having new clothes and never wearing soiled clothing. They thus frequently change the color and design of their dresses, and we must remember that Louisianians are French. The inexpensive English material feeds this avid taste for novelties. Every two weeks, or at least every month, bales of it arrive by way of Phila-delphia or New York. The ladies crowd to the sale and fashions that are three or four months old are to be found adorning the ladies of the colony. Muslins also are quite inexpensive. A dress of the French type, called in this country *romaine,* costs from twelve to twenty-five francs, either plain or embroidered. These, too, do not wear well. They are also made by machine. The thread is weak, that is to say, not enough cotton is used, and it is not spun as much as is hand-made thread. Dresses worn a few times or washed only once become loose and flacid and tear almost at the touch. The tears are concealed rather than sewn up, and soon the dress is discarded or given to the Negro slave.

Silks are hardly ever worn except to balls or performances, and I presume that calico and muslin will continue to predominate be-cause of the heat of the climate.

Footwear is not a particularly brisk item of trade. A great number of the ladies go barefoot around the house for a part of the year on their wooden floors; especially in the country.

The English are sending their knitted goods, and Boston has already begun shipping cheap shoes, which are inferior to ours.

Hats are even less important. The ladies here have the desir-able custom of always going bareheaded in the summertime. They wear bandanas made of English cloth. These are constantly changed, and they appear in new colors, shades, and stripes. These bandanas retail for about four or five *livres*. Jewelry is simple, consisting only of necklaces, earrings and rings, these last actually without stones. I repeat, I do not believe that there is a worse commerce to encourage with the colonies (especially Louisiana) than that of the export of jewelry. These objects are seldom worn, they do not wear out, and people are not in a hurry to replace them if they are lost. The goldsmiths can manufacture jewelry on the spot, according to local taste. They can, moreover, put in as much alloy as they please, since the colonists pay little attention to this, and the local goldsmiths work mostly in melted-down *quadruples* [*Spanish coins — the double pistole.—Tr. note.*] For all of these reasons jewelry exports to the colonies would not be profitable, besides which, this miserable industry, so much vaunted, is not worthy of the resources of a nation like France.

CHAPTER XXXVI

Contination of the same subject. Fashions. Observations on their influence on Commerce and customs.

Men's clothing shows very nearly the same disadvantage of French goods as did women's and for the same reason, the expensiveness of manufacture. I arrived in Louisiana in the hottest season. I was not a little surprised to find men completely dressed, the neck covered with a high collar, arms lost in long sleeves so that even the hands were invisible, the chin buried in a triple cravat and legs sheathed in high boots, the facings of which were drawn out even higher. I was tempted to believe that a whirlwind had brought these men suddenly from the far north and deposited them on this stifling coast, buttoned up as they were with their red faces, their labored breathing and the sweat flooding the folds of their collars, a sight really painful to see. But when I was assured that these were the gentry of the country, voluntary slaves to our fashions which in this place formed a cult of imitation as painful as it was slavish, I said to myself, what explains this servile imitation even to the point of endangering health and well-being? Especially in an age whose impetuous character seems to indicate so little restraint? Ignorance. False ideas of the good and the beautiful. This ignorance explains why men will accept, without examining, fashions from a country which they consider more enlightened, even if it means ignoring the obvious differences that climate should make.

If there existed, not in the colonies of course, but in some corner of Europe, a truly excellent education which would imbue young people with a sense of the dignity of man, which by means of the principles of fine arts explained how magnificent are the natural shapes which nature has given to our species, would these young people take up fashions which conceal the heavenly features of the face, which muffle the harmonious proportions of the body? If they wanted new fashions, would these people at least adopt those fashions, comfortable and healthy, which would accentuate the charms and beauties of nature? Out of respect for nature, would they not reject those fashions which make an ignominious travesty of nature or merely deform? Yes, fashions reflect the condition of the soul of a people more faithfully than people think. If a society is gentle, benign and full of well-being, its fashions will show pleasing variations. If a society is stained with vice, if it falls into debasement, its fashions will acquire a low and hideous character. In the same way that fashon becomes insignificant when society falls into the worst state of all, that of nudity, where there is neither virtue nor vice. I find that historians have not paid sufficient attention to this correspondence between fashion and the character of societies. They have thus missed one of the surest means of learning about them. In France today ladies' fashions have improved. Light, pleated materials gracefully cover the ladies' figures. They are no longer stiff and rigid in appearance and, if I am not mistaken, the ladies act more naturally and pleasantly in society.

More than one politician sees in our fashions a source of industry and riches from export to many nations. For myself, I see in our fashions the greatest obstacle to the perfection of our art, to domestic industry and foreign commerce.

Let us return to suiting. The material of which the men's clothes are made is English, not as good looking or as well made as ours, but of good quality and light, suited to the climate and above all infinitely cheaper. This material costs only three or four piastres per ell, at most five, while ours costs from ten to fourteen piastres. The sale of English material here is prodigious; one seldom sees a suit of French material made locally. French woolen goods, like cotton, stay on the shelves and are finally sold at a loss. There are some things of which perfection is not to be perfect, but to suit the largest number of people. This principle may not apply in exact science, but it is essential in the manufacture of objects in trade. In Louisiana, as in all colonies, people do not like to keep their clothes for a long time and they could not anyway, for the moths do so much damage to woolen goods that it would not be possible.

Nankeen is a material which is almost universally used for pants and suit coats. This again comes from England, but already the Americans have begun to import it themselves from the Orient. It is used a little by both sexes on farms in the interior.

Our hats maintain their predominance over those made in England or the United States, being better felted and thicker, although more expensive. Their durability makes them really less expensive in the long run, in spite of their higher initial cost. They are more resistant to rain and to the accidents of long trips. Our hats have only one defect. They are often heavy; a serious inconvenience in this climate where the heat can make a hat unbearable. It would be better to pay a little more for a lighter hat, that is to say, one with less sizing. Some individuals make hats locally, without style, to be sure, but light and so flexible that they can be stuffed in a pocket. They last through several years of continual wearing. They are not dyed and they cost 10 piastres.

Our linens must compete with the Irish linens. They [*The same ambiguity of pronoun is found in the original.—Tr. note.*] are superior in quality, but just as expensive. Because of the difference in price, almost everyone, from slave to master, has shirts of Irish linen. Our linens, however, are not as decisively rejected as some other objects mentioned above. Their high quality insures that they are sought for various household uses, such as bed linen and table service, but the high cost of these objects restricts the volume of the trade. We shall see how the Louisianians supplement imported linen by use of the unbleached grey product of flax for coats, shirts and pants.

A considerable article of trade in this country is woolen blankets. English blankets sell fairly well, but their wool, if beautiful, is sparse. The weaving is too thin and they are napped only on one side; on the other they are almost bare. Thus they are neither durable nor warm, and, although their prices are a quarter to a third lower than ours, ours are preferred. Our large and beautiful blankets of the first quality sell easily for from 18 to 20 piastres. One need not fear importing the best quality available. There is, however, a particular style of ornamentation, much in vogue in this country. That is, that the two ends of the blanket should be bordered by a band of blue, three or four inches wide. The small blankets, of high quality, are proportionately less well sought after. The common blankets which are used in trade with the Indians are worth more than those of the English, but ours could not compete with those imported from the north of Europe, from Danzig, Frankfort, Hamburg, and Holland, where the Americans and the English themselves seek them out. These blankets are well woven, better than ours, made of a less curly wool, but longer and better suited for resisting water. The retail prices range from 8 to 15 francs, those having the finest wool being the most expensive. The sale of the large bed blankets does not compare in amount to the sale of these. Every sailor, every traveler, has one to cover himself at night. Aside from this, all colonists, men, women and children, have these capes for wearing in the wintertime and the slaves as well.

This cape is made of a single blanket, large enough to approach an overcoat in form. It is not cut behind. At one end it is split so as to form sleeves and a collar or hood. At the bottom end is found the blue band of which I spoke earlier and the same band at the front end is used to make cuffs for the sleeves. The Negroes have a hood instead of a collar, like Chartreux or Trappist monks. This is the first comparison that occurs to a European who sees groups of Negroes working in the fields during the winter. The capes of the masters differ from those of the slaves in being more ample, in being of finer wool and in lacking the hood. This useful garment, which alone has withstood the tides of fashion, has been used in the colony since its inception. It is indeed extremely useful. It is warm without restricting activity: it does not restrict walking, moving, or working. In a country where, within a few hours a cold morning may suddenly succeed hot weather, where one can be sweating in a sheltered place, but shivering if exposed to the wind, a garment that can be put on and taken off without a lot of trouble is a necessity. You who are coming to New Orleans, if you intend to visit the interior, do not forget your cape.

Quite aside from this sizeable market for common blankets, these articles are useful in the Indian trade. If one reflects that every individual of all of the tribes within seven or eight hundred leagues who trades with Louisiana has at least one blanket, one will see how important is this trade, and it will grow in proportion to the increase in the numbers of the colonists and their slaves. It could grow to be counted in millions from the borders of Louisiana to Mexico, from the sea to the sources of the Missouri, or even to the Pacific Ocean. There exists, in addition, a multitude of Indian tribes who have never had dealings with Europeans, a large number of them armed only with arrows which would offer sizeable new markets for this trade.

Let genius invent what it will to satisfy vanity and luxury. These inventions will produce modest workshops where thousands of hands will be at work spinning and weaving these sturdy woolens, and the secret of diminishing the price of them so that no nation could compete in their production with France would produce for him riches more than the product of the mines of the universe. The secret is bound up with the numbers of herds which could be made to yield a higher crop of wool by fertilizing the fields.

A type of coarse cloth, dyed blue, known in this country as *Limbourg*, coming chiefly from Germany, is an item of trade almost as brisk as that of blankets. This cloth, five quarters wide, costs from 15 to 20 piastres for a bolt of sixteen ells. It is used for making shirts and pants for winter wear for the colored people, workers, and the poorer colonists in the countryside. This article has an immense sale among the Indians. These people use it to make mantles and skirts for the women, as well as *braguets* and *mitasses*. *Mitasses* are rather like leggings attached to the knee and lower part of the leg. The thighs are always naked. The *braguets*, or loin cloths, are made from one quarter of these cloths, passed between the thighs and tightened around the back like a girdle. The women's skirts are made from a piece of material about half an ell long reaching from the waist to the lower part of the thigh. The mantles, which consist of about an ell and a half of material, they use instead of blankets. The women, particularly, wear them. They decorate the edges as they do their skirts, with wide woolen ribbons of yellow or red, upon which they make a kind of mosaic out of white pearls, or braid them together, to make a very pretty effect. One can see how the market for these coarse goods will grow as the population of this part of the continent grows and as the commerce with the Indians grows.

A little of this is manufactured in Canada, but if the European nations have the good sense not to increase their prices too much, they will always have an advantage over the inhabitants of the New World because of the lower labor costs. And if a nation engages in manufacturing not only for domestic consumption, but for the export market as well, one can be assured that the nation which enriches itself by a favorable balance of trade with specie payments flowing in will see its manufacturing fall off, as these riches drive up the cost of raw materials and labor. For this reason, England is near her downfall, and after her will follow her imitators. [*A bit of wishful Napoleonic thinking.—Tr. note.*]

CHAPTER XXXVII

Continuation of the previous chapter. On commerce and in-
dustry. Guns. Powder. Locksmithing. Hardware. Agricul-
tural instruments and trade. Labor. The effects of its high
cost. Hospitality.

In this country hunting is more important than with us. The Indians live entirely on game, and the colonists in the countryside
also live on it for a part of the year. The guns, the only arms
which are employed for this purpose, should have a brisk sale, and,
in fact, they do, but it is so important to the hunter to have a good
weapon that price does not matter to him. Nowhere are badly
made guns so poorly received as here. They are not wanted at all.
The guns exported here should be carefully chosen as of the best
quality. Luxury ornaments are hardly considered and do not repay
the cost of their labor and material. The colonists pay only for
a good quality firearm. Double-barreled guns do not sell well. The
preferred gun has a single barrel of about six feet long, of a type
called London, no doubt because they are made there. Carbines
also sell well; the Indians hardly use anything else. They buy
them for the equivalent of thirty piastres (50 écus). The humidity and salt sea air are so corrosive that they require especial attention be paid to the protection of guns during shipment from
Europe, in order to prevent rust. Even a good barrel can be so
corroded that it cannot be safely fired. Among the precautions to
take, one must rub them with grease and to plug the barrel and
the touchhole with tallow.

Powder must be of first quality in a country where everyone
hunts. It sells in the city at retail ordinarily for 1 piastre and
wholesale for five or six *escalins* per pound. However, already
some manufacturers in Kentucky can furnish it to hunters in bulk
for three *escalins* per pound. Once again, we note that if the price
is not kept low this branch of trade will also be lost to Europe.

Locksmithing and hardware are almost entirely English. This
trade, even including nails, is very slow. Louisiana has only a
moderate sale of these objects. If one leaves aside the city it is
rare to find panes in the windows even a few miles away. Often
the hinges and even the locks are of wood, and the house may not
have a single iron nail in it.

Agricultural instruments are few and simple. Light plows,
harrows, some tipped with iron, ordinary spades, flat wide picks

of medium size such as one might expect to be used in a land with no rocks which is not worked very deeply, both because it is fertile and because it is so wet. All of these except the picks and spades are made locally.

All of the tools of wheelwrighting, carpentry, woodworking and coopering are of English manufacture. It must be admitted that these are better shaped and better finished than ours. These advantages are so marked that even Frenchmen who arrive here soon adopt them. All tools brought from France are a dead loss. Indeed, I do not see why we do not adopt these English tools in France. The hand saw, made large something like the saw our gardeners use, is much less fatiguing to use than our saw with a frame and is less clumsy to use. I have often myself verified the usefulness of this saw.

The bits of the augers, cleaning out the hole as the work proceeds, makes the job of boring easier and more exact. The planes and instruments for millwork may be disassembled and reassembled with admirable facility, so that the same instrument can be used for different operations, grooving, rabbetting, or making molding. One can import from Philadelphia a chest containing a complete set of carpenter's tools which ordinarily costs about 100 piastres.

The price of Negroes is higher in New Orleans than in any other colony. The fear caused by the insurrection in St. Domingo has made the importation of this merchandise extremely difficult, and there is so much land to cultivate that nobody has enough. They rent for more here than even at Martinique. A Negress rents here for 12 to 15 piastres a month, while at Martinique it would only be six to eight piastres. A large number of these Negresses sell calicoes, muslin handkerchiefs and the like in the streets and the neighboring countryside. Negroes rent for even more. Those that know trades and are good workers can earn up to twenty or thirty piastres a month for their masters.

A wild Negro, that is to say, one straight from Africa, will sell for five hundred piastres, while a creole Negro, who has some working skill, will bring from a thousand to fourteen hundred piastres. One can see what enormous sums are tied up in individuals that may be carried off by death at any instant and many people have indeed been ruined by these too-frequent accidents. The result of this high price of sale or rental of Negroes is that labor costs are very high in this country because they are almost the only workers. Only a very small number of whites do any work, and they only work long enough to make enough to buy slaves of their own to work for them.

The high cost of labor is reflected in the high price of vegetables in the markets, where fish, game, and meat are very cheap, these not being the product of much labor. Vegetables are so rare that sometimes they are lacking altogether. In the spring there are no first fruits, although the cold spells are so transient that with a few precautions one would hardly notice the winter. No one knows anything about seed beds, greenhouses or shelter, nor anything at all of the art of vegetable gardening. In the dry periods of summer there are no lettuces or other leafy vegetables, because no one waters or protects the young plants. Notwithstanding the fact that a person near the city can make six, seven, eight, nine, ten piastres a day from the sale of vegetables, not even these exorbitant prices have stimulated anyone to perfect this branch of agriculture.

I have examined several of the large vegetable gardens. They are shameful, not to the slaves who cultivate them; they don't know any better, but to their masters who hardly bother to oversee work outside of the fields. The expense of slave labor on the one hand prevents the introduction of new products, and, on the other, stunts the ingenuity and industry of the masters themselves.* The abundance of meat and fish does not prevent inns and boarding houses from being expensive for foreigners, for the reasons I have indicated. A room costing one piastre a day is mediocre. To get a passably good room, one must spend fifty to sixty piastres a month. Louisianians, whose tables are always loaded,

---

*I find proof of this assertion in the *Travels of M. Michaux to the West of the Alleghany Mountains*, for in speaking of the products and industries of the cities of America he compares conditions in regions which have no slaves to those in Charleston, which has about the same number as New Orleans. "The port of Charleston," says this traveler, "is constantly filled with little ships from Boston, Newport, New York, Philadelphia, and ports in between, which are loaded with grain, salted meat, potatoes, onions, carrots, beets, apples, pickles, corn and hay. Lumber is an important importation and *although all of these products are imported from three or four hundred leagues away, they are cheaper and of better quality than those produced locally.*

"In winter the markets of Charleston are provided with living fish that are caught in the waters off of the northern states, brought in, in boats which are provided with sea water tanks which are open to the sea. The boats which engage in this trade carry, on the return trip, rice and cotton, most of which is re-exported to Europe, produce *always being cheaper in the northern states than in the south.*"

welcome foreigners. Before the disasters of St. Domingo brought so many to the country, foreigners were welcomed daily in people's homes. Some still are welcomed because of their misfortunes. I myself have witnessed this welcome of unfortunate people in several houses.

These hospitable customs, which do honor to their humanity, especially characterize the French. No modern people carry this virtue so far. No people of antiquity practiced it so magnificently as the colonists of San Domingo. Inns were superfluous in all that large island for the colonists immediately took in all travelers and sent them, in their own carriages with their own servants and horses, from one dwelling to the next. One could thus visit hundreds of places in the island as though visiting friends. The splendor of San Domingo will astonish posterity, but the memory of its hospitality will always mix with our admiration, tender regrets for the past . The list of the sins of the unfortunate inhabitants was long, but one must say of them that, more than any other people known, they were hospitable.

CHAPTER XXXVIII

Customs. Gambling. Necessity for spectacles. Religion. Laws.

After the affairs of the day the businessmen of New Orleans go to gambling houses, where admission is all too easily accomplished. Well-established fortunes are thrown away, and those that are just beginning to be established are wiped out even more quickly. Here a ship captain loses more than he made on his voyage and sometimes embezzles the cargo with which he was entrusted; here a simple shop-keeper loses the remnant of the resources which have taken him across the sea; here another traveler, who had returned with his gains bought by long journeys, by so many dangers and fatigues, no longer has even the capital to begin again, and here the planter who came to the city to sell his harvest, on the proceeds of which he must buy provisions for his family and clothing for his unfortunate Negroes, must return without provisions or clothes unless the ruinous usurers come to his rescue (for this country abounds in Jews who are not Hebrews). But indeed, what is there to do in the evenings? Converse? About what? Louisianians are strangers alike to art and science or even to the most ordinary items of knowledge. Therefore they play, and play heavily, seeing that the course of business puts into their hands a great deal of money. They are disgusted by a game in which the stakes are too low.

The women have the usual feminine disposition. They are not motivated by the desire to please and while there are a reasonable number of flirts, they hardly have the flirtatious spirit. Imperious with their Negro servants and totally at the mercy of the whims of their children, they would do better to turn the latter over to the former in order to be less sedentary. The men, wearied by the monotony of the company of their wives, seek solace in the company of the Negresses and especially of the mulatto women. A great number form liaisons with these lascivious, coarse, and lavish women and are ruined, to be dismissed and replaced by others or end vilely, living with these women with swarms of children, who, condemned by original sin to abjection, become what they can.

Winter is the season of balls and they are very frequent. There are public balls, both for ladies of quality, which means the whites, and for the colored women. The men go to both. The stiffness and aridity of the great ladies make these balls extremely dull for those who do not gamble. The others show much more vivacity, but not the kind that everyone likes.

The Ladies' ball is a sanctuary which no women even suspected of mixed blood may enter. Not even the most pure conduct or most eminent virtue could wash away that stain in the eyes of these implacable dowagers. One of these, married, and known to be indulging in intrigues with various men, one day entered a ball and announced loudly, "There is mixed blood here!". The remark was picked up and was passed around the ball. There were noticed two quadroon girls, known both for the excellence of their education and the blamelessness of their conduct. They were warned and obliged to retire, hastily, from the company of a lewd woman whose company would really be a humiliation for them. These girls had two brothers who were officers in the merchant marine. Aboard ship these two could order twenty lashes for white sailors whom on land, they could not even look in the face.

The citizen of Geneva had no need of pageantry in his industrious town where the moderate return for his labor necessarily stretched out his working day, where religious and civil instruction imbued that education which perfects the family spirit from within, but the cities of the colonies, especially New Orleans, lacking establishments of public instruction, lacking that urbanity which gives rise to taste in arts, the culture of literature and good society, where the function of the priests is reduced to holding brief masses, where the ease of large profits tend to make assiduousness in manual labor unnecessary, where slavery debases the customs of the country, and where a continual stream of strangers, particularly sailors, introduces to the community every kind of vice; here pageantry would provide the means to escape the dangers of these idle evenings, and of the ruinous gambling societies, to make up for that instruction which is supplied neither in churches nor in private or public assemblages. By these spectacles morality, being represented in all its appealing aspects, would recall to the citizens the eternal laws of humanity, the duties of paternity, and filial submission. At least pageants would halt the progress of evil if they could not exterminate it, and would render the manners less coarse and dissolute and induce inward gentility and outwardly a toning down of the manifestations of misconduct.

The immense region of Louisiana has no more than a dozen priests, secular or ordained; and for this tiny number of ecclesiastics the Spanish Government has established a Bishop at New Orleans with a salary of fifteen thousand piastres, while the governor makes only six thousand and each parish priest only thirty a month, plus his fees and perquisites which amount to very little. The isolated and sparsely populated regions see a priest only accidentally, no more often than our rural communities in France see a bishop. In the absence of priests, he is baptised who wishes it, and according to his own ideas, and although the colony is under the Spanish government, people die without priests as elsewhere and they are hardly in evidence at all. As for marriages, they are performed by the chief officer of the district. Otherwise the intended spouses would lose in waiting too many days of love. When a priest does go through the countryside he regenerates with the water of baptism men who are already enfeebled by old age and he calls upon couples to be fruitful who have long ago lost the capacity of fructification. Religion in this colony is all a matter of form; of substance there is nothing left. By substance I mean those ideas that religion gives on divinity, on the nature of the soul, on the destination, on the duties of society and, especially on the art, not of extinguishing the volatile and admirable passions of man, but of directing them. These ideas are not to be found in the religion of this region and I doubt if the ministry here could expound them.

The colonists are quite satisfied with the Capuchins who perform the functions of parish priest in the city; they leave the conscience free. In no country in the world is tolerance so broad and in no country is it appealed to so much. Women, Negroes and officers of the governor's staff are almost the only people who go to church. Here one doesn't even have to know how to read to become a philosopher and scorn the popular prejudices. These Capuchins, who are now so tolerant must have once been less so, so powerful is the force of the clergy or rather so much is man inclined to that hard despotism that attempts clumsily to force its desire on others while truly what is required is much circumspect persuasion in order to peaceably achieve an end. One day the chief of the Capuchins notified the Governor of his receipt of an order to establish the Inquisition. This caused an uproar in the colony, which was almost all French. For answer to the order, the Governor deported the putative inquisitor to Spain, an unheard of thing under this government. This Capuchin has returned and taken up his pastoral functions, but has forgotten his projects for an inquisition, at least in public, even if he still nurses them in secret. [*This is the famous Père Antoine.—Tr. note.*].

When the *mores* are corrupted by so many things, when religion, or at any rate, its ministers, have compromised the fundamental principles of morality, which they reduced to jejune practices affecting neither the mind nor the heart, the only force remaining to direct the activity of men is law. But when laws themselves are given over to magistrates who, holding supreme authority, can alter or violate the laws they administer, then laws become instruments of oppression, whatever their wisdom and moderation. That is the situation in this country. No country has more laws and no laws show a greater concern with preventing abuses and protecting innocence, and in no country are the laws more vexatious and excessive. And this is so because the judge disdains to learn or consult the law. One day I had occasion to ask an *Alcalde* what his duties consisted of. My question embarrassed him and he asked me to return later. The baillif had notified an individual verbally that a judgment had been given in a certain matter, whereupon, he had me go to ascertain its contents. It had not yet been written in the court register, but existed only in the judge's head.

Corruption, that monster that feeds on the unfortunate, that springs up in decaying nations and hastens their destruction; corruption, that, according to Tertullian, did more damage to the Roman Empire than the barbarian armies, makes frightful ravages here in disregard of the law. This Don André of whom I spoke earlier [*Don Andreas Almonaster.—Tr. note.*] who, having arrived poor in this country, built churches and hospitals and left the richest fortune in the country, achieved his great wealth through the shadowy paths of corruption. It is true that in the outlying districts of the colony justice is summary. The local magistrates [COMMANDANTS.—*Tr. note*] most of whom can hardly sign their names, decide matters at the lowest level which can then be appealed to the only tribunal, in the city. This court was composed originally of several judges, but for some reason has been reduced to a single one called the *Auditeur*. He would have been better named the *Preneur* [taker]. If by chance this gentleman and the lawyers have left some plaintiffs the wherewithal to make a final appeal to Havana, the money they must squander to do it will likely finish them. The excess of evil is sometimes its remedy. Here justice has resulted from injustice, for the inhabitants have lost their taste for litigation and have adopted the habit of accepting the decisions of arbiters. I have often heard the colonists lament these depredations of justice and blame themselves for not having deputized some of their number to carry their complaints to the court at Madrid. They relied upon the benefits that the government has heaped upon them.

CHAPTER XXXIX

M. Laussat, Colonial Prefect takes possession of the colony. Provisional organization. Twenty days later the Prefect cedes the colony to the United States. The author present at this proceeding. Evidences of grief of the French and Spanish during the ceremony. Principal themes of the Prefect's remarks. Reflections on this subject. Celebrations that took place during the short possession by France. Proof of the attachment of the Louisianians to the Spanish Government.

M. Laussat, the *préfet*, was already at New Orleans when I arrived. The functions that this administrator were to have fulfilled were extremely important. He was to stimulate this vast country; to encourage the colonists in their various endeavors; to encourage the immigration of new colonists to hasten the clearing of the land and to enlarge the population; to stimulate commerce in the interests of both the mother country and the colony, and to eliminate the competition of the English, to build roads and bridges over the streams and bayous,* to clear these same streams of obstructions of mud and snags, to dig several canals (an easy matter in this flat, soft earth); to reserve forests for the future and for the needs of the state; to reestablish healthy conditions in the city and to preserve it in the countryside; to establish education in all its branches from the most elementary on up; to perfect the mapping of the region, to make important observations on the natural history of the region; to prospect for minerals and to study innumerable plants in order to enrich medicine, arts, and agriculture.

To accomplish so many objectives M. Laussat was embued not only with a zeal for glory and a desire to be useful; he was prepared for his job by administrative experience, acquired before the revolution, by his membership in various legislatures, by a taste for study and the habit of work, and he had brought with him the largest library ever seen in this country which he intended to be a public establishment for the use of his colleagues in the diverse branches of administration and instruction. Upon his arrival, he especially sought out those colonists whose plantations or places of

---

*Construction of bridges, so necessary for communication and so lacking everywhere, is here a simple matter. Tall trees are felled across the streams from one bank to the other and these are subsequently covered with smaller logs and a little dirt.

business, or whose journeyings were in distant regions of different climate, in order to solicit information about them. Convinced of the meagerness of information on that score, he was preparing to visit these regions himself when he learned that reasons of state had altered the destiny of Louisiana; that she was to be ceded to the United States and that the French Government had delegated him to oversee the transferral. M. Laussat could not but be moved by this unexpected development which demolished at one stroke all of his plans. I had heard him discourse on them with such enthusiasm! His stay in the colony now having been reduced to a short period, his duties now were reduced to leaving among the Louisianians memories to cherish of the French Government, showing itself among them.

On the 30th of November, 1803, in his capacity of Commissioner of the Government, he took possession of Louisiana from the Marquis de Casa Calvo and M. de Salcedo, Governor in the name of the King of Spain, and on the 20th of December following he ceded the colony to Messrs. Claiborne and Wilkinson, Commissioners of the United States. During this brief interval M. Laussat presented to the public in a series of brilliant receptions an affable wife provided with the grace of beauty, enhanced by vivacity and charm which is so often the elegant companion of French genius.

[*Daniel Clark, that advance agent of the American government in Louisiana, offers the following* VIGNETTE *of Loussat: "His naturally irritable temper was last night roused afresh, and his hatred of the Spanish authorities augmented tenfold, by a refusal of a dozen officers and her families to assist at a fete given by his lady. This being attributed to orders or hints from the Marquis de Casa Calvo, so transported Mme. Laussat, that she expressed herself before the whole company in terms of the greatest rage and indignation at the conduct of the Spanish officers, whom she called 'souls of filth,' and 'mean slaves' and this scene was carried to the highest pitch, to the amazement of all present."*—TERRITORIAL PAPERS OF THE UNITED STATES, *volume IX, "The Territory of Orleans, 1803-1812, p. 201-121. Clarence E. Carter, U. S. Government Printing Office.—Tr. note.*]

The Louisiana ladies for whom she was the model of taste appeared with a magnificence which was astonishing in such a colony. This magnificence could compare with that which could be offered by the principal towns of France. The Louisiana ladies are usually tall, and this height, with the whiteness of their complexions which was accentuated by their light-colored dresses adorned with flowers and rich embroidery, gave an unreal air to these festivities. The last of these especially astonished one by its magnificence. After a tea, a concert, and dances, at midnight we went down to a room where was laid a table for from sixty to eighty people in the middle of which stood a temple of good faith surrounded by columns capped by a dome under which was found the allegorical goddess of that attribute. But apart from this room, the brilliance of light beckoned from beneath an enormous balcony closed off from the outside by drapes, and here were forty or fifty tables provided with different dishes offering a choice to four or five hundred convivial souls who were seated in small groups.

These entertainments doubtless served to disseminate taste, finery, and pleasure in a fledgling colony whose actual needs are economy and work, but under the circumstances they served a useful function, that of renewing the bonds of attachment of the colonists, in making them cherish what is French and in impressing upon them the greatness of the mother country.

M. Laussat, to console the grieving Louisianians for their separation from the mother country, said in his proclamation: "Considerations of prudence and humanity, allied with considerations of policy even more weighty, worthy in a word of the genius who even at this moment sways the destinies of nations; these considerations have given a new direction to the beneficient intentions of France for Louisiana. France has ceded Louisiana to the United States of America. You, Louisianians, will thus become a living monument to that friendship between the two Republics which cannot but increase from day to day and which must strengthen so powerfully their common peace and common prosperity.

"You cannot fail to note Article 11 of the treaty. 'The inhabitants,' it says there, 'of the ceded territories will be incorporated into the union of the United States and admitted as soon as possible to the enjoyment of all the rights, advantages, and immunities of the citizens of the United States, in accordance with the principles of the Federal Constitution, and in the meantime they will be protected and guaranteed the enjoyment of their liberty, prosperity and in the exercise of the religions that they profess.'

"Thus Louisianians, you are raised at once from the status of colonials to that of metropolitan citizens with a constitution and a free government.

"By the nature of the Government of the United States and of the guarantees whose protection you receive immediately even the provisional regime under which you find yourself will be governed by popularly elected officials subject to your recall and censure, who will always need your esteem, your votes, and your affection.

"The time will soon arrive when you will be given your own permanent government, which, while it will incorporate those sacred principles laid down in the social compact of the Federal Union, will, at the same time, be adapted to your customs, your manners, your land, and your localities.

"But especially, you will be quick to appreciate the advantages of a justice with integrity, impartial and incorruptible, where the invariable forms and procedures and their publicity, where the carefully laid down limits to authority and the application of laws combined with the moral and national character of the judges and juries, will assure the safety and prosperity of the citizen.

". . . The Nile of America, this Mississippi, which washes, not deserts of burning sand, but extensive fertile plains, the most fortunately located in North America, will see thousands of ships filling the wharves of this new Alexandria.

"Among them, I hope, Louisianians, that you will always note with pleasure the French flag, and its appearance will, I hope, never fail to lift your hearts. That is our hope; I solemnly declare it here in the name of my country and its government.

"Bonaparte in stipulating in Article VII of the treaty that for twelve years Frenchmen will be allowed to trade in the colony under the same conditions as citizens of the United States without paying other duties, had as one of his principal ends that of giving to the former ties of the French of Louisiana with the French of France, opportunity and time to re-form, to grow stronger and to perpetuate themselves. A new correspondence of ideals would spring up between one continent and the other, all the more satisfying and durable because it would be based upon a reciprocity of sentiment, services, and common ideals. Your children, Louisianians, would become our children and our children would be yours.

"I have described this picture at some length as some consolation for this abandonment and to offer it in answer to the reproaches and regrets of you Louisianians, the product of the ineffaceable attachment that you feel for the country of your ancestry, reproaches natural under the circumstances and which the French Government hears with love and sympathy.

"The French Republic sees in this event, for the first time in modern history, an example of a colony voluntarily emancipated by the mother country, an example paralleled only in the golden ages of antiquity. May Louisianians and Frenchmen always call one another by the sweet name of 'Brother' no matter where on earth they may meet and may this title alone from now on describe the relationship between them in their eternal attachment and free dependency."

In the months to come I had too many occasions to observe how many violations soon occurred of the "rights, advantages and immunities" of the Louisianians in the enjoyment of the "liberties and properties that were especially reserved," and to see how the inhabitants were disappointed in the expectation of receiving "leaders, solicitous of their approbation, their votes, and their affections." I saw the application of that justice which was "impartial, incorruptible and with integrity" and I saw day by day the hope fading that the citizens would have a "constitution adapted to their manners and customs, etc."

On the morning of the cession I went up to the City Hall where the respective commissioners were to gather. During the preliminary formalities I walked with M. Laussat, the Prefect, on the broad gallery where we looked out on the town square. Our conversation was of the consequences of the transferral that was being completed. The Prefect was moved and so was I, but when, as was his duty, he proclaimed in a breaking voice that the French inhabitants of Louisiana were relieved of the bonds of loyalty to France and had become American citizens and that new bonds of citizenship now bound them to a new country, I was overcome by unexpected thoughts and emotions which had never come to my mind before this moment. What! I thought to myself, this country that I have so loved, in whose bosom I have always lived, to whom I owe everything that I value; which possesses all that I hold near and dear; this country whose name alone flatters my pride and awakens in me such noble sentiments; could it cease to be my country? Could I break the ties that unite it to me and all at once become indifferent, or perhaps even its enemy? Could I take up arms against it and cease to wish it well?

During these reflections I observed the French flag slowly lowered while at the same time the American flag was raised. Presently a French soldier stepped forward, took the flag, folded it and silently returned to the ranks. But the American flag jammed and for some time refused to rise in spite of the efforts to raise it, as though it were ashamed to occupy the place of the flag to whom it owed its own independence.

An uneasy silence reigned during this interval among the spectators who flooded the square and filled the galleries, balconies and windows and it was only when the flag was finally fully raised that suddenly piercing "huzzas" arose from a certain group of spectators who, at the same time, threw their hats into the air. These cries and this animation only high-lighted the lugubriousness of the silence and immobility of the rest of the crowd. These were the French and Spanish, all heavy-hearted, mingling their sighs and tears. However, what had not been done to alienate the colonists from the French administration and its representatives? How many absurd stories had I not heard on that subject and about the Prefect himself when he, withdrawn and isolated, could not and did not take part in the administration?

This transition from one government to another did not cause any difficulties or even a slowing down of the administrative machinery. It seemed even to speed up so that the new organization established by M. Laussat was wisely and promptly installed. After functioning only twenty days the government was turned over to the United States. M. Laussat, no longer exercising any authority, received in several tributes, unequivocal testimony to the affection of the Louisianians, for him and for the mother country.

At the same time the Louisianians paid tribute to the Spanish government for the favors and benefits of the Spanish king and promised to remember them always.

Here, among others, are the remarks of M. Leblanc, Commandant of the Post of the Atakapas, the most important post in the colony, a gentleman, be it noted, who had been disgraced by this same Spanish government for a matter that I shall speak of shortly.

"Louisianians, my fellow citizens, as Commander of the Post of Natchitoches, founded by my ancestor*, and afterwards commander of this post, I reappear today among you briefly, charged with this honorable function by the munificence of the French Government. I am flattered to be selected for this function which makes me the conveyor of sentiments of honor and gratitude to the best of princes. We are gathered here together to promise eternal remembrance of the unceasing paternal affection of His

---

*By the celebrated Saint Denis, who first opened the route to Mexico by land and had that foresight to establish commercial relations with these rich countries, knew how to retain the friendship of the Indians, and who was much mourned at his death.

Catholic Majesty, manifested by acts of beneficence for the general prosperity of our country and for the individual well-being of all of us. This gratitude will remain unalterable in our hearts under another suzerainity, even as we have retained the love of our country, under 33 years of Spanish rule and as we have never separated in our hearts these two sentiments let us repeat together *Vive la République Francaise; Vive la monarchie d'Espagne."*

CHAPTER XL

Natural History. Remarkable insects. Decree of the Prefect. Its consequences.

I call the attention here of my readers to some observations whose importance they will appreciate.

Among the major scourges which afflict humanity there is a species of insect, greedy and gaudy always choosing to attract the most conspicuous of prey to batten on. This insect continuously attends its prey and the better to devour it, lulls it, deceives its senses with false appearances, until, drained of all of its vitality the parasite abandons its prey worn out and overwhelmed by the ills it has been done.

These insects who, although greedy, are finicky in the choice of victims are indigenous to the Old World and thrive especially in populous places or rather find suitable victims there most easily.

The first explorers seem not to have encountered them in the New World, but today they are fully naturalized. I have observed traces of their existence in New Orleans itself. A singular feature of these creatures is their ability to take whatever form is required by the nature of their prey. All that Réamur has told us about the metamorphosis of caterpillars is nothing in comparison to these, for even more than they, these insects creep and are extremely flat. That is their salient characteristic. They have certain instincts, but it is certain that they have no soul.

Although naturalists maintain that all life must come from pre-existing life, these creatures are not so engendered, but are the product of decay.

Other insects are armed with teeth, saws, pincers or stings, but these have only one weapon, a tongue, which penetrates only through its thinness and flexibility. The tongue secretes a colorless fluid which soon produces stupor, fantastic illusions and eventually, gangrene. These insects are not found in cottages and humble dwellings, they are found only in palaces, castles and imposing mansions and it is always the master of these places who is their intended victim. Thus they are seen at New Orleans dear readers, and you know these obnoxious insects under the various names of flatterer, toady, and sychophant. Happy those who have escaped their wounds, for to be wounded is to already harbor the germs of gangrene. And if you have had no experience with them avoid them even to observe them. Being forewarned does not always remove the danger.

Before my arrival these creatures had already taken over the seat of government and shortly before had attacked the Spanish Governor Salcedo, an old gaffer, of whom they deprived the little sense he had left (without gaining much nourishment from that since this old fellow was so tight). But the appearance of a new victim, plump and healthy, upon whose table appeared good food and fine wines quickly made them drop the doddering old man who, disillusioned and ashamed, hastily departed the colony, incognito. The newcomer was the Marquis Casa-Calvo, General in the Army of His Catholic Majesty and Special Commissioner charged with ceding Louisiana and fixing its boundaries—and very rich into the bargain. M. le Marquis loved entertainment and so these insects managed to surround him solicitously, their buzzing announced his presence from afar. They followed him hunting, fishing, on his trips, on his walks, in his clubs, to public festivals and, I believe, in even more private places. These fickle insects, however, left him quickly enough when a new and more promising victim appeared. This was the Colonial Prefect. The abandoned Marquis quickly recovered. He could easily have warned the Prefect, but the venom of these insects has the dire property of inspiring a stong dislike of their victims for each other. The Marquis and the Prefect, therefore, felt an antipathy for each other without knowing why and everything they did was at cross purposes. The Prefect, trained as he was during the storms of the Revolution, and having seen these creatures under so many different forms, should have easily recognized them, but they traded upon his complacency, born of the idea that such creatures did not yet exist in these regions. We shall see what were the dire results.

Upon the arrival of the American Governor the scouts of the band immediately provided themselves with new uniforms and a new appearance and went out to gain a foothold with him, but they found him so dry and were so revolted by the vapors of grog and whiskey, that for the moment, at least, they suspended operations. Then seeing no further prey some of them took ship for the home country, returning to the putrefaction from which they sprang.

It was in this state of illusion and prejudice that the Prefect issued the following decree on the 3d of December, 1803. In doing so, animated as he was by sentiments of patriotism and hatred of crime, he took up the cause of the worst enemy of society, a rascal more fertile in criminal schemes and accused of more crimes than even the famous Desrues, and in doing so, called down anew suspicions on innocent and virtuous families, subjecting them anew to calumnies and humiliations and shames. He disseminated errors in the colony which fomented dissensions which on several occasions had the parties ready to cut each other's throats and to upset and destroy the largest business house in Louisiana. I was myself deceived. I regarded innocent persons with abhorrence, as though they had about them the foetid odor of crime and I only gradually perceived the truth, comparing accounts, disentangling the passions of the principals in the affair and finally obtaining original documents which had been hidden up to then.

PROCLAMATION

Placing at liberty M. Saint-Julien on condition that he will present himself to the authorities whenever they shall require it.

In the name of the French Republic, Laussat, Colonial Prefect, Commissioner of the French Government, after having deeply deliberated on the affair of M. Louis Saint-Julien, native of Bordeaux, inhabitant of the town of Carencro in the Atakapas district, an affair which was notorious in this country when we took possession of the colony in the French Republic;

In view of a continual stream of documents, official and unoffical, which relate directly or indirectly to his conduct which have the ring of truth, from Floreal (April) last to his transferral to the prisons of this city in the month Fructidor (August) following, which throw a light upon the subject which cannot be denied;

Considering that, in origin the only crime of Louis Saint-Julien was obviously having felt and communicated the joy of a Frenchman who always loved his country when the news that Louisiana would return to the suzerainity of the land of his fathers was confirmed and the news quickly followed that a French expedition would arrive, or at the publicity attending our proclamation on this subject and the preparations that went forward following it, on the part of the Spanish governor and ourselves;

Considering that the murderous attack then committed on his person and on that of his wife on the 28 Prairial (17th of June) at eight o'clock in the evening in his house, having left his wife wounded by a bullet in the breast of which she later died and he himself struck down, stretched out unconscious on the ground for several hours in front of his house (such is the unanimous finding of the preliminary hearing and of the succeeding dispositions); this event alone delayed the execution of the first order for his arrest and called forth another, based upon this horrible attack and which upon his recovery caused his incarceration and he has been strictly confined as if accused of the murder of his wife;

Considering that the scandalous discord and implacable hatreds which have raged in the Atakapas and Opelousas have profoundly infected and denatured the feelings of the inhabitants that, because certain inhabitants professed a strong attachment for France while others declared an intolerant and exclusive attachment for Spain, as if the two nations were not united in amity and alliance [*Good rhetoric, but poor logic. Spain was the enemy of France in 1791-92 and her ally in 1794, but Napoleon invaded Spain in 1807 and the alliance was never easy. Reinforcing nationalistic differences was the animosity between Republican and Monarchical ideals.—Tr. note*] that when an offence occurred to trouble public order, neither faction hestiated to attribute it to the other;

Considering that this circumstance must have resulted from this ferment of passions, manoeuvering and intrigues which could have easily deceived the authorities; that the evidence does not seem sufficient, that the appearances, presumptions and proceedings have turned public opinion and raised a universal clamor, it is time to repair this error without delay;

Considering, finally, that the origin of this affair lies in the attachment of the Sieur Saint Julien to France, his country and that this fact notoriously had the effect of rendering him suspect and was regarded as criminal although the least discreet of his words could, under the circumstances in which the colony found itself hardly have been called imprudent by even the most sensitive authority, that in consequence for the national honor, it falls to the French authority during its brief tenure of office in this region, to liberate the innocent in chains in the name of the French people and only to accompany the measure with such reservations as are necessary in this delicate situation to show the government's sagacity and circumspection;

It is therefore decreed that the Sieur Saint-Julien, presently imprisoned in the city jail, shall be set at liberty before the close of day.

He will, however, first give assurance that he will appear before the public authorities whenever and however often they shall require and to this end he shall post a bond of 400 piastres.

The municipal authorities are charged with the execution of this decree. It will be printed and publicly posted.

Issued at the City of New Orleans, the 11th Frimaire of the twelfth year of the French Republic and the 3rd of December, 1803.

The affair which lies behind this proclamation, one of the most tangled that I have ever seen, I shall reveal to the reader in the pages that follow in order to show to persons in power that they may come to grief from the influences that surround them and even from the impulses of generosity. I shall reveal it in order to draw from it new observations on the human heart and to show that only public-spiritedness guided by knowledge can enlist the enthusiasm of men for the good, the beautiful, and true virtue. I shall reveal it to make solemn amends to the respectable families that I have baselessly suspected and scarred and finally, I tell the story to attack as vigorously as I can, the audacious scoundrel who, since my return to France, again escaping punishment, continues to outrage the innocent and weave anew his devious plots.

CHAPTER XLI

The author prepares to travel in the interior of the colony.
Preliminary observations. The Canadians first discovered the
interior of the country and comprised the first settlers. Their
customs, their courage. Obligations that the mother country,
commerce and science owe to them. Indifference of the Gov-
ernment for the colony. The colony is deeded over to an indi-
vidual, then to a company. The strange reason why the Court
of France was interested in the colony. Grants established by
courtiers.

While these things were going on in New Orleans, I made frequent trips, not all around the environs of the city, for just behind the city were impenetrable swamps, but along the high
ground along the two sides of the river, which, as I have noted,
formed a strip of inhabitable land only half a league wide. The
clearing of the land around the buildings there permitted me
only a limited opportunity for observing nature. I had to go
much further from the city in order to find sites wider and more
elevated; more diversified and still covered with native vegetation. I therefore made the necessary arrangements for a trip to
the interior. I had observed as much as I could of what had appeared to be interesting of the commerce and manners of this city
which promises to be one day one of the largest cities of the world.
The time that I chose for my trip was doubly fortunate. It was
at the beginning of February, which is the time in those regions
when spring brings out the flowers and leaves [*Important for a
botanist—Tr. note*], and, although the colony had been ceded at
New Orleans, the transfer of government had not been effected
in the distant settlements. I should, therefore, find the Spanish
Government still in operation and could be a witness to the effects
of the changeover to the very different government of the United
States. Indeed, I did observe at several places during the three
years of my stay in the various regions of the country with what
astonishing rapidity this new nation expanded and forced these
people, whom it called fellow-citizens, to its views of this encroach-
ment. I shall faithfully relate the story together with observations
on the natural history of the region, but before doing so I want to
recapitulate the history of the colony up until it was ceded to Spain
and during the 33 years that it was under the Spanish government.

My readers will then be able to follow with greater interest the details of my observations.

The French Canadians had accustomed themselves in their bitter climate and long winters to traveling in the woods for long distances for hunting and fishing. These activities were a necessity for them, or rather a passion much more satisfying to their ardent characters than the regular and peaceful activities of agriculture. Their explorations stretched to the north to the rocky coasts of Labrador, the country of the Eskimos, and at the same time they explored the wild coasts of Hudson's Bay, where they extended their efforts to see if that bay communicated with the Pacific Ocean. To the northwest, still audacious, they went up the rivers in light bark canoes, surmounting rapids and discovering new lakes, crossing mountain chains and bringing astonishment and even horror among new Indian nations, different in their manners, origins and languages from those they had known before. The Canadians familiarized themselves with them and married their women. By these means they opened up new possibilities of commerce. But that propensity which always leads men to seek out southern regions led them to push southward in even larger numbers. [*This is quite untrue.—Tr. note.*] Near that great system of lakes with whose navigation they were so familiar, which feeds the Saint Lawrence River, they found a large number of streams whose course was to the south. Pushing down these they saw the plains around them spread out and reveal that they were rich in game, especially wild cattle [*Buffalo.—Tr. note.*]. These lands were fertile and the climate milder than those to the north. Thus they reached the *Meschassepi*, that general confluence of waters of which so many streams are tributaries, and they explored it to its mouth in the Gulf of Mexico. While they did use the route of the broad and winding Ohio, to which they gave the name of *Belle Riviére*, along whose banks, alternately bordered with hills and plains, they hunted; they especially used the route of the Illinois, which crosses more spacious prairies with less winding, and whose mouth is less distant from its origin. This route brought them more promptly to the Great River. Six leagues to the south of the mouth of the Illinois, the Missouri discharges its muddy waters into the Mississippi. This Missouri, which runs so far and along whose banks wander so many peoples, who descend to its confluence with the Mississippi, forms an immense outlet for trade. Thus a great number of Canadians settled on both banks from the mouth of the Illinois to several leagues below the Missouri, calling the country Illinois after the name of the powerful nation who lived there and allying themselves with these gentle, but brave, people. Soon they founded several mixed settlements. They also settled on the St. Francis River lower down on the same side, but a more important site was at the mouth of the Arkansas, 300 leagues below the Missouri. This river rises in the mountains of New Mexico not far from the capital at Santa Fe. [*This branch of the Arkansas is now called the Canadian River.—Tr. note.*] In its long course it crosses immense prairies and is swelled by several rivers, particularly by the White River. The river flows through country where buffalo and mountain sheep are abundant and along its banks beaver and otter, whose fur is so valued in the trade, are numerous.

Finally, lower down on the same side the Canadians reached the last tributary of the Great River, a tributary whose reddish waters caused it to be named the Red River, also joined by several other good-sized tributaries. This river system stretching to the west again offered them an avenue of communication with many more Indian tribes. [*Actually the Red River was blocked from about the neighborhood of Alexandria to that of Shreveport by a huge impaction of vegetation called the "Great Raft." This was not finally cleared away until Henry Shreve did it in 1836.—Tr. note.*] Several Canadians settled there and established commercial relations with the natives.

On the east bank these enterprising explorers did not establish themselves as firmly. The long Ohio River was a slower communication route and more difficult to navigate, although they had familiarized themselves with its course and with the regions that bordered it. They explored also, without settling there, the small streams which join the river on that side, but when they found Bayou Manchac to the east of the Mississippi and realized that it ran through Lakes Maurepas and Pontchartrain to the sea, they left the mainstream of the river which was too sinuous and whose banks were covered with dense vegetation and the approaches to whose mouth were drowned in vast uninhabitable marshes or trembling prairies and followed this branch, the Iberville River, whose name they gave to one of their illustrious compatriots. Its easy passage led them in a few hours to those beautiful lakes whose waters teemed with fish, whose bordering lands attracted many Indians for the hunt. Arriving at the sea they found the Pascagoula and the Mobile Rivers. Going up these to their headwaters, they found the country which was the headquarters for a number of Indian nations, covering all of West Florida and communicating to the north with the tributary of the Ohio. [*This country was explored, not by Canadians descending the River, but by the French-Canadian expedition of Iberville exploring upward from the coast. The Iberville River was discovered by Iberville in 1699. After he had, with great difficulty, found the mouth of the river and painfully made his way up as far as Baton Rouge* (ISTROUMA), *he was told by the Indians, who had heard of his settlement at Dauphin Island, that he could return to his ships more easily via the lakes, which he did. The countryside along the banks of Bayou Manchac and the lower reaches of the Amite River is even less inviting than the banks of the lower Mississippi.—Tr. note.*] Over and above the advantages of this situation for fishing and the mildness of its climate and its ease of communication with so many Indian nations, there was another. This was the possibility of shipping the furs traded from the Indians directly to Europe without the difficulties and dangers of taking them up the river to Canada. That is why, as I have noted above, that the Canadians preferred this situation to the places through which they had passed, although the soil was really poorer than in the lands further north. These were the motives which induced a number of them to settle at Dauphin Island as a trading post for their compatriots. [*The settlement of Louisiana did not originate with Canadian* VOYAGEURS, *but with King Louis XIV's farsighted Minister of the Marine, Jerôme de Pontchartrain, who was anxious to take advantage of the opportunity offered by the Peace of Ryswick to carry out de La Salle's project of establishing a series of French posts from the Great Lakes to the Gulf, in order to check both the British and the Spanish colonization in North America. The expedition set sail from Brest in 1698.—Tr. note.*] Thus these audacious Canadians forged a chain of communication running 1800 leagues from Montreal to Mobile, of which the Illinois establishment was the central pivot, which finally ended at the south on the ocean, and this project was completed in just over twenty years. Who can describe the obstacles which greeted them at every step? The ever-present dangers that they surmounted, the suspicious or hostile tribes that they had to intimidate, fight, or entice. Who knows what unknown rivers they had to navigate, what rapids they had to shoot, what portages they had to make, what new bayous they had to probe, those sinuous, labyrinthine streams, where one must search long, probing and retracing one's course again and again before finally discovering their end? Who knows what mountains they explored, what rivers they traced, following their twisting banks or fording them, what swamps they had to cross or find a way around, what dark forests they had to become familiar with without a compass, without even a view of the sun to orient themselves by; what numberless vines they had to extricate themselves from; what dense canebrakes they had to cut trails through by ax? How often they faced thirst and hunger, sometimes living on nothing more than roots and green fruits and at the best of times living off the game that the country afforded. What heavy burdens they carried or dragged; what hardships they bore, sometimes broiling under a burning sun, sometimes burying themselves under the snow to ward off the cold; passing nights in the storm, huddled beneath a tree, or sleeping sitting up on guard against a wily foe, a loaded rifle in one hand, the pack in the other, and a mouth full of bullets.

These *Canadiens* were conquering warriors, without generals or even armies; navigators without ships, merchants without wealth, and geographers without compasses or geometry.

They made immense conquests for their country which knew nothing of them. They discovered an incalculable source of trade, and the merchants never knew it. They pushed back the frontiers of geography and made other scientific discoveries and the scientists paid no attention. Poets sang of the passage of the Rhone by an army as a prodigy to be celebrated in statuary, monuments, and painting, but all were silent on the innumerable feats of these *Canadiens*, more memorable than those recounted of old of Theseus and Hercules, who are remembered as demigods.

One must question whether that palace that Louis XIV had built at such great expense, surrounded by the illusion of artifice, whose narrow horizon was hemmed in by low hills covered with pleasant glades, could kindle in the monarch and his ministers the grand designs of empires. Was this palace of indolence and ease a fitting place where the soul might stir at the recital of the incredible deeds of the hardy Canadian? Could the admirer of those diminutive garden cascades, whose diminutive waters are encased in marble and lead, have the spirit to admire the prodigies of navigation of the Canadians? On those sanded avenues among the glades, coldly symmetrical, could the imagination grasp the reality of those frightful wildernesses which, however, cry out for settlers to fructify and enrich them? The very word hunting in this seat of boredom only implies a languid pleasure in which the piled-up game hardly leaves even the monarch any freedom of choice, and here the Canadian *chasseur* conjures up a picture of a happy sybarite usurping pleasures usually reserved for the great.

CHAPTER XLII

Continuing the preceding. The feeble efforts of the French Government to establish the colony of Louisiana. Their slowness, their lack of coordination. Strange reasons why the great courtiers supported the project.

In vain, the good priest Father Hennepin, after a long stay among the Illinois Indians, during which he had traveled extensively, came to relate at court the marvels of the country he had explored. He was listened to with that indifference all too common where interest in the trivial leaves no room for interest in important matters. Even though offended, Father Hennepin published an account of his travels dedicated to the great Colbert [*Jean Baptiste Colbert, 1619-1683, Louis XIV's chief advisor and Minister of Marine.—Tr. note*], in which he pointed out that the country he had claimed for France was larger than Europe itself. He was so overwhelmed by the indifference in his audience that he retired to end his days in bitterness in Holland.

Thereupon Cavalier de La Salle, a Canadian gentleman who had learned from Father Hennepin the potential of this vast country, resolved to explore it himself. He left Quebec in 1679 with a large party of men, went up the Saint Lawrence, past Niagara Falls, crossed the lakes, and went down the Illinois to the Mississippi and then down it to about three leagues above the Missouri. Here he constructed a fort, the first French fort in this country, which he called Creve-Coeur [*Heart-broken.*—Tr. note], no doubt in memory of the hardships he had to surmount on his long voyage. This fort later was called Fort Saint Louis, which name it still bears today. [*Fort Crève-Coeur was near the site of present-day Peoria, Illinois, not St. Louis, which was settled much later in 1768-1764. Robin's confusion probably arises from the circumstances that in 1765 the British took over the country east of the Mississippi, whereupon the French garrison commander, St. Ange, retired across the river with his troops to St. Louis, where he remained until the Spanish finally took possession in 1770.—Tr. note.*] La Salle continued his exploration to the mouth of the river, which, in order to flatter Louis XIV, he called the St. Louis River (for which reason also Hennepin had already called the surrounding country Louisiana).

After having made observations and fixed the latitude, La

Salle went back up the river to Quebec, from which he sailed to France.

The discovery of the mouth of the Mississippi in the Gulf of Mexico which opened far easier communication with the interior of the continent than the route through Canada, and the continued navigation of both the Mississippi and the St. Lawrence, which between them formed an immense chain through this region that could restrict the growth of the already powerful English colonies, would have made a strong impression on a government more aware of the importance of its colonies. Colbert, however, did authorize at the entreaties and urging of La Salle, a fleet of several vessels carrying about three hundred people, soldiers, volunteers, hired laborers, women, and clerics. This fleet left La Rochelle in 1684, and everyone knows the story of how they missed the mouth of the river and were carried too far to the west, where La Salle landed at the Bay of St. Bernard. His hard character had already antagonized the naval officers and inflamed still more those who had to share hardships with him. Several of them conspired to murder him, and only seven of the original party finally reached Canada, some having died of hardships en route, but most of them having been killed by the Indians or the Spaniards, who considered the French interlopers in their colonies.*

*The snobbishness of the court of Louis XIV had spread like an epidemic in all classes of French society from the throne down to the humblest village, where the petty noblemen scorned his bailiff; the latter in turn looked down upon the attorney, and he, in his turn, despised the sheriff, and the sheriff finally scorned the peasant, the least of all, victim of all and he who fed them all. The effects of this snobbishness were felt especially among those who attended the court. How many evils sprang from this cause, especially in the Ministries of War and the Marine! Cavalier de La Salle, simple Canadian gentleman that he was, with his great vision, his courage, and his energy, was lost and lost his patrimony from breathing for only an instant this pestilent atmosphere. Having received the title of Governor of all of the country that he had explored from the Gulf to the Illinois, he thought himself the superior of all who were with him. He abandoned the simple manners of his native country and adopted those of the court, where everyone was either master or servant. He became difficult and despotic. During the crossing his arrogance alienated the naval officers, themselves an arrogant lot, who were perfectly willing to sacrifice the interests of their country to strike at him. After realizing that they had missed the river's mouth, they refused to sail back to it and stranded in the Bay of St. Bernard [Matagorda Bay] the fleet which contained the provisions necessary for his settlement. It is true that when he found himself with his expedition stranded in that inhospitable wilderness he gave an example of constancy and courage for all, but his stubbornness and pride turned the men whom he could have saved into base murderers.

The court then seemed to lose all memory of that region and the great river which flowed through it. Fifteen years later, in 1698, another Canadian, Iberville, since then a Commodore in the Navy, instructed by his compatriots settled on the lakes, finally found the mouth of the river from the sea. During the interval the Canadian *voyageurs* had continued the exploration as I have outlined above. Iberville was named Governor and brought in colonists by sea. Iberville's colonists were Canadians. At the death of this good man, however, Louisiana was again abandoned. Thirteen years went by before Crozat, a rich individual, obtained for himself the grant of this enormous country. He claimed the additional privilege of the exclusive rights of trade there in all lands, coasts, ports, islands, and harbors to be found in that colony, to be enjoyed in perpetuity, in fee simple, with the sole obligation of liege homage and faith. Thus, just twenty-eight years after the enterprise of Cavalier de La Salle, the French Government was reduced to abandoning to a private owner one of the most fertile regions of the world, larger than Europe itself! What reflection this state of things brings to mind! How deplorable are the causes which brought the government to this. Even so, the concession of Louisiana to an individual could have been advantageous to the colonists and to the mother country and a source of glory and prosperity to the concessionaire, but it would have required an individual of extraordinary shrewdness and local knowledge, not a person whose only interest was to enrich himself by forcing on the colony a tyrannical monopoly, to make them sell at low prices and buy at high ones; a scheme that forced upon the colonists a trade in contraband, which in turn forced the company to set up customs, guards, and offices and to burden the colony with these unproductive mouths. He should have encouraged the colonists to export and import and to have levied on only those exports which the colonists could sell at a profit. Then settlers would have flocked here in even greater numbers than in the territories of the United States. The prairies of Louisiana can be cleared with less difficulty, the soil and the climate are more productive and the resources more numerous. By the rapidity of the growth of the population of the United States one can see what would have been Louisiana's: It would have been, in truth, a New France which would furnish the mother country with almost all colonial goods, timber, naval stores, etc., and which would absorb all of the excess of her manufactures, provide her merchant marine with sailors and increase it because of the necessity for the transportation of colonial goods.

Crozat, if he created such a colony, would become the father of one of the greatest people in the world. If his fortune kept pace with that of the colony, it would be one of the greatest any individual ever had. It would have come only through the wise distribution of land to the colonists. The first settlers in each district would be given land free, the others would be charged a moderate fee, which would be raised gradually with discretion as the neighborhoods became more settled. But, instead of this, Crozat exhausted himself in squeezing the sponge before it was moistened, and four or five years later he abandoned his concession, discouraged by his unavailing efforts.

A new company, called the "Company of the West," in 1717 succeeded to Crozat's concession, but still with the same monopolistic point of view, to sell dear to the colonists and buy cheap from them. They apparently knew no better. They began with great expenditures, niggardly ones to be sure for populating the colony, but extravagant for receiving, keeping and inspecting records of transactions which could not last long, down to each Canadian who, bringing in his furs by incredible labor, was forced to sell them to this company.

But ends very far from the prosperity of Louisiana were the secret aims of the Company of the West; it wished to profit from feeding speculation, that fever of exhausted states which only whips them up at the expense of paralyzing industry and altering the very *mores* of the country. Thus Law promised with his bank to rid France of her weight of debts, to bring back prosperity to agriculture and commerce, and he probably would have succeeded had he not been saddled with the prodigalities of a dissolute court and forced to make promises beyond his capacity to fulfill. In order to give the public new grounds for enthusiasm and investment, he directed their attention to the banks of the Mississippi, from which were to come incalculable riches. Thus was organized this Company of the West whose stockholders were invited to share in the inexhaustible treasures of the Mississippi. In order to lend credence to these inflated promises, the great courtiers were invited to participate and were given concessions in different parts of the colony and sent out agents to establish them. Law, in particular, had a concession styled a duchy on the Arkansas River (about 250 leagues from the projected city of New Orleans) of four square leagues, where 500 hired laborers were to be sent with a company of dragoons, and, indeed, almost a thousand were sent there, Germans for the most part. With the fall of this minister, these laborers came back down the river with the intention of reembarking, but those who survived were at liberty to settle along the river eight leagues above the city, where they are found today in the most populous district of the colony called the *Côte des Allemands,* a district that feeds the city with rice, corn, beans, chickens, etc. La Renommée deliberately circulated the story that at the source of that same river, the Arkansas, there existed a boulder of emerald. This was an obvious come-on, but it so excited the stockholders that the commander of the nearest post was ordered in 1721 to go look for it. He traveled about three hundred leagues, taking with him workers, engineers, and soldiers to guard this treasure. LeBlanc, Minister of War, had a concession on the Yazoo, Marshall Belle-Isle had one lower down including the Natchez; the brothers Pâris, who founded their fortunes at court at that time, had two concessions, that of *Pâris du Vernay* was at Bayougoulas and that of *Pâris Montmartel* at Illinois, a country of mines, and rich mines it was said. Also a large number of miners went over to exploit these riches, and, in order to show what an interest the Regent himself had in the Mississippi country, the capital was named New Orleans. [*Philip, Duc d'Orléans, was Regent of France during the minority of Louis XV, until 1723. One of the worst decisions of his tenure was to countenance John Law's operation of the Mississippi Company.—Tr. note.*]

These great persons and financiers vied with each other in placing their relatives and protegés in regiments destined for service in the colony. Most of these officers settled permanently in the country. One sees numerous descendants of *Pelletiers, de la Houssayes, d'Apremonts, Macartis, Leblancs* (these last, more noble than their ancestors, have become Deblanc, as the relatives of Pâris also gave up the plebian name of *Bernard* to take that of *Dubuclet*) and others. It must be admitted that this spirit of nobility was not conducive to the progress of the colony, for many reasons. It perpetuated in the new colony a taste for luxury, for good cheer and leisure, and, aside from graciousness, this took the form of pride and arrogance from which in ten or twelve years resulted riots, plots and wars with the Indians which cost so much blood and just missed destroying every Frenchmen in the colony. The simple Canadians in thirty years had never been treated as anything but friends, companions, and relatives.

The first war with the Natchez, a people who had done important services for France, arose from the disdainful refusal of a commander to avenge the murder of one of their warriors, killed by a French soldier. Their plot to exterminate all the French, executed in part, was inspired by their despair at an order from a French commander to evacuate their village. The commander wanted the site of the village to erect his house, and this ground, under which reposed the ashes of their ancestors, was the site upon which the Indians had never ceased to offer hospitality to the French. Thus all the wars against the Indians in Louisiana had their roots in the same cause, the haughty character of the French officers who believed that to these people they owed no duties of humanity, justice, or faithfulness to treaties.

The agents of the company destroyed the Natchez nation, and destroyed also one of the most considerable branches of trade in Louisiana, as the Natchez were numerous and powerful. Expeditions against the other Indians had the same effect. This state of war at the same time necessitated frightful expenses for troops, provisions, and munitions and reduced the number of workers in the colony to a small number. The profits of the company's monopoly which ruined the colonists and which they still remember to this day* were far from offsetting the losses of the Company of the West, and in 1730 it was obliged to return the colony to the King after 13 years of possession. In that interval the city of New Orleans had been founded, the fort of Illinois, called Fort Saint Louis, had been built of stone; that of Balize at the mouth of the river, which served as a guide to ships entering the river as well as a defensive structure, had been built at great expense on piles in the middle of an uninhabitable marsh. At Natchez a fort called *Fort Rosalie* was built; a simple palisade on a mound. The fort of Arkansas was even less formidable and that of Natchitoches on the Red River, established by the celebrated St. Denis was equally trifling. At Mobile a stone fort had been built which still exists today. These different forts had only a few people living around them; poorly because they had so few outlets for their products, and because of the high cost of the goods furnished by the company.

The only products of the land were a little rice, corn, tobacco, and furs, some *merain*, and a little salted meat for the colony. The Canadian St. Denis, who had opened a route to Mexico from

*Objects sent from France by the company were sold to the colonists at 300% of the French price.

Natchitoches across unknown wildernesses, a statesman, as well as an explorer, had pursuaded the Spaniards to establish a post at *Assináis*, fifty leagues from Natchitoches, from which they moved to within about ten leagues of Adaïes. He hoped thereby to open up large outlets for our French goods and to receive in exchange money which the colony badly needed. These sagacious views had the double advantage of usefulness to both Spain and France. These two peoples, drawn by their mutual needs, would have populated their respective lands. Spain would have had a large population north of Mexico which would have formed a powerful buffer, and the more the French settlers flocked to the region around Natchitoches, the more the settlement of the Spanish area would be stimulated.

I cannot repeat too often that nations need the help of each other in the same way that men need the help of other men. However, the principle followed by the Spanish Government of being always isolated was here, as elsewhere, the great obstacle to this population growth and the French were only able to initiate a furtive and trifling trade with these regions.

From 1730 to 1769, the time during which the colony was administered by the French Government, the products were about the same and the population growth was small.

Finally, the disastrous war of 1756 resulted in the treaty, so dishonorable for France, by which she ceded, on the one hand, Canada to the English, and on the other, abandoned Louisiana to the Spanish, already possessed of so much useless wilderness. Thus was dispersed and destroyed that important belt of territory which had restricted the English colonies in North America to relatively inferior land and had reserved to France regions which could have absorbed a larger population than that of France itself; would have assured to her dominance in the New World forever and, I venture to hope, would have rendered the commerce and navy of the mother country indestructible even supposing that the colonies, like those of the English, had subsequently become independent*

The loss of these colonies, so unfortunate for France, was not much felt by the country, and we know with what impudence

---

*One should never lose sight of the fact that the independence of the United States brought about an increase in English power instead of weakening her, on account of the volume of trade between England and the United States. Everything worked out to the advantage of England. Important truth for the colonizing nations.

Louis XV's mistress announced their loss to the king, who expressed the ordinary transient regrets of a sensitive person, but soon forgot them for the pleasures of love.

The colonists, however, whom this feeble government sacrificed, showed a heroic devotion comparable to any in history.

During the war, the English had tried to force the Acadians to fight against the French, although under the Treaty of Utrecht, by which they had been transferred to English suzerainty, they had been assured of neutrality. The refusal of the Acadians to bear arms against their country brought down upon them persecutions which they bore with constancy. These persecutions forever blackened the reputation of the English Government, who inhumanly dragged from their homes these people faithful to the sacred love of their country. Ten to twelve thousand were seized and dispersed through the English colonies. A large number of these escaped and wandered, old men, women, and children, for more than six years, across the empty solitude of these regions, living on wild fruits, game, and vegetables with a little grain that was sowed and reaped hastily, harried by English detachments like wild beasts. These were the colonies which had given birth to such Frenchmen that the government cast adrift. Louisianians, on their part, were no less dismayed to find themselves separated from the mother country; for a long time they refused to believe it, or deceived themselves into believing that the disposal would be reversed. They were nourishing these hopes when several years after the conclusion of the treaty, *Ulloa* appeared to take possession of the colony in the name of the Spanish Government. But the Louisianians had not yet received any official notice from their government to obey a Spanish commander. They refused to accept him until the French Government should send them instructions. They addressed a request to the French court asking for instructions. What could these petitions accomplish if even the heroic devotion of the Acadians had been useless? The Louisianians did not even receive an answer.

CHAPTER XLIII

Continuation. Arrival of O'relly [O'Reilly] at New Orleans. Twenty citizens shot. Unzaga Governor. The qualities that made the colony love him. Don Galvez succeeds him, changes the manners of the colony. His conquests, his holdings in Louisiana. Observations on his death. Miro, his successor. His holdings. Burning of the city.

In 1769, only six years after the treaty, General O'Reilly appeared and finally took possession of Louisiana on the 19th of August. Everyone submitted; he did not meet the slightest resistance. However, several days later he invited the principal inhabitants to come to his house. They believed it to be an invitation to lunch, but upon arrival twenty among them were arrested, the others sent away. The former were taken out and shot immediately. This was nothing but murder, for, indeed, the colonists could not be charged with disobedience, for their government had not informed them that they had been placed under a new government, and, finally, if they had been guilty, they should have been tried under the laws of their country. They could not be tried under the laws of Spain, which they did not yet know. The treaty which gave them to the Spanish monarchy expressly stated that Louisianians were to be governed according to their own laws, usages, and prerogatives, the letter that the Duke de Choiseul, who was a minister, wrote on the subject reaffirmed these conditions. This wound still bleeds. All Louisianians feel strongly about it and only speak of it with sorrow. The Spaniards themselves share their sentiments and do not fail to observe that this blood was not spilled by a Spaniard. O'Reilly, who had advanced through the military service, was an Irishman, narrow-minded and bloody. He could not see the difference between a company of insubordinate soldiers and sensitive colonists, raised under the mild laws of the French monarchy. This was the only act of which all Louisiana could complain under Spanish domination. O'Reilly, whom the very ground, soaked with the blood of twenty worthy heads of families, reproached for his crime, soon left the colony, leaving to fulfill the function of Governor, Don Louis Unzaga, under the dependency of the Captain General of Havana. [*This is a most inaccurate and perjorative account. The Louisianians had been fully informed that they were to be ceded to Spain. The difficulty with Ulloa arose from the fact that he would not take over the full re-*

sponsibility for governing the colony. Having brought few troops with him, he wished the French troops to continue to serve as garrison and for the French officials to continue in office. He thus refused to formally present his commission to the Superior Council and insisted on acting as a governor, who did not take full responsibility for his administration. The colonists finally tired of this and ordered him either to present his credentials or leave. He left. The colonial leaders were thus technically guilty of rebellion and sedition, and, whatever may have been the wisdom of O'Reilly's act, his legal grounds were impeccable. Incidentally, only six were shot, and they after a fair trial.—Tr. note.] This governor at once set about to make the unhappy Louisianians forget their distaste for the change of government and the shocking loss of their countrymen. Louisianians recall that he enriched the colony by winking at the clandestine trade with the English. The colonists were able to buy goods at a lower price than they had ever before known, not only necessities, but Negroes on credit which they paid for with their own produce.

The inhabitants of Pointe Coupée, who were the remnant of those who had escaped the massacre of the Natchez, today form one of the richest settlements of the colony, and they owe their fortunes to this period. The credit extended by the English enabled the Louisianians to increase the acreage under cultivation and thus to diversify crops. If it is true that only the English reaped the benefit of the increased production of the colony, at least the mother country stored up future benefits for itself, because of the growth of the colony stimulated by this trade. A weak colony needs a greater liberty of trade than a well-established one.

I wish some casuist would resolve the case of Governor Unzaga. Should he have obeyed the laws of his country to see Louisiana languish and dwindle, or was he right to infringe those laws in order to see the colony prosper? It is always unhappy to see a man placed in the position of only being able to do good by violating the law, or to do much evil by enforcing it. Perhaps there does not exist in the social body a more dangerous cause of demoralization.

Don Bernard Galvé [*Bernardo de Galvez. Henceforth the usual Spanish form will be used.—Tr. note.*], a young colonel, the nephew of the Minister of War, succeeded to the gentle and tolerant Unzaga. His agreeable manners, extremely popular, quickly won the heart of the fickle Louisianians. His taste for pleasure and pomp led him to increase the number of celebrations and idle gatherings which distracted the colonists from their simple customs and useful occupations. It must be admitted that, in this respect, the governor was not good for Louisiana, for when he left the colony his light-minded ideas remained.

Galvez loved martial glory and, desirous of hastening his advancement, found the means of seeing both purposes in the war which France and Spain declared on England in support of the Revolution of the American colonies. He made use of his popularity among the Louisianians by raising a corps of militia and attacking neighboring British posts. With a few troops he attacked and carried the fort at Manchac on the river at the entrance to the Iberville River [*Bayou Manchac.—Tr. note.*], and the fort at Baton Rouge, five miles further up. The first was a simple palisade, but the last consisted of earthworks. These victories were a source of great joy to the Louisianians, notwithstanding the fact that these forts were the source of that useful contraband which caused the colony to flourish. They did not consider that aspect until later. It is not the first time that a people has rejoiced in victories that were, in fact, detrimental to them. The following year Galvez attacked with equal success the much stronger fort at Mobile. His troops being unequal to the task of taking Pensacola, he sailed to Havana and to French Saint Domingo [*Haiti.—Tr. note.*], from which he obtained the necessary troops and ships. The forts of the city of Pensacola, which were awaiting the attack, surrendered after little fighting. Galvez was rewarded for his successes by the appointment as Lieutenant-General and Captain General of Havana. Shortly afterward he was raised to the rank of Viceroy of Mexico, where he died. It was believed in Louisiana, especially, that he was poisoned along with his uncle, the Minister, when a plot miscarried that would have led to an uprising in Mexico which was to lead to his election as king. The best answer to this rumor is that his widow, a native of Louisiana, who would hardly have had a sympathetic welcome at court under the above circumstances, was well received there and granted a considerable pension. She died a lady-in-waiting of the queen.

This governor founded Valenzuela-la-Fourche in Saint Bernard Parish at English Turn and Galvestown on one of the branches of the Amite River, of which he was made the Count. [*Valenzuela, according to other authorities, was along Bayou Lafourche. Henry M. Brackenridge, VIEWS OF LOUISIANA, 1814, in an appendix prints a letter of Dr. Perry, dated Natchez, Mississippi Territory, Jan. 12,*

1813, describing Madisonville and Vicksburg. In it he says that Galveztown is on the Amite River on the southeast bank below the mouth of Bayou Manchac. This would place it between the modern towns of Denham Springs and Port Vincent in Livingston Parish. No trace of it appears on the U.S. Geological survey topographical sheets for this area today. The name has a curious English ring. Why should a settlement of Canary Islanders in a Spanish colony acquire a typical English town suffix?—Tr. note.]

Colonel Miro, one of Galvez's companions in arms, succeeded him as Governor. He governed tranquilly from 1783 to the beginning of 1792. He established the city and fortifications of New Madrid and Nogales [*Vicksburg, miscalled Walnut Bend.—Tr. note*], a little below the mouth of the Ohio, a favorable site for agriculture because of the excellence of the soil; for the fur trade because of the large number of Indians still inhabiting this region and which in case of war with the Americans could serve as a bulwark against them, or at least could serve to cut their communications from the river.

The fort and settlement of New Madrid were placed facing a bar which protrudes into the bed of the river in such a way as to narrow the channel during low water, rendering this fort the master of the Mississippi. The terrain upon which the fort is built is elevated and only rarely subject to flooding, but the river's current washing against the friable earth of the bank erodes three or four hundred feet a year [*60 to 80* TOISES. *An old French measure of about six-and-a-half feet.—Tr. note*.]. The fort was originally 2,000 feet from the bank of the river [*300* TOISES.—*Tr. note*.], but the successive yearly erosions have brought the river up to the fort and have begun to cut into it. The population of this district has grown considerably. However, the dampness of this flat site, which has been neither drained nor shaded by planting trees, makes the site very unhealthy.

In 1788 a fire destroyed one-third of New Orleans. It was Good Friday, and the devout Royal Treasurer, called Hacienda, had had a chapel constructed in his house. The virgin, robed in finery very different from the garments she wore on the day of Our Lord's death, surrounded by lights, caught fire while the devout gentleman sat at table with numerous companions drowning his sorrows. One can imagine what a fire this must have been in a city of highly combustible wooden houses. In the place where a few hours before were populous neighborhoods, streets filled with carriages and pedestrians, stores filled with goods and bustling with trade, now was to be seen only a sterile plain whitened with ashes. The citizen could not even recognize the house from which he had just escaped; he wandered bewildered through his former neighborhood, carrying the pitiful remnant of his property, having not even a place to rest his head. The Governor spent his personal fortune unstintingly for the relief of the victims of the fire, and his wife, perhaps even more remarkably, abandoned from that time on the finery so dear to her sex to offer to the unfortunate city an unparalleled example of austere simplicity. Even during state functions one would have thought she was a nun in her plain dress and white smock. This disaster was followed by another, less extensive, but more callous. Colonel Maxent, in the circumstances, had opened his house to the fire victims. For several months he fed them and he had stored in a warehouse at his country place the belongings which they had salvaged from the fire. Some scoundrels, who have never been identified, burned this to the ground during the night, and the last resources of these unfortunates were consigned to the flames.

CHAPTER XLIV

Baron de Carondelet succeeds Miro. His sagacity saves Louisiana from the troubles of the Revolution. His actions on that score. His moderation and his activity. He fortifies the city, constructs several forts in different parts of the colony. The achievement during his administration of several objects of public utility. His conduct towards General Collot. Gayoso and Salcedo, last governors. General observations on the way in which Spain has governed this colony. Products of the colony. The cost of its maintenance. Its population.

M. Miro was succeeded as Governor by **Baron de Carondelet**, who was born of Flemish stock and who had campaigned with Galvez. This governor, in the difficult circumstances caused by the Revolution, conducted himself with the ability of a statesman and a wise administrator. The revolutionary explosion ready to break out at any moment was checked or nullified by the combination of measures that he took. He saved the colony. Every ship brought fresh news of events in France, exciting the mobs of the people, officers, sailors, and travelers decked in the national colors, sang and danced on the levees and in the streets, inciting to insurrection a city where the majority favored this step. The news of the execution of Louis XVI deepened the crisis. Baron de Carondelet did not deceive himself about the dangers that surrounded him, but hastened to secure the means of defense. At the same time he exhibited a wise moderation toward the firebrands. The least sign of harshness, or, on the other hand, of weakness, could have lost everything. He avoided both. In order to control the river he had a fleet of galleys constructed. He surrounded the city with fortifications, paying especial attention to those that commanded the river. Guards and patrols were stepped up. Cannons were loaded as if the enemy were at the gates. The Council, heretofore composed of six *regidors*, was increased to twelve in order to secure the backing of a larger number of citizens to give this body more influence in maintaining public order. He installed street lighting in order to better control incidents at night. He established a militia throughout the colony which, divided into local corps, could move promptly and render aid if needed. At every post he set up officials charged with examining the passports of foreigners, with maintaining patrols and sending out detachments if necessary, and especially with preventing gatherings of Negroes and arresting all runaway slaves. His precautions were extended to the farthest limits of the colony. He had constructed on the river on the tributary called Margot [Wolf River] a fort named Varanca [*San Fernando de Barancas, better known as Chickasaw Bluffs, the present site of Memphis, Tennessee.—Tr. note.*], and another a little lower down on the other side on the St. Francis River, which he named Feliciane. These were way stations for the forts higher up at St. Louis, Illinois, and New Madrid, while protecting the lower forts of Nogales [Vicksburg], Natchez, and Baton Rouge. [*The fortification of Chickasaw Bluff was established by Gayoso at Carondelet's orders. There is a River St. Francis and a stream named Margot here, but* FELICIANA, *of course, referred to the district around present-day St. Francisville. Earlier, French commanders had established temporary fortifications at Chicasaw Bluffs, notably La Salle and Bienville. I cannot find any other authority for more than one fort here.—Tr. note.*] At the lower end of the river [Mississippi] he built a fort at Plaquemine to protect the city in case the fort at Balize, situated several leagues below, should be forced. [*Fort St. Phillip.—Tr. note.*] Above Mobile at "Tombecbec" [Tombigbee] he established another called Fort Confederation.

Baron de Carondelet, at the same time, took care to inform himself about everything that went on in public meetings (which, on account of the political ferment, were frequent), and he discovered what was happening even in private gatherings where his conduct was the subject of all conversation. Calumnies about him were mixed with dire threats against him. He had the most extreme agitators brought before him and repeated to them verbatim what they had said and, after a few calm observations, often mixed with pleasantry, sent them away with an exhortation to be more moderate. Some were won over by these moderate and straight-forward proceedings, but those who hoped to benefit from turmoil in the colony, aided perhaps by other fearful persons, spread the rumor that the Baron intended to exterminate the French in the colony and that his military preparations were for the purpose of slaughtering them all at the same time. These rumors were current even in the remote districts of the colony and were so believed that every Frenchman had his arms ready and slept with them at his bedside. I found in various districts in the colony, and even at New Orleans itself, Frenchmen who still believe that such an atrocious plot existed. Our revolution caused so many rumors to circulate among us that it is hardly surprising to find that Louisiana had her own rumors. I compared the accounts of this plot with the testimony of knowledgeable people and I saw how baseless were these stories. In particular, I interviewed the person who was particularly in the Governor's confidence and the candor of his remarks would have left me no doubts if I had had any. That the Baron de Carondelet, himself a Frenchman [*He was, in fact, a Spanish Netherlander, or as we should say today, a Belgian.—Tr. note.*], should wish 'to exterminate all the French! He, whose administration was unfailingly mild and benevolent! He did not lock up a single person. Two hotheads he did deport to Havana for two years, I believe, but their properties were preserved as if they had not been absent.

It was in these circumstances that General Collot, accompanied by Adjutant-General Warin, a distinguished Engineer, arrived in the United States. After a short stay, they proceeded to Fort Pitt, where they embarked upon a voyage down the Ohio and Mississippi, making soundings everywhere, sketching the principal settlements, drawing plans of all of the forts and posts and making side trips up the principal tributaries. These activities caused alarm to the English in Canada, to the United States, and to the Spanish in Louisiana. The first two of these powers issued orders for the arrest of these two officers. Baron de Carondelet received daily accounts of their doings, which caused his anxiety to mount and, at the same time, information from the Spanish Ambassador to the United States, M. de Jaudenés, which compelled him also to issue orders for the arrest of General Collot, upon his arrival at New Orleans. As for Adjutant-General Warin, he had just been murdered by savage Canadians on the Arkansas River near the mouth of the White River. There are grounds for believing that the English administration in Canada was a party to this murder* In arresting the General, Baron de Carondelet showed him all of the courtesies due to his office. The morning after his arrest he visited the prisoner in his cell and chatted amiably with him. Later he allowed General Collot to return to wherever he chose.†

---

*I obtained several of these details from Don André, an estimable Spaniard, who, for twenty-five years, was Secretary-General to the Province of Louisiana under different governors down to the retrocession of the colony to France.

†An account of General Collot's journey from the United States to New Orleans and his descent of the Ohio and Mississippi was printed several years ago, with numerous plans and maps.

These plans to preserve the colony had also a second object, that of increasing its prosperity, and some of his measures served both of these ends at the same time. He had constructed the canal, of which I spoke earlier, which, running from the back of the city to Bayou St. John, facilitated navigation from Pensacola, St. Marks, Mobile, and Galvezton by way of Lake Pontchartrain. The administration of justice was improved. He gave the *syndics* the right of assessing judgments up to the sum of ten piastres. He obtained from the central government a reduction in duties which, however, were already moderate. The city owes to him the establishment of a theatre, a French troop composed of actors who had escaped from San Domingo. Certainly, these were not the actions of a man who nourished in his heart a desire to exterminate all Frenchmen. A second fire in 1795, having consumed everything that escaped the first, the Baron forbade the use of inflammable roofing material.

Agriculture, that great objective of all colonies and all countries of the world, made remarkable progress under his government. The culture of cotton and sugar cane repaired the fortunes of planters ruined and discouraged by the fruitless harvests of indigo, which every year died suddenly in the fields before reaching maturity.

In 1797 M. de Carondelet was named to the residency of Quito in Peru and left Louisiana, where the remembrance of his benefits still draws praise from the mouths even of his former enemies.

His successor, Don Gazioso [*Gayoso. One cannot but be bemused by Robin's distortion of Spanish names. "Gazioso" would mean "the gaseous one" in Spanish.—Tr. note.*], formerly commander at Natchez, had in his short administration time only to cause regret for the passing of Carondelet's. Gayoso, as poor an administrator of his own affairs as of those of the colony, died insolvent. He was replaced by Don Salcedo, last of all of the governors who returned Louisiana to the French commissioner.

During the thirty-three years which the country was under Spanish domination, French customs and manners were always dominant, and the Spaniards who came here were Frenchified, rather than the French inhabitants becoming Spanishized. The governors themselves, as well as the commandants under them, adopted French manners and they, or at any rate, their children, married French women. The Spanish language was so little used and the French so generally adopted, that the majority of Frenchmen born in the colony during the Spanish rule did not need to learn this foreign tongue. I saw these Frenchmen who had lived since infancy under Spanish governors, related or married to them even, who did not understand a word of Spanish, an interesting observation I think as it shows how well the Spaniards took the measure of French character and how they respected, according to the letter of the treaty, our most sacred possessions; our laws and customs.

All lands were granted free to the colonists, except for a small fee for drawing up the deed, and if we must reproach the government for anything in this practice, it must be for having made grants to persons who used them to the detriment of the progress of the colony instead of helping it.

The Acadians and others, in addition to free land grants, received an annual stipend for the first years of their colonization. These expenses, plus those of the construction of forts and the maintenance of about two thousand troops, cost Spain annually five to six hundred thousand piastres. The custom duty of six percent did not produce more than one hundred thousand (because of the prevalence of fraud). The government, thus, had expenses over and above revenues of four or five hundred thousand piastres a year, which money increased the amount of specie in circulation. These four or five hundred thousand piastres, spent principally by the military which produced nothing, insured that the colony's imports exceeded her exports, because it was necessary to import goods 1] for the colonists, who paid with their goods in exchange, and 2] for the soldiers who paid in cash. The products of the colony, even at the end of the period, scarcely reached the total of five to six million *livres Tournois,* of which sugar and syrup make about a third. [*Here, as elsewhere, Robin's comparisons are obscured by a change in monetary unit. 500,000 piastres would equal about 2,600,000 livres.—Tr. note.*] This value of goods was not enough to offset the double importation, once for the colonists and the other for the employees of the government, and the payment for imports perforce had to be supplemented by cash. This was not necessarily a bad thing, for if cash had become too readily available in the colony, the cost of labor would have gone up and this would have been harmful, especially to agriculture.

I will complete this rapid recitation of the most interesting events of the Spanish administration of Louisiana with this tabulation of the population of the colony, according to geographical subdivisions, made by the Spanish government.

POPULATION
Lower Louisiana

			Remarks
New Orleans and Its Suburbs	Whites	3,948	This is the count of the Census of 1803. It is obviously too low. The population has noticeably increased even in one year.
	Free Men of Color	1,335	
	Slaves	2,773	
	Total	8,056	
Saint Bernard or Terre aux Boeufs		661	The population here consists of colonists transplanted here from the Canary Islands. They have few slaves.
Lower Coast (From the City to Balize)		2,388	Of which slaves make up an estimated 1200-1500.
Gentilly and Bayou St. John		489	Of the total of 1,933 individuals in these two settlements, 1200 to 1500 are believed to be slaves.
Upper Coast or Chapitoulas		1,444	
Coast of St. Charles First German Settlement	Whites	689	Census of 1803.
	F.M.C.	105	
	Slaves	1,620	
	Total	2,414	
Coast of Saint John the Baptist, Second German Settlement	Whites	1,161	Census of 1803.
	F.M.C.	48	
	Slaves	1,204	
	Total	2,413	
Cabahanocé or First Acadian Settlement [St. James & Ascension Parishes]	Whites	1,584	Census of 1803.
	F.M.C.	19	
	Slaves	1,139	
	Total	2,742	
Lafourche de Chetimachas, or Second Acadian Settlement	Whites	677	Census of 1797. One could reasonably suppose an increase of about 1/6 from that time to now.
	F.M.C.	13	
	Slaves	464	
	Total	1,154	

Valenzuela de La-fourche	Whites	2,367	Census of 1803.
	Slaves	375	
	Total	2,742	
Iberville	Whites	778	Census of 1797. Again, one may reasonably infer an increase of 1/6.
	F.M.C.	8	
	Slaves	314	
	Total	1,100	

[Baton Rouge is omitted. Martin gives about 1,500 as its population, so Robin's figures are off by that number.—Tr. note.]

Galvezton	Whites	213	
	F.M.C.	8	
	Slaves	26	
	Total	247	
Point Coupée or False River	Whites	547	Census of 1791. In 1785 1,521 were counted and lately the rate of growth has accelerated. One can thus confidentially expect a population today of 3,000 souls.
	Slaves	1,60?	
	Total	2,150	
Attakapas	Whites	2,270	Census of 1803, that of 1789 showed 2,017 souls.
	F.M.C.	210	
	Slaves	1,266	
	Total	3,746	
Opelousas	Whites	1,543	Census of 1797. This post at this time consists of more than 600 households and 4,000 people, of which only about 300-400 are slaves. A third of the population is American.
	F.M.C.	103	
	Slaves	781	
	Total	2,427	
Concorde			A new settlement where there are at least a few inhabitants, as well as at Catahoula.

Arkansas	Whites	340	Census of 1791.
	F.M.C.	3	
	Slaves	47	
	Total	392 [sic]	

Total .... 37,697 people

Upper Louisiana

New Madrid		1,500	In 1803.
Cape Giradeau	)		
Sainte Genéviève	)		
Carondelet	)		
Portage des Scieux	)—	5,500	In 1803.
Saint Charles	)		
Saint Ferdinand [Memphis]	)		
Saint Louis	)		

Total 7,000

Lower Louisiana 37,697
Upper Louisiana 7,000

Total 44,697

[*It is interesting to compare these figures, gathered, according to Robin, from Spanish sources, with the figures given in Martin,* HISTORY OF LOUISIANA, *page 300, which he ascribes to the American counsul. Obviously, they derive from a common source. The figures for New Orleans and the suburbs are identical. But there are discrepancies. Robin gives Chapitoulas (the area of the present city business district) as only 1,444; while Martin gives it 7,444. I suspect that Martin's figure is a misprint, since Robin goes on to give an approximate white-slave proportion. If Martin's figure were correct, it would mean that even at this date the population of the future American city was almost as great as that of the Vieux Carré itself. This seems unlikely. Robin inadvertently omits Baton Rouge and lumps Valenzuela with Lafourche. There are minor discrepancies in most of the remaining posts. Martin does not break down the figures for Upper Louisiana, and Robin leaves out Mobile and Pensacola, but for good reason. They remained under Spanish dominion.—Tr. note.*]

CHAPTER XLV

Trips to the interior. Details on methods of travel. Different types of boats. Oarsmen or hired help. Dangers of river navigation.

People in this country are so accustomed to travel by water that the generic term *"voiture"* [standard French for "carriage"] is always applied to a boat. If a Louisianian says to you "I brought my *voiture"*; Can I give you a lift in my *voiture"*; he is referring to his pirogue or skiff as a Parisian using the same word would mean his coach.

These *voitures* in use on the river are extremely variable in shape and size. Many are made from a single tree trunk; others from two or three, firmly joined. Others are real skiffs made of planks of varying timbers in the European manner; some are flat-bottomed, some are rounded and some are provided with a keel like ships. Some can contain only two or three people; others up to thirty or forty and can carry 100 barrels. Some are elongate and pointed at each end; others are broad and rectangular like those called *chalans*. Those made of a single tree trunk are called *pirogues*. Some of these are forty to fifty feet long by six feet wide and four to four and a half feet deep. These craft are made from the poplar, a tree which in these regions reaches an enormous size. [*Presumably the swamp cotton wood,* POPULOUS HETEROPHYLLA *is meant.—Tr. note.*] Ordinarily, however, boats are made from cypress, a lighter and more solid wood, which warps less and will last a long time in the water without rotting. The ribs of the larger boats are of oak of those species which have a hard wood and are naturally gnarled. A few are constructed entirely of oak, but these have come from far-off regions to the north where the cypress does not grow. In this hot climate oak shrinks and cracks and will not last long.

The great diversity of these "water carriages" is not due to the caprices of fashion as is the diversity of our land carriages now built high, only to be suddenly meanly disparaged; now decorated with embossed bronze, replacing the older thin plaques and slender chips; now built square and sharp-angled, now rounded like a gondola. The untutored artisans here have not yet learned to fashion at great expense new shapes in order to replace them with still newer ones.

This diversity of shape of these boats comes from the diversity in their usage and in the places where they must go. Those that come from the far-off rivers that are wide and shallow are wide and flat in order to draw little water, while those that navigate the surface of the deep rivers and must overcome the swift current, are more elongate and draw more water and are heavier. Their thick, rounded bottoms glide over the snags and logs which are found in all parts of the river bed. The narrow bayous where the water sometimes rushes in torrents require boats that are shorter and lighter, whereas others still require very light skiffs in order to shoot the rapids or to be dragged over the river bed in low water.

Luxury craft, however, do exist. They are used by the rich planters to travel to town. At the stern is a kind of pavillion under which the stern master sits. The rest of the deck is open and filled with benches upon which the rowers sit; twenty silent and morose slaves sitting under the eye of their master, striking the water with their multi-colored oars. Their master's vanity has taken them from the fields in order to parade them before the city, as in France useless lackeys might be hired to run behind a carriage. Fifteen to twenty slaves, in order to display in this lugubrious manner, two or three masters. Our bourgeois at Paris on Sundays in September gather together in groups of 15 or 16 at four or five sous a head in order to boat down to St. Cloud and they require only two boatmen who get them there fast and join themselves in the merry making above the market. Need we ask which is more pleasing to the gods?

The boats designed to go up the Mississippi to the far corners of the colony in order to bring to the planters the goods that they require, have a covering at the stern called the *tendelet,* sometimes made of wood, but more often consisting of a pole frame over which is thrown a tarpaulin to make a shelter from the sun and rain. Sometimes, instead of a tarpaulin, it is covered with oxhide. This tendelet is for the boat's captain and his party. It is raised above the rest of the deck and it is a comfortable place from which to observe the countryside. One sleeps there at night and eats there during the day in bad weather. One must stay there all during the trip no matter how slow, for in many places there are no roads. Another tarpaulin called the *prélat,* covers the cargo in order that it will not be ruined by bad weather. The rowers are divided evenly on each side of the boat. In the stern is the captain and in the bow a man called *bosman* [*boatswain.*

— *Tr. note*] sounds the water ahead in doubtful places. The number of oarsmen varies according to the size of the boat from three to four up to twenty or twenty-five.

Navigation of the Mississippi is not like that of European rivers emptying into the ocean, which can be navigated to a great distance upriver by using the tides. Tides are low on the Louisiana coast and while they may slow the current slightly, tides never reverse its impetuous current. To go upriver one must use either sail, a rope, or oars. Sailing is so tortuous that it is seldom done. The tall trees in the uncleared stretches of the river stop the wind anyway. Hauling by rope is only practical in the cleared stretches of the river where the trees have been cut down from the shore where the men can walk freely and again on the wide *battures,* that is flat built-up shores extending outward from the bank. Boats are obliged to stand so far offshore that hawsers would be of little use. After much of the river bank has been cleared doubtless it will become practical to establish relay stations for horses. Such an improvement would speed up transportation and decrease its cost. At the moment oars are most often used and sometimes, exclusively.

A fully loaded boat with a full complement of oarsmen cannot make over six leagues a day and to do this it must be under an experienced captain. He must know on which side of the river the current runs swiftest in order to avoid it, and how to take advantage of eddies and counter-currents. These eddies are sometimes an eighth of a league long and can almost carry the boat upriver themselves. He must know where the main current takes up again in order to cross the river in time to take advantage of the next eddy.

These crossings are difficult and dangerous. In the middle of the river the current can push the boat back down a mile or two before the crossing can be made. The voice of the captain can then be heard urgently exhorting the oarsmen, to whom he has not neglected to distribute earlier a *filet,* the usual ration of *tafia* [rum]. If a strong wind is blowing from the shore they wish to reach, this adds another reason for wishing to reach it, for the bank and trees will shelter the boat. However, if the wind comes up suddenly while the boat is midstream, it is necessary to return to the side from which the boat came, for the waves may swamp it. If the boat is lucky enough to reach the shore from which it came, other dangers are waiting. The wind being from off the water piles its waves against the boat and tends to drive it to the shore even if moored and if the boat cannot find a sheltered creek or inlet, the roaring waves will drive it on the bank and break it up. I have seen those enormous barges, their shape reminding me of moving houses, slowly floating along on the smooth surface of the quiet river, that had been suddenly blown ashore by violent winds, lying high and dry in pieces on the bank more than 25 feet above the water line and their cargo of cotton floating on the now tranquil waters.

The boats fear storms, but even more they fear those bends which form eddies beneath bluffs towering above, bearing trees to their very rims. Fly, fly from these treacherous retreats. Soon the bluff, undermined by the seething waves, will break off and slide into the abyss, carrying those great trees to the bottom still standing so that only the tips of their branches and their superb crowns protrude from the water.

Calm itself has its dangers. While the eager oarsmen ply their oars on the tranquil surface of the eddy, the boat may strike upon one of those treacherous floating tree trunks in the river. Often the oarsmen attempt in vain to pull the boat off. In vain do they attempt to push the log down and push the boat off. The bottom is pierced and the water rushes in, boiling up inside and the boat must be abandoned.

The volume of travel on the Mississippi which goes upward from New Orleans over so many rivers hundreds of leagues to the north, the west, and the east, increases from day to day, and makes the services of those who ply this trade ever more desirable. For the most part, the sailors are European, Frenchmen and a few Englishmen, and for short trips local inhabitants, who disdaining agriculture prefer this type of life. However, the majority of the oarsmen are French Canadians. They have preserved their national character in their language, which they speak quite well, and in their impetuousness and ardency. They are the best boatmen on the river. One can recognize their boats from afar, from the sound of their oars and from the songs and cries which resound through the sonorous woodlands.

These boatmen are hired by the month or by the trip and from this circumstance are known throughout the country under the generic term, *engagés,* [hired hands.] The average cost for each man, including his food, is about one piastre per day.

They would make their fortunes in short order if they were not almost all drunkards, gamblers and wenchers. A few days after finishing a trip they no longer have a sou. I have seen them lose, on the very night of their being paid off, all that they had made by so many fatigues and dangers. In order to rehire them one must always give them an advance, for often they have gambled away their very clothing and too often a number of them decamp after receiving these advances. In the city they are to be found in certain particular inns where almost all of them owe something. The troubles of their trips and the excesses of their dissipations wear them out early and few of them reach middle age.

A boat trip begins regularly at dawn. Every two hours there is a pause to catch one's breath, which is what smoking a pipe is called. At least three times a day the *filet* [ration of tafia] is distributed. Breakfast is ordinarily on board, but at noon, everyone goes ashore to eat lunch and to rest until two o'clock. As soon as the boat is made fast by double hawsers, everyone disperses to gather wood for the fire. Dinner is prepared. It consists of salt pork or beef with rice or *gru* (ground corn). [*Probably a short form of standard French* GRUAU, *c.f.* gruel. *Etymologically related to "grits," which it is.—Tr. note.*] Also, everyone is provided with biscuit. The captains, in addition, have chicken or often wild game. In the evening the ship is moored at sunset and the crew camps near the boat, as close as possible so as to be ready in case of bad weather. Supper finished, everyone goes to sleep around the fire, which they are careful to maintain all night long. Those *engagés* who are prudent always have a bear skin to sleep on with a couple of blankets, according to the season. Whatever the weather they never sleep with anything else and, what is remarkable, they never have any colds. The captain and his staff sleep under the *tendelet* and keep guard on the boat. This mode of travel can be very agreeable to those inquisitive persons who are suited to it by taste and character. A boat of light construction, lightly loaded will go faster and nature offers everywhere so many varieties of points of view of different objects, that one always has something new to observe.

I made my first trip on the boat of one of those lost Frenchmen who left Paris at the time of the Revolution for the Promised Land, the district of *Scioto* [*In the present state of Ohio on the Ohio River. Approximately the present-day town of Portsmouth, Ohio.—Tr. Note.*] in the United States. The sharpers who sold him this land told him that crops grew there as if by magic, but what they did not tell him was that, first, he would have to rebuy the land and then, log off the trees which were so large that it would have taken years for this unexperienced Parisian to cut down as many as twenty of them and, in the meantime, he had to fight off the continual attacks of the disgruntled Indians who saw themselves despoiled of forests in which they had been accustomed to hunt. This Parisian, disheartened by these enormous trees and the attitude of the Indians, took to the Ohio River like many others and sought a better fortune at New Orleans. Restless again after a stay of several years, he was going to try his luck in the regions bathed by the Ouachita. The desire to cut down expenses on this trip and other considerations with which he did not acquaint me, made him urge me to make my trip on his boat and my arrangements with him were too advanced when several people in the city gave me some information about my choice. At any rate, we left and soon I was able to contemplate from the river the pleasant spectacle of the houses on the cleared bank.

I said to myself: Not eighty years ago these banks were covered with trees, jagged, raised, drooping, or lying on the ground, enormous logs piled up everywhere, obstructing and retarding the flow of the river. This tangle of vegetation retarded the run-off after the floods and caused the land to be flooded longer and thus to acquire a greater coating of river sediment. The dull roar of this impeded run-off, mingled with the cries of innumerable water birds, re-echoed unceasingly in these lugubrious solitudes and the wandering Indians could make themselves heard only by their piercing distress calls.*

Those audacious Canadians, who were the first to navigate the river in search of new routes, at first dreaded to approach these forbidding banks, and often traveled at night, their oars muffled to insure silence. Now these menacing trees have disappeared, children of the centuries, who reared their crowns above the brownish waters. They have disappeared under the hand of civilized man! Today I can look over the pleasant banks along the river's sinuous curves without obstruction.

Those heaving, tangled logs have long since floated down, the playthings of the current, to the ocean, and now the traveller may move everywhere along the river in safety. Even the Indian, unafraid under our benevolent laws, no longer fears the river. The river, free from this choking vegetation, widens its bed and its

---

*The Indians call to each other in the forests by means of piercing cries which can be heard at a great distance.

majestic current now runs more peacefully. But Man, its master, has marked its limits and forbids it to cross them. In vain do the many tributaries gather their waters together from so many cloudy mountain ranges, from the melting of so many snows under the breath of spring. In vain do they increase in size and become impetuous currents, and in vain do the winds and tempests bestir them. No longer may the waters cover the plains they have created, where formerly they stretched at will. The river now flows more rapidly between two levees, and behind them, below the level of the menacing current, are raised in perfect safety, a long succession of neat and pleasant houses, surrounded by fields of corn, cotton, indigo, rice and sugar cane; and there, where once the mire gave rise to the disgusting races of reptiles, today man and herds of useful animals live and multiply. [*The idea that mud and slime gave rise by spontaneous generation to the animals living therein, is an ancient one. It may be found in Pliny. It is perhaps surprising to find this idea in an eighteenth century naturalist with scientific pretensions.—Tr. Note.*]

You detractors of civilization, come to this prosperous settlement and then, enter the neighboring swampy solitudes. Must you not then admit that by human artifice man is happier, nobler and better, and nature itself richer? Let your bitter censure be reserved for the ostentations of cities, where the abuse of artifice endlessly creates useless desires, keeps the indolent in idleness, puffs up the pride with perfidious flattery, and leaves to poverty only abjection and despair. But in these places where man by glorious labor makes nature fertile and has created new riches for himself, for generations to come, in these far-off regions, be respectful and show only admiration.

CHAPTER XLVI

Naturalization of Sugar cane; Useful innovation in its culture, Establishment of Sugar Refineries, Obstacles opposed to this, their production. What it could be.

Near New Orleans are to be found a number of sugar refineries. The naturalization of this plant (sugar cane) in Louisiana is a triumph, for it is a native of the tropical regions, and in Louisiana the cold weather, while not of long duration, is irregular in appearance, bitter and sudden. Even more important for the prosperity of colonies in general, is the fact that up to now sugar cane has been cultivated by hand, that is the ground is worked by a mattock. In Louisiana, ploughs have been introduced in cane cultivation. Thus the number of men necessary to run a sugar plantation is reduced and the general advantage will be shared by all colonies, so that sugar will be cheaper in Europe as a consequence of this discovery.

The culture of sugar cane has been attempted in Louisiana for a long time, for the fact that sugar cane was planted as a garden herb, gave rise at an early date to the speculation that it might be cultivated on a large scale, and as long as fifty years ago, the first attempts were made. What appeared to be an invincible obstacle was, that while in tropical colonies the cane requires from 14 to 18 months to mature, the intermittent cold spells in Louisiana restrict the growing season to about nine months. By that time the juice of the cane is not thick and grainy as in the tropical colonies, but is still watery and will not make good sugar. Moreover, if the cane is hard frozen, its juice deteriorates completely, and this reduces even further the chances of making sugar here. But a light freeze, that is, one which will kill the leaves to keep the cane plant from making more juice without altering that which is already formed; such a freeze will favor the maturity of the juice instead of hindering it.

The sun, still hot in the intervals between freezes, evaporates the excess water from the cane, draws the sugar particles nearer together in the juice, begins their fermentation and brings the juice to the point where granulation begins. Therefore, in Louisiana, it is necessary to recognize the time of maximum maturity of the sugar cane. The cane should be cut after the light freezes of November, and piled up and covered to protect it against the hard freezes later on. [*Known today as wind-rowing the cane. —Tr. note*].

Once the discovery was made it was only necessary to construct the necessary buildings and to obtain the proper instruments; expensive and difficult things to do, since the objects were not immediately obtainable, and it was difficult to know where to turn to learn the rather difficult art of sugar making. These considerations halted the Louisianians and it was only ten years ago, that fugitives from San Domingo persuaded some of the planters in Louisiana to try again.

It was necessary to make an investment of two or three thousand piastres, pay four or five hundred piastres for the mechanism of a mill driven by animals over and above the nourishment of the workers and the transport of the materials. The masonry alone for the mounting of the sugar cauldron costs 300 piastres. Those San Domingans who direct the harvest are paid from 1,000 to 1,500 piastres for about two months' work. The yield is about 100,000 lbs. of raw sugar.

The prohibition of the importation of Negroes into Louisiana rigorously enforced by Carondelet (who nevertheless was credited with intention of encouraging the Negroes of Louisiana to revolt in order to slaughter the French) caused the price of Negro field hands to rise from a thousand to 1200 piastres apiece.

These high costs did not deter the Louisianians and several saw their efforts crowned with success.

Sugar cane, this reed that Nature has destined to grow in cool places [sic] grows in heavy humid soil with a surprising rapidity. Planted in January, February and March, it grows rather slowly until the hot rainy period of the solstice, but then its stem rapidly thickens. It attains up to two inches in diameter, and by October reaches a height of eight or nine feet, and is mature and ready for cutting by the first of November.

A single arpent of cane can yield two thousand pounds of sugar and two barrels of molasses. A hundred pounds of sugar brings about 8 piastres, a price which it has never yet dropped below, and a barrel of molasses brings 15 piastres (although it sells today for almost twenty piastres). Thus the arpent of land above yields 190 piastres or 1000 livres. (A piastre is worth 5 livres, 5 sous) and prices are more likely to rise than to drop.

However, the stubble cane, that is to say cane planted the previous year, gives thicker growth but shorter and smaller canes. One third are newly planted, one third are one year old, and the one third two years old is not so productive. The yield is reduced to 1200 pounds of sugar and one and one half barrels of molasses per arpent. That comes out to 118 and ½ piastres per arpent, or for 100 arpents 11,850 piastres or 61,212 livres tournois. Forty Negroes are enough for this cultivation. Each slave, thus produces about 300 piastres per year. The Louisianians, stimulated by these successes, will soon have acquired the know-how themselves to construct the necessary buildings. The cauldron and other necessary utensils are now available locally, and in such quantity that the prices are modest. The planters' running expenses now only amount to about 1000 or 1500 piastres. Since they no longer have to pay the sugar makers and builders, their only expenses are the salary of an over-seer, extra help during the grinding season, and the cost of maintenance.

The local soil is suitable for brick-making, and wood is readily available for construction, fuel and cooperage. The ditch that is dug in order to drain the land, serves also as a canal for transportation, and even as a passage to the lake where one can procure shells to make lime. All construction work is done by the Negroes on the Plantation and it must be admitted that some of the Louisianians show much intelligence in this work. Here is a remarkable example: The San Domingan who directed the construction of the first sugar houses built the grinding mill in a hexagonal or octagonal form. A Creole named De Gruise, a descendant of one of the French officers who came out at the founding of the colony, without instruction, but by native ability, found that an angular edifice was both displeasing to the eye and wasteful of material, but circular construction was too difficult for the local colonial laborers. M. de Gruise had heard of la Halle in Paris [*The central market of Paris now knows in the plural form "Les Halles" — Tr. note*] and from descriptions of it, he had built in brick two leagues from the city, on his house, a rotunda so like it, that on seeing it I expressed astonishment. I was even more astounded upon learning how M. de Gruise had conceived and executed the work.

Sugar cane is not subject to the diseases of indigo, nor to being eaten by insects like cotton and thus presents a prospect of a more certain return. The number of sugar plantations, therefore increases daily and soon sugar will be the principal crop in regions where the climate is favorable. In 1802 there were 75 sugar plantations. The largest of them produced over two hundred thousand pounds of raw sugar and the total production in the colony is estimated at five million pounds of sugar, not to mention the molasses. Five million pounds of raw sugar at 1200 pounds per arpent, were produced on 4,166 arpents of land which averaged 55 arpents for each of the 75 plantations.

[*An Arpent equals 1 and ¼ acres — Tr. note.*]

Sugar cane can be grown on both sides of the river, from about 10 leagues below the city to above Pointe Coupée. This is over sixty leagues, and even considering that along this stretch the cultivated land extends to a width of only a quarter of a league, that amounts to 123,000 arpents, suitable for the cultivation of sugar cane. Let us reduce the amount to half of that to allow for subsistence farming and other needs. That leaves us 61,500 arpents upon which to grow sugar cane, whose annual production at 1200 pounds per arpent would come to 73,000,000 pounds, over and above the molasses production which would increase correspondingly. [*This would amount to a total producti n of 37,000 short tons, and 1200 pounds per arpent would amount to 1500 pounds, or ¾ of a ton per acre. In 1959 the total production in Louisiana was 441,000 tons of raw sugar at an average yield of 3 or 4 tons an acre—Tr. note.*]

Thus half of this land, from 10 leagues above the city [*About the site of present day Moisant airport. — Tr. note.*] to Pointe Coupée, costing 1000 livres per arpent, would yield an annual revenue 61,500,000 livres, to say nothing of the other half. To the west of the river, the Attakapas and Opelousas regions have a variety of prairies at the same latitude of which only the parts closest to the sea are under water. This land could be also utilized as the cultivation spreads. As the land is cleared, the less stagnant air will expel the excess humidity and extend the capability of this cultivation to the North, but even neglecting this, if one considers all the plains which stretch along the coast westward from the Attakapas to Mexico, a distance of 300 leagues, how immense is the possible yield!

Everywhere in this region there are numerous waterways leading to rivers which can be used for transport. Thus as the culture of sugar cane spreads it will always be simple and cheap to secure wood for construction, and fuel from the forests to the north, provided of course, that the government of the colony prevents the destruction of the forests by timely regulation.

The quality of Louisiana sugar has won it a place in the world market, but it must be admitted that it should be boiled down longer and stored for a longer time in order to completely drain off the molasses which would then thicken. The sugar would, it is true, lose its attractive blond color, and would become browner, but it would store better and would spoil less in transportation.

CHAPTER XLVIII

Saw Mills—wood used. River Floods. Rice Plantations.
Quality of the rice appropriate to the places where grown.
District of the Germans. Their Character, their customs.
Pointe Coupée, other customs. Richness of the Settlement.

Across the city are found several very productive saw-mills. These mills make up to thirty or forty thousand francs per year. The mills are built along the river bank and can only operate when the river level is above that of the surrounding land. A trench is dug in the levee and the water wheel of the mill is set into this as deep as possible. The river water rushes through the trench to find its way into the swamp and lakes, and it runs as long as the river level remains above that of the lakes. The high water lasts roughly from April to August, and during this time the mill runs night and day. In years when the river remains low, the mill runs little or not at all. The cypress, a wood much used in this country, is the only one sawed into boards.

The rice plantations which are operated mainly by the Germans, whom I mentioned earlier, along with a few others, are watered in the same way by trenches cut in the levee, and they also can only be watered during the period of flood. The river spills into the fields but never drains them. In lower Egypt, the Egyptians water their fields during the flooding of the Nile, and a lack of flooding means a failure in the harvest. Just so in Louisiana, a failure of the river to flood prevents the saw-mills from turning and the rice fields from being flooded. Rice cultivation could be much extended in Louisiana. All of the plantations slope away from the river and at their back is drowned land which could be used to grow nothing else. However, for a long time yet, a lack of labor will prevent this fertile land from producing everything of which it is capable.

What is particularly harmful to the progress of rice culture is the lack of a marketing outlet, the fruit of an ill-advised policy which is supposed to benefit the poor man and the merchant even more. Rice had fallen to two and a half piastres a barrel weighing 190 pounds. This low price discouraged the growers. Today rice sells for eight to nine piastres and rice culture is reviving. I do not doubt that rice will become a major item of agricultural commerce. Its consumption in this country is prodigious. It is seen on all the tables of the Creoles instead of bread. Boiled rice and cornbread replace wheat completely. Louisiana rice is very white. A half hour at the most is enough to cook it, which would seem to show that it is less substantial than other rices, especially those of the Levant. Perhaps the water of the Mississippi which nourishes it, being so soft and soapy, communicates to it the property of being promptly soluble upon cooking.

Our doctors tell us that rice destroys the stomach. However, a number of people on earth live principally on rice—actually more than live on wheat. The people of Africa live on rice and corn, those of Asia, the Indian sub-continent, almost all of China, Japan, Indo-China, Siam, Madagascar, Borneo, and Ceylon all use rice as their dietary staple. Several European countries use it extensively as do the European colonies of America. Louisiana, which produces it in large quantities consumes a lot of it too. It is the bread of most of those who cultivate it. But it is true that everywhere, where it is the principal nutrition, it is prepared very differently from the method used in France. They take care not to cook it in too much water, nor to let it cook too long, for this will dilute the mucilage which thereupon loses its nutritive quality and prevents the action of the digestive juices and at the same time relaxes the fibers of the stomach. These effects do not appear when it is prepared in the simple and rapid manner that so many rice-eating people use. Louisianians cook it in a closed vessel with a little water so that it is concentrated. (In Louisiana a cast iron pot is used.) The rice swells up without being diluted and it is served without any other preparation in a mass like bread. It is eaten in combination with other food. Rice thus prepared is healthy nourishing and agreeable. It refreshes the blood giving it that fluidity so necessary in Southern climates, and I cannot too strongly recommend its consumption to everyone newly arrived in the colony.

These rice fields submerged for a part of the year in so many countries with hot climates, sometimes give rise to contagious maladies. I observe that this occurs only occasionally and could be avoided, for it is always the fault of the cultivators, who expose to the action of the sun the reservoirs of water and the canals which water the rice fields. The mud washed in by this water causes the trouble when the fields are not dried out enough at harvest time, but as long as the rice or the stalk shades the water that nourishes it, it is salubrious, not harmful. It refreshes the air, purifying it by its emanations. How can one fail to see in this production, evidence of the continuity, the admirable economy of Nature. Rice grows on these drowned lands where other grain will not grow.

It grows without rain in torrid climates, in the seasons of the river floods, and in regions where the equinoctical rains pour in torrents that would destroy other crops, but which fortify and invigorate rice. Its lax, resilient head, its more numerous stamens* than are found in other grains, its thick and fleshy leaves—insure that neither heat nor heavy rain will prevent its setting fruit. Covered by a tough dry envelope, the grains are neither swollen by the humidity nor cracked by the heat. Its nutritious substance, greater than that of wheat, so suitable the putrid maladies so frequent in these climates. The crews of ships fed on rice are never attacked by scurvy, and the Indians' most efficacious remedy for dysentery and maladies of that sort, is a dish of rice-water. Thus Nature offers rice to man in these regions where wheat and other grains could not grow, and it has exactly those qualities most necessary in climates where one is forced to make use of it.

These Germans living among the French have retained their taciturn character, their language and their manners. They do not have that open and affectionate countenance of the French. They are stingy but well behaved. They work their own farms, without Negroes, and although originally northern they have become well acclimated. Yellow fever never bothers them because they work. This malady strikes those who in New Orleans live in inactivity or in the too active state of passion and intemperance.

These Germans, who are the food suppliers of the city, (as I have already observed) live well, without however having made any fortunes. This is hardly astonishing when we consider that the city market is not large, that the price of meat has always been low, and that the artificial restrictions of commerce have prevented the development of other outlets.

Twenty leagues above the city the Acadian coast begins and runs about another twenty up from there. Like the Germans they work their own farms. Only a few of them have Negroes. Already the population has risen so that the farms are sub-divided into strips of two or three arpents of frontage. You must remember that each plot ran back forty arpents from the river. Only about

---

*They number six or more, whereas in other grains there are never more than three.

half that depth, however, is under cultivation, the rest being inundated and covered with cypress and similar swamp vegetation.

Rice, corn, several kinds of beans, melons (in season) pumpkin, salted pork and beef make up their principal diet. Their customs can be compared to those of our farmers of Beauce and Brie [*The region around Chartres, and the region to the east of Paris respectively.—Tr. note.*] Good fellows! They do not show the zeal in their work that their European confreres would, for on the one hand, they are not pressed by necessity, and on the other hand, the lack of outlets for their product discourages them from greater efforts. However, they are still Frenchmen, passionately loving their country, proud to work for it, and showing a great predeliction for its products.

Ordinarily their manner is reserved but they are no strangers to gaiety. They love to dance most of all; more than any other people in the colony. At one time during the year, they give balls for travelers and will go ten or fifteen leagues to attend one. Everyone dances, even *Grandmére* and *Grandpére* no matter what the difficulties they must bear. There may be only a couple of fiddles to play for the crowd, there may be only four candles for light, placed on wooden arms attached to the wall; nothing but long wooden benches to sit on, and only exceptionally a few bottles of *Tafia* diluted with water for refreshment. No matter, everyone dances. But always everyone has a helping of *Gumbo*, the Creole dish *par excellence;* then "Good Night," "Good Evening," "So Long," "See you next week" (if it isn't sooner). One shoves off in his pirogue, his paddle in his hand; another gallops off on horseback, others who live nearer walk home singing and laughing. The Carmagnolle [*jacket. — Tr. note.*] is the usual garment. Clean clothes are a great luxury for them. The women wear a simple cotton dress and often in the summer they wear only a skirt. They go to the dances barefoot, as they go to the fields, and even the men only wear shoes when they are dressed formally. As for learning they don't know what it is. Most of them cannot read.

Once past the Acadian coast the houses become more and more spaced out. Forty-five leagues from the city, on the right bank, is located the city of Baton Rouge. The people in this region are a mixture of Germans, Acadians and Irish and the farther one gets from the city the more primitive are the living conditions. Finally fifty leagues from the city is found the settlement of Pointe Coupée, a region of great fortunes and also of very diferent customs. Here is dignity and ostentation, but no more pleasure, no more simple clothes, no more dancing. The owner of a hundred Negroes scorns the company of him who owns only fifty, and he in turn, despises the man who owns still fewer and so on. Pride isolates everyone from his neighbors. However, the hospitable custom still prevails and the traveler is cordially received by almost everyone. Meals are served with a European opulence that is astonishing in this remote district.

The more elevated ground (higher than on the opposite bank), the spacious well-built dwellings with their surrounding settlements of Negroes, the large gardens and orchards nearby, all give to this settlemnt a bustling and prosperous appearance not seen elsewhere in the colony.

The land, back from the river, is more elevated and in this respect the region is more favorable for agriculture. The English were on the opposite side, and their tradesmen, traveling down from Natchez to Baton Rouge (as I noted previously) furnished the settlement with the goods that it needed, especially Negroes, at a very good price, on long term credit, and took their payment in kind. Originally the principal products of the region were indigo wood, furs, bear-oil, and some game and salt-meat. These planters, encouraged by credits during the failing harvests, were the first in the colony to attempt to grow cotton, when the low price of indigo, and the ravages of the diseases to which it was subject made it necessary to look for another cash crop. They were successful. Near the city, the low wet soil is not suitable for cotton, which requires drier soil, and only up-river is this culture possible.

Some of the plantations at Pointe Coupée have more than one hundred Negroes, among which there may be only one or two white people with their wives and children. One cannot but experience uneasiness at this great disproportion. Here the white inhabitants are not, as in the city, in a position to aid each other. Dispersed on the plantations, they could not put down an uprising in a single place. They would be slaughtered one after the other. Without effective intercommunication, the uprising would spread without difficulty from plantation to plantation. After such an uprising, the Negroes would have an immense country into which to retire. They could place vast regions of forests, lakes and river between them and these settlements. Going to the northwest they would reach regions inhabited by Indians who have little to do with Europeans whom they fear and dislike. There the Negroes would be safe, mingling with the Indians and enflaming their hatred for

[margin note, handwritten: fear of slave revolts]

the white man and discouraging them from permitting either settlement or trade.

Something like these reflections are felt by the inhabitants of Pointe Coupée. They live among continual alarms. At night they patrol the countryside and everywhere they spy and listen in on the Negroes. The least suspicious matter, a few more fervent meetings, say, among the Negroes, redoubles their fears and multiplies the nocturnal patrollings and espionage. In 1796, at the time of the ravishing of San Domingo, when the inhabitants of all the colonies were struck with terror, those at Point Coupée who were already terrified because of the great danger that surrounded them, thought that they discovered evidence of a conspiracy among their Negroes, evidence which may well have existed only in their excited imaginations. From the discovery of this conspiracy, probably false, resulted the hanging of at least 12 Negroes and the condemning of two white men to the mines. The mysterious forms of Spanish criminal justice leave us no way of ascertaining the evidence upon which the existence of the conspiracy was based. One can see how gnawing is the anxiety, which far from diminishing with time, is growing, because the colored population is growing faster than that of the whites.

Two or three years before my trip to Point Coupée, an event occurred which shows how slavery must influence the behavior of the masters. A man of the region, whose character was haughty and evil, raised among Negroes, whom he made a game of cruelly whipping, was famous as a bully throughout the colony. He quarrelled frequently and his quarrels could only be settled by the sword. More than that, he intervened in other difficulties, and forced to fight those who had every intention of reconciling. A young man of the city, the apple of his mother's eye, had some insignificant difference with one of his friends. The bully intervened and proclaimed that only blood could wash away the affront. The mother who believed that her son would be dishonored if he did not fight, herself girded on his sword. A few minutes later her cherished son was carried in, covered with blood, and dying of his wound. His bereft mother flung herself upon him, pressing him to her breast, calling his name. He was no more, and his mother took leave of her senses, a condition that lasted so long that it was feared that it would be permanent. I saw this sensitive lady, the victim of the most atrocious prejudice, her face lined by her terrible affliction.

The bloody bully quarrelled at Pointe Coupée with his brother-in-law. He had become the scourge of the colony and a tyrant over his family. The brother-in-law ridded society of this wretch, by still another crime, that is, by shooting him to death in the woods. A mulatto woman in the house, who knew all the circumstances of the murder, was thereupon poisoned. She died in horrible agony, but no one has been punished and the whole affair remains shrouded in mystery.

These crimes were not conceived and executed in the heat of a great city, where extreme corruption, misery or heightened passion inflamed the principals. They took place fifty leagues from a little town, in the peacefulness of the countryside, surrounded by immense solitudes where most of the inhabitants have never seen even a good sized village. They took place in the midst of abundance, where everything appeals to the tranquility of the soul, where gentleness and humanity are necessary virtues, almost involuntary ones. Our populous districts hardly offer comparable examples among their worthy families. Do we need to seek any other cause for this anomaly than the existence of the condition of slavery which accustoms the free man to sacrificing his fellow creatures to his passions as a child sacrifices his toys to his tantrums?

The hospitable customs of the country insure that no inns can be established there. There are, to be sure, here and there, some low taverns, the meeting places of the idlers of the countryside, the drunkards and the gamblers. Stores, however, are springing up daily, and these nearby sources of merchandise, which offer credit to the planters, make it no longer necessary for them to go down to the city for their necessities.

A second type of merchant, increasing even more in numbers, has also its advantages, although mixed with some inconveniences. These are the *caboteurs*, boatmen peddlers, who, two or three in number, navigate the river in pirogues carrying sugar, coffee, tafia, china and some cloth goods. These *caboteurs* are, for the most part, French sailors, stranded in Louisiana by the war, a few Catalans and also a few English. They sell their usually low-grade goods at low prices because of the competition, among them. There are so many of them, that they are met with continually on the river, coming and going. They take in payment, chickens, eggs, tallow, lard, hides, honey, bear-oil, corn, rice, beans, in fact anything that they can sell in town, and they are the principal victuallers of the city.

These *caboteurs* do not confine their commerce to the masters. They maintain an illicit trade with the Negroes that is much more lucrative. The latter steal chickens from their masters, and whatever else they can take, and trade them for *tafia*, sugar, canvass, handkerchiefs and knick-knacks. True, the Negroes do have chickens and pigs of their own, but they can sell nothing without the permission of their masters. It is better for both the buyer and seller to do without the permission. The inhabitants complain continually of the thefts committed by their Negroes encouraged by the *caboteurs*, and they curse and revile the latter. They do not see at all that these boatmen give them a market for goods they could not otherwise sell, and by their competition, engendered by the numbers of them, get the planters a better price for their produce, at the same time giving them the opportunity of obtaining small luxuries daily, just as if they were in town.

A third type of merchant comes daily to the inhabitants of the countryside. These are the peddlers, some in carriages, with one or two horses, others on foot, carrying on their backs hardware, clothing and jewelry. The majority of them are young men of French families, who having received a good education, have been reared in indolence. For this reason or that, lack of room for them at home, because they are so numerous, the impossibility of returning home at the moment, the lack of means for returning because their resources are exhausted, by imprudence or calamity, these young men are reduced to this painful state, which at least, is not regarded here, as degrading.

One of them, who came to Louisiana by way of the United States, had come down the river to New Orleans by way of the Ohio from Fort Pitt. Upon arrival, he found himself penniless. With much difficulty he obtained the credit, with which to buy the goods to fill his pack. He had not gone a league from the city when the difficulty of the road, which was slippery, discouraged him. Cursing his destiny, he told me he was tempted to jump with his burden into the Mississippi. In this state of mind, at about midday, he arrived at a stately mansion about four leagues from the city. He approached and displayed his few wares. He sold a few trifles and then the owner said to him "It is time for dinner. You must stop with us." The young peddler accepted with reluctance. The planter and his family put him completely at his ease. The cheer was excellent. The wine was an old Bordeaux and was poured freely. While dinner was progressing, the sky became overcast and the weather turned bad. "You will stay with us tonight," said the planter. "You will rest, have breakfast with us tomorrow, and then you can take up your route again, refreshed. You must accustom yourself, a little at a time, to the weariness of travel." The young man then showed his thanks with a gesture. He was too choked with emotion to speak. "To think," he said to himself, "they do not look down upon me for being a peddler. I am given the same consideration and extended the same courtesies as the foremost citizen of the colony! I shall never be humiliated again! Fatigue is nothing to me now." He slept soundly that night, and the next day his pack seemed easier to carry. Things went so well for him that soon he bought a horse and wagon. Then a second horse, and finally a Negro helper. In five years he had saved five to six thousand piastres.

The planter who gave encouragement to the young man, who still perhaps does not know all the good he did by his hospitable action, is one of the leading men of the colony and he is named *Maccarti* [*Macarty plantation is the site of present day Carrollton. According to Grace King the name is that of an Irish family that fled to France with James II, presumably after the Battle of the Boyne in 1690.—Tr. note.*]

Bad weather likewise caught me at his house, and I also was treated to a cordial reception. It is not always money that people down on their luck require. A kind word and good counsel may be enough to settle the destiny of such a man and to transform him into a useful member of society.

However, one should not expect to find rich sugar planters as hospitable as Mr. Macarti everywhere. Often one finds rich people much less cordial. At the home of a poor Acadian, or a miserly German, or an Irishman (who is still more so), one may expect only coarse corn bread, *sagamite*, grits with salt meat to eat, water to drink; only the floor upon which to sleep, wrapped in one's cloak and blanket. The bear-skin that travelers almost always carry with them, is the usual bed in the outposts of the colony.

Those merchants who travel by carriage, have a more difficult life even than the peddlers. At every house they must carry in their wares to tempt the buyers. The merchants must, themselves unhitch the horses, and re-harness them in the morning, and lead them out to pasture. In short, the merchant must be his own groom, often during the hottest hours of the day. Let the carriage become stuck in the mud, or broken, or let the harness be broken and the unfortunate merchant must be porter, wheelwright, saddlemaker and harness-maker all rolled into one. Notwithstanding this, I have met merchants of this sort who had been born in Paris raised by blind parents who schooled them to indolence.

[*This suspiciously large number of young men of good family whom Robin met in humble stations of society makes one wonder if they were not more likely the prototypes of The Duke and the Dauphin of Huckleberry Finn, spinning a good yarn for the ear of a sympathetic traveler. However, this was the period just after the Revolution and it is possible that some of them were telling the truth—Tr. note.*]

What a rich patrimony does that father leave to his children, who steels them against the vicissitudes, who habituates them to the privations of life, who teaches them to bear the adversity of the weather, to sleep on the ground and to endure long marches. Those of war itself are no longer nor surrounded with more difficult and unremitting labor.

CHAPTER XLVIII

Houses of the countryside. Their construction, their distri-
bution, materials; fencing; destruction of the forests, Obser-
vations on that subject. Description of the still uncultivated
land along the river; Obstruction of Navigation. Walks of
the author among the primitive forests, principal types of
trees observed there.

From the city to Lafourche [Donaldsonville] both banks of the
river are lined with houses. From Lafourche to Point Coupée the
interval between houses becomes longer. Beyond Point Coupée
there are no houses outside of the few settlements at long distances from each other designated on the map until the Illinois.
The houses close to the city (especially those of the sugar planters) are sumptuous. Farther away they are smaller and simpler.
Some of the houses are of brick with columns, but the usual construction is of timber with the interstices filled with earth, the
whole plastered over with lime. These houses have ordinarily only
two or three large rooms, but the heat of the climate makes galleries
around the houses a necessity. All of them have one, some around
all four sides of the house, others on two sides only, and, rarely,
on only one side. These galleries are formed by a prolongation
of the roof beyond the walls, but the prolongation forms a break
in the angle of the plane of the roof so that the gallery roof rises
instead of falling. This produces an effect opposite to the appearance of a Mansard roof. These attached wing-like roofs are supported by little wooden columns, an agreeable effect for the eyes.
The galleries are usually eight or nine feet wide. These wide galleries have several advantages. First, they prevent the sun's rays
from striking the walls of the house and thus to keep them cool.
Also, they form a convenient and pleasant spot upon which to
promenade during the day (one, of course, goes to the side away
from the sun), one can eat or entertain there, and very often during the hot summer nights one sleeps there. In many houses the
ends of the galleries are closed, to form two additional rooms.

Houses are built either on the ground or elevated on blocks.
The most miserable and poor ones are built on the ground, especially those of the Negroes, which are called *cabanes* or *cases à*
Negres. Their construction is cheap and quick. Cypress posts
about three inches square and about ten to fourteen feet long
(somewhat thicker at the butt end) are driven into the ground to

a depth of about two feet, to form the shape of the house. The roof tree and joists are pegged to these posts and hold the house together. The vertical posts are slatted and the chinks filled with earth mixed with the plant called Spanish beard [Spanish Moss]. It is fine and black like horse hair and never rots [*this refers to the inner core of the moss, after the soft grey outer covering has been rotted away.—Tr. note.*] and makes the caulking quite stable. The red earth found in several regions of the colony dries to an extraordinary hardness and takes a nice polish. I do not doubt that when the population rises, and wood has become less abundant, the art of pisé will come into its own and beautiful and agreeable buildings will be erected by this means, more comfortable, healthier and less expensive than stone buildings would be, stone being absent everywhere in lower Louisiana. [*Pisé is rammed earth construction of walls. Mud, alone or mixed with gravel, is pounded in forms and allowed to set to a rock-like consistency. Afterwards the forms are removed and the mud surface painted or white-washed to protect it from rain. The method of construction is almost unknown in North America.—Tr. note.*]

The roofs of the houses are covered with bark, with *pieux* (a sort of plank) or with shingles. The bark is always made of cypress, which is smooth, flexible, strong and durable. These *pieux* are loose shingles eight or nine feet long and about ten inches wide, and from ten to fifteen lines thick. [*12 lines equal one inch. —Tr. note.*] They are pegged to the roof beams, or nailed down by cross-pieces. These big shingles are not displeasing to look at, but their long length makes them split easily and fall off, so that houses so roofed are liable to leaks. Conventional shingles give less trouble in this way, although they do give some.

The doors are also simple, pieces of *pieux* held together only by cross pieces, made entirely without iron, not even a nail. Bolts, locks, even the keys, are made out of wood. The chimney, again, is made of four posts tilted inward toward each other, with slats nailed across the posts, the whole covered with a wide coat of mud, and oddly enough in this country, where in the winter large fires are kept going day and night, where the cooking fire is always lit and tended by improvident Negroes, chimney fires are rare.

Houses on blocks are much more expensive to construct. One must have a floor beneath, supported by strong floor joists, and the construction must be more solid. Chimneys in these houses are brick. The piers upon which these houses are raised are sometimes nothing but sections of large tree trunks, and sometimes blocks of bricks. The more houses are elevated, the more they are cooled by the wind, and their especial advantage is that they are much less bothered by mosquitoes, which are continually blown away by the wind.

All of the fences are made of these same *plat pieux* or cypress planks. The ends of these *pieux* are cut into tenon which fit into mortises in *other pieux* which are driven vertically into the ground. A fence made five or six of these *pieux* high is an excellent barrier for animals. These fences are not bad looking, but are not nearly as pleasant to the eye as a hedge would be. Some of these fences enclose more than 100 arpents. *Pieux* cost from six to ten sous apiece, according to where they are bought, but almost all of the planters have them made locally by their Negroes. The trunk of a cypress tree may rise sixty to eighty feet high. After it is cut down, it is sawed into nine-foot lengths which are easily split, like our staves.

If one wanted to use them, there are plants suitable for making strong hedges which would be impenetrable even to Negroes. The Mimosa with its ivory thorn, or the locust with its long thistle-like thorn, would bush out promptly to form an impenetrable barrier, but this would of course take time. The hedges have to be pruned to keep the plants from throwing out suckers. The inhabitants would rather have their cypress board fences, which require only a minimum of indifferent attention. However, the time is not far off, when, in some districts anyway, the farmers will have to turn to living fences. The woods behind the plantations are being logged off at a surprisingly rapid rate. The cypress does not grow from the stump and the young trees grow very slowly.

The inhabitants are preoccupied with the present and have no regard for the future. They push this short-sightedness to the extent of not even leaving one tree in open fields to shelter the animals and men. Only occasionally do they leave trees along the paths and roads. The inhabitants of this land seem to see in trees only obstacles of their labors. They do not see them as attractive to the eyes, nor do they see the necessity of these majestic plants for shade and for purifying the air. I do not believe that in the entire history of the colony any inhabitant has ever planted a cypress tree, a tree so useful to the inhabitants that they scorn to use any of the many others that cover the land. It seems that these people would find a treeless plain entirely satisfying to view. I have seen respected citizens, in choosing a cypress for some purpose, make a game of cutting down a large number which they simply left dying. Once when I was in the Atakapas, a certain man sent to ask my permission to cut down a large gum tree (it was about eighty feet high) which grew in a wood that I owned. I asked the Negro, "Why does your master want to cut it down?" "To get the moss that covers it," he replied. This behaviour is no better than that of the thoughtless savage who cuts down the tree in order to get the fruit. Indeed his behaviour is often less destructive of Nature than that of civilized man.

I find this taste for destroying native productions stems from the maxim that we teach to children that the earth is given to man to enjoy. From this teaching, the child concludes that he is at liberty to change, upset or destroy anything he pleases, according to his whim. Instead of this erroneous notion he should be taught that man is the foremost of creatures only because he is the foremost conservationist; that the most meritorious of activities is the preservation of his environments; that he should enjoy everything; but misuse nothing; and that even in the least of creatures he should recognize the work of the creator. Then he would submit to authority in the wilderness as in human society. Then he would do good everywhere, more from good habits than through obedience to commands. What a heap of dull moralizing could then be consigned to oblivion!

CHAPTER LI

Red River. Flooded Lands. The Rabbits of Louisiana. Dif-
ferent customs. Black River. The Quality of its water. The
Wilderness along its banks. Prairie. Meeting with the In-
dians. Trade with them. Property among these people. Ob-
servations on this subject. Error of Philosophers about Prop-
erty. Dwelling at Cataoulou. Remarkable Monument of the
Indians. The Tinsa. Extent and effects of the river on these
countries. Different Products.

When one leaves the Mississippi and ascends the Red River, one
must take care to ascend along the bank opposite to the *Chafalaya*
[Atchafalaya] where the current runs swiftly. This is the Charybdis of the region, respected by all the boatmen who go up and down
the river. One must be certain in going from one river to the
other that the weather is good and the wind moderate, for while
the water is quiet near the banks, in the center of the river, where
the two currents flow together, the water is extremely choppy, and,
with the slightest wind, very dangerous. I well recall the perilous
passage I had at this spot on one of my trips, and I can still see
the pallor of the captain's face and feel the consternation of the
oarsmen. The waters of the Red River are seen long before one
comes to the River. The Red River water is dark and reddish.
It does not have either the taste or the beneficient qualities of the
Mississippi water, of which the inhabitants rightly boast. They
attribute to it the capacity for increasing fertility (and they may
be right), and especially of increasing the frequency of the occurrence of triplets. Does the habitual eating of fish have anything
to do with this? The water of the Red River is not only disgusting
to see but has a brackish taste which becomes more noticeable when
the water is low. This is to be attributed to the salt springs that
feed into it.

The land at the entrance of the Red River is so low that it is
flooded for several months to a depth of from fourteen to twenty
feet. One can estimate the height of the water by the marks left
on the trees; the reeds and water left tangled in the branches of
the crown, and the hairy-looking detritus left so high up on the
willows. The traveler at this time, loses all sight of land, except
for the tops of the trees. When the boatmen stop for the night,
they choose a spot where the current has jammed some uprooted
trees together into some loop of the river to form a sort of plat-

form. There they tie up their boats and light their fires on the gently heaving platform, and sometimes even stretch out their bed-rolls there. There is only one known point of land on the left as one ascends which is usually out of water when the river is high. Formerly there was a little fort on it. Someone told me that he had camped here when the river was in flood and had found a large number of rabbits, which had been forced up on it by the water, and they could be taken by hand. To think of rabbits in this swampy region where there is not so much as a hillock! These rabbits, however, are different from ours. They do not dig burrows; they could not, the water would flood them. They live in the fields, and make nests covered with a little vegetation. As we see, Nature varies the species and diverts their instinct according to the region. Their meat is good, but not as good as that of our wild rabbits. It is not as white. This rabbit seems to me to share characteristics of the rabbit and the hare and to tie together these two genera. [North American rabbits are of the genus SYL-VILAGUS, *quite different from the European genus* ORYCTOLAGUS, *which is the wild ancestor of the domestic rabbit. Hares are members of the genus* LEPUS, *and are represented in North America by the Western Jack rabbits and Northern Snow-shoe rabbits.—Tr. note.*]

The trees are not very tall, except along the banks of the river, no doubt from being submerged so much. Many of them are covered with a white lichen, both leafy and filamentous. The curves of the Red River are frequent and curve more sharply than those of the Mississippi, forming continuous turns in and out, limiting to an extraordinary extent the view of the traveler, searching for the infrequent spots that are suitable for mooring. The winds blow less forcefully here, but navigation still has its danger. One may be proceeding smoothly on the quiet waters, when, making a turn, one is suddenly surprised by surging waves. This takes place when the wind blows against the current.

Ten leagues up from the mouth is found the Black River on the left [*On the left bank. Actually on the right if one is proceeding upstream—Tr. note.*] whose waters are darkened by its shaded banks topped with still higher trees. The water looks and tastes alkaline, no doubt on account of the large number of leaves and wood which rot in it, and the large amount of vegetation which is on the banks. Travel is faster along this stream, sheltered from the wind, but everything is lonely and wild and the traveler soon tires of this monotony. One is oppressed and longs for a wide horizon and less still air. We began to encounter patches of prairie of various sizes, surrounded by forests. The curve of the river makes a most agreeable picture through these prairies. It was Spring, and I noticed that as we got further North that Spring was not as far advanced as it had been in New Orleans. In these prairies the grass was still a dry stubble. Our sailors amused themselves by setting it on fire at different places in order to drive the game to their guns, and during a part of the night the light that all of these fires gave would equal that of the greatest cities in the world.

The swiftly moving flames enveloped everything in sight. We could see nothing but an immense pall of fire in the dark night from which the smoke billowed and eddied into the sky. The banks of the river became higher as one goes upstream, and the vegetation also becomes more and prettier. The cane brakes, it is true, are not as large or as thick as those along the river. This reed only grows on land that is never (or almost never) flooded. Its roots, forming runners along the surface, make tangled knots like bamboo, which send out a host of suckers, and it springs up everywhere when the ground is cleared. These cane brakes, on account of the large amount of humus that they deposit, make the soil very fertile, and the farmers regard their cane brakes as the best possible land; in fact, they judge the quality of the soil by the thickness of the cane.

A slight wind had sprung up to aid our oarsmen, and while we were proceeding at a good pace on the quiet water two fine pirogues decorated with deer heads sporting long branched antlers suddenly darted out of a nearby bayou. They were manned by Indian families. Women seated nonchalantly near the steersman directed him with comely outstretched bare arms, while the men manned the high oars. We hailed them and invited them to come ashore with us, after which we treated them to a few glasses of *Tafia*, which they accepted willingly, the women as eagerly as the men. A few words of French, which they understood, a few words of their language, which one of our sailors understood, and many gestures at which the Indians are past masters, enabled us to get along. They traded us half a deer for a handful of salt. Their pirogues were loaded with bear and deer skins, deer, tallow and bear oil. They were on their way to the posts at Rapides and Avoyelles to trade. It is when the hunting season is finished that trading is mainly done.

In exchange for powder, ball, handkerchiefs and wool blankets we got deer and bear skins, oil and fat, at quite a good price. They told us that we would come to an encampment of a dozen families two days' travel away. We stopped there. The men were away hunting, scattered throughout the countryside. Each family had its own hut, which consisted of a few poles stuck in the ground, arched over to form a low-roofed hutch about four feet high, in which one could only fit sitting or lying down. These huts are only about nine feet long and six feet wide. They are thatched with palmetto leaves. Outside, a fire burns night and day. The Indians like to sit around a fire, especially at night when they do not sleep. These fires are never large, and everyone crowds around them. This custom traces to their habit in wartime of never speaking loudly, so as not to be heard, and of never building large fires so as not to be seen. Nearby two forked sticks stuck in the ground supported a cross piece upon which hung drying pelts and meat.

These women were impatient to see what we had to trade. Ornaments were what they most wanted. This desire, the source of luxury, is often seen to characterize the fair sex as much in these somber forests as in the heart of great cities.

I tasted a reddish gruel, which I saw the Indians eating, and it tasted like a gruel made of potato starch. It is, however, made from the bulb of a smilax or sarsaparilla which appears to be related to the yams. This plant is very common; its bulbs, as big as a fist, and made of a tough substance, may be seen on the surface of the ground.

The Indians extract the starch by mashing the bulbs and letting the starch settle in water, as we obtain starch from potatoes. They make delicate little cakes out of it, and it is also used in medicine. A tea made from it is used to induce sweating. [*This plant is* SMILAX PSEUDO-CHINA, *and the suggestion that it is related to yams is a botanical absurdity. William Bartram describes its use among the Florida Indians thus: "There was a noble entertainment and repast provided against our arrival consisting of a variety of dishes and a very agreeable cooling sort of jelly, which they call* CONTE. *This is prepared from root of a china briar (*SMILAX PSEUDO-CHINA*) . . . . They chop it in pieces, which are afterwards well pounded in a wooden mortar. Then being mixed with clean water, in a tray or trough, they strain it through baskets; the sediment which settles to the bottom of the second vessel is aftrewards dried in the open air and is then a very fine reddish flour or meal; a small quantity of this mixed with warm water and sweetened with* *honey when cool becomes a beautiful, delicious jelly, very nourishing and wholesome. They also mix it with fine corn flour, which, being fried in fresh bear's oil, makes very good hot cakes or fritters."—Tr. note.*]

Each household has its hut, its chickens, its dogs, some iron, copper, wooden and clay pots. These last are made by kneading ground-up shells into the clay before firing.

Where then are the traces of communal ownership of goods among primitive societies? Does not every individual wish to be the owner of property, and the master of what he needs? Would he wish another to have his wife at his beck and call? Would he wish his weapons, fashioned to his own use and measurements, to be as much another's as his, when driven by hunger, he must hunt in order to live? The sense of property is born of a sentiment existing in all creatures, even the meerest brute. Herbivorous animals only go in flocks or bands, because there is enough for everyone, and even here, in time of scarcity, the stronger will drive away the weaker. What a chain of false reasoning, what errors are born of this false supposition, that property is a product of civilization! Property is developed, ramified and strengthened by civilization, but it is not the product of civilization. It existed before all civilization, even among scattered individuals wthout even a rudimentary civilization.

It is true that individual ownership of land does not exist among the Indians, because they do not cultivate the land, or, at most, only grow a little corn in temporary plots, and their dwellings are only miserable hovels which they are always ready to abandon. Under these conditions, land ownership is a matter of indifference to them and would even be a burden. On the other hand, national property rights, those that assign to each nation where it shall hunt; such rights are vigorously maintained. It is in defense of these rights that the Indians make their terrible wars, in which the stronger tribes exterminate the weaker ones, slaughtering women and children as long as the weaker tribe exists as an entity until its pitiful remnants are absorbed in some other tribe.

Philosophers are wrong in attributing to property all of the calamities and crimes which sully the earth. It is rather the abuse of property, not property itself, which is responsible for the disorders of Society. Property is the energizing principle of virtue, ability, and enlightenment. It is a perverted sense of property which is destructive.

We arrived at last, at the dwelling of a colonist in this vast wilderness. It was a wretched shack, leaky and badly furnished, but we were in need of provisions, so our stay there was prolonged more than usual, although we were still fifty leagues from the Post of Ouachita, our destination. The proprietor was a native of Bordeaux, named Ébrard, married to a Canadienne who had borne him several children.

Long a resident of the colony, after many journeys, unfortunate enterprises, and, especially, heavy gambling losses, he had just retired to this sombre wilderness, surrounded by water. I asked him why he had chosen to come to this wild spot, without the comforts of civilization, or the company of men, which, however worthless they may be, one can hardly do without. He answerd me: "While this spot may seem lonely, I am visited here more often than I would be almost anywhere else in the colony. Few days pass that some traveler does not stop here. You see that Bayou that enters the river near my house? It runs to the west, where it communicates with a large lake called *Cataoulou* [Catahoula], which means, in the Indian language, *place of great value.* The bayou likewise is called Bayou Cataoulou. [*Today called* LITTLE BAYOU.—*Tr. note.*] The coves of the lake are bordered by hills already occupied by a large number of Anglo-American families. These restless souls love the solitude of the wilderness and make a living by clearing virgin land, selling it, and then moving to new virgin land.

"The number of these settlers is growing daily and will grow still more, now that the country is owned by the Americans. Even at this moment a large number of new families is *en route* for the region. There are some settlements not a dozen leagues from here. The only route of communication that the settlers on the lake have is the bayou which passes my door. If you go up the Black River about a league, you will find the *Tinza* [Tensas], a branch of the river. If you go up the Tensas you will find on the right side a little natural canal which has been artificially enlarged (I myself assisted in this work) which leads to the river a short distance from Natchez. Natchez is the settlement of the Americans who were originally settlers in the old French colony and the last Spanish acquisitions. Today it is a considerable trading post for English goods, cheap and convenient for the inhabitants of Cataoulou. [*The site of Ébrard's cabin is that of the present day town of Jonesville—Tr. note.*]

"Moreover," continues M. Ébrard, "I operate a road overland which leads to the River. It is the only route suitable for the droves of cattle, the *cavaillades* coming from the Spanish provinces to Natchez. These animals, if they could only get past the Spanish customs guards (bribery was the usual method) would bring a return of three or four hundred per cent in Natchez.

These droves of animals must cross the river here on a ferry I maintain for the purpose, and it is rare that the travelers themselves do not require provisions or a guide in these difficult regions. At the same time, those coming up from the city have not seen a human dwelling for a hundred leagues, and do not fail to stop here to fulfil their various needs. Thus you see, all of these routes make the spot a well travelled one and my modest investment has paid off well."

M. Ébrard, a true Gascon, would naturally boast of the advantages of his property and he would naturally wish to convey his enthusiasm to interested travellers. What is remarkable in this is that he was perfectly truthful, besides which, M. Ébrard is one of the most obliging men that I have met. I have noted this upon every occasion that I have visited him, and I have always had a pleasant visit there. All that he requires to become a rich man at that location is more diligence.

In examining a little house that he had constructed I noticed that it was raised on an earth platform, which is level, and perfectly square. It measured about fifty feet on a side and was about twenty feet high. I told him that I did not think that such a regular platform could have been the work of nature and I asked him if he knew anything about its origin. He answered, "Since you are one of the few people to make that perceptive observation I will show you something that you will find both interesting and surprising. Follow me". We walked across some cane brakes with enormous canes, through which passed several roads. I then saw three other earth platforms, of the same shape and elevation as the first. They are equally spaced and were connected by a large ditch, whose earth had been thrown up into a high parapet. I recognized then that this work, several arpents in extent, was a true fortified camp. Even more surprising, was a structure placed as at the head of the camp, on the landward side, a cone-shaped elevation which I estimated as at least a hundred feet high, whose summit was reached by a spiral pathway. From this eminence one could see far across the tops of the trees. The sinuosities of the Bayou Cataoulou [Bayou Little] were spread out before us as well as the Black River turning upon itself in such a way that its turns communicate with those of the Bayou, so that the little tongue of land upon which M. Ébrard's house stood, was a little island of eight or ten arpents. Canes, bushes, even trees were growing on this artificial hill, and remarkably enough several long leaved, trees which are found nowhere in this region.

This site protected on the west behind by swamps, to the North by Bayou Cataoulou, and on the east and south by the Black River forming a semi-circle was admirably chosen as a fortress, but by whom and when? I could not get any answers to these questions from M. Ébrard. This type of fortification is nothing like those of Europeans, and besides, none of them had a post in this region. M. Ébrard thought that the people might have been refugees from Mexico, driven out by the Mexicans, who had come here to find a safe refuge, but between here and Mexico are numbers of other tribes who have never been under Mexican rule. Why would such refugees have come this far in order to escape them? [*The reference is of course to the Aztecs, not to the Spanish Mexicans.—Tr. note.*]

In consulting the notes which I carried with me on the different places that I traveled, I found that Dumont a contemporary, and LePage-Dupratz, who had written some memoirs of Louisiana, stated that the Natchez Indians, after massacring the French abandoned their fort on the river (The Mississippi) and retired to the banks of the Black River and there constructed a fort similar to the one they had abandoned. I could no longer doubt, then, that this was that last retreat where the unfortunate Natchez were massacred by the French and most of the survivors taken as slaves to San Domingo. How could these people, ignorant of architecture, without instruments, and who did not usually work, have moved so much earth, carried it so far, and raised such an imposing structure? The love of independence, the hatred of tyranny had made these miracles.

This monument to despair brought home to me the injustice of the French to the Natchez. Did the misfortune that the colonists experienced, the massacre they suffered, and the ruinous expenses of the armies which bankrupted the company, did these expiate before the eternal justice the crimes which the French committed upon this hospitable nation?

If, in Nature, there does not exist a leaf, whose venation, whose scalloping, whose hairs and petioles are not provided for its usefulness in the sacred schemes of Nature; if there does not exist an animal whose stomach, teeth, claws and talons whose instincts even, are not provided in conformity with the wise plans of the creator; is man alone, better endowed than any other creature able to abuse his gifts? Ah—the author of Nature, so sparing in his gifts towards all beings, could not have been too generous to man except in the expectation that he would conform all the more strictly to the sacred order. If man, on some occasions, appears to run counter to the sublime order, on some other occasion he will be required to pay for this dereliction with interest.

In Tensas, the last western branch of the Mississippi communicates with the Red, Black and Boeuf Rivers by small channels, difficult to navigate, and swamps. When the Mississippi rises, it discharges into these streams, which are then swollen, their currents halted and finally reversed. Everywhere in its course the majestic river imperiously dominates his tributaries who yield to him and draw back from his presence like the lackeys of a potentate.

Thus the river is not really contained in a narrow bed of perhaps four or five hundred *toises* [2400-2000 ft.], which would be astonishing when one considers the quantity of water coming down from so many regions through so many channels. But like the Spirit of God, of whom the river is the sublime work, the river conceals its extent. It spreads out all through the region, feeding those streams which seem to be feeding into it, and spreading out over enormous areas under the eternal cypress trees, filling the numerous lakes to be found in this country, and thus the full width of the river approaches fifty leagues by the time it reaches the sea. The sea itself, receiving the water from so many channels, yields to the river and modifies in its presence its beaches, its currents and its winds and storms.

This region has some special commodities. The edible pecan is found in great abundance along the Red River and its tributaries. It is a kind of a walnut of excellent flavor and quality, but of a very different shape from ours. It is elongated like an olive and of about that size, with a single shell, about as thick as that of a hazelnut. The fruit, like that of our walnut, is separated by membraneous partitions into four lobes. Its taste is the same but better.

The persimmon tree multiplies by suckers whenever the forest is cleared, and becomes abundant. Its golden fruit resembles that of the greengage [*reine Claude*] and tastes like that of the service berry [*Pyrus domestica, also called the sorb.—Tr. note.*] but sweeter. Its meat is nourishing but astringent. The Indians make a paste of this fruit which, dried, serves them as bread.

The wild cherry whose fruit is better than that of Europe, has an agreeable taste and is especially used to make a rich and fruity cordial. The tree reaches a height of about fifty feet with a well shaped trunk and its wood is one of the most important products of the region. It is an excellent hardwood, taking a good polish and showing a pleasing pattern in the grain. It does not, like our European Cherry wood, lose its color with age, but on the contrary becomes redder and redder, never however, attaining the dark color of mahogany. It rivals this last in fineness of grain and it is superior to it in color. [*This apparently refers to the Black Cherry* PRUNUS EXIMA—*Tr. note.*] These forests contain a tremendous diversity of wild plums, none bushy in habit like our sloe, but all large trees with fruits that are yellow, red, purple and many of them too bitter to eat. The best of them taste very different from European plums and all of them are more watery.

With culture, doubtless better varieties could be produced to enrich the agriculture of the region.

These trees are not tall but the crowns spread out much like an apple tree. In early spring they are covered with flowers, and this makes a pretty picture in the still leafless woods.

Cephalanthus, vulgarly known as button wood, here grows to a greater height than the plum trees. It also in early spring is covered with white flowers even more striking. Our botanists state that it grows to a height of only four or five feet, but here it reaches more than thirty. Its flowers, packed in globular heads spread out their common calyx, which is green at first, but soon becomes a brilliant white, and it lasts a long time. In autumn the ripe fruits formed in little heads, are of a brilliant red, and add still more color.

[*The button-bush,* CEPHALANTHIUS OCCIDENTALIS, *is of a bushy habit in the northern part of the range but reaches the dimensions of a tree in southern areas—Tr. note.*]

And everywhere in Spring one sees the beautiful red blossoms of the Judas tree covering the boughs of the trees [The *Redbud, Cercis canadensis*].

The oaks are more numerous, more diverse, taller and straighter than those along the lower banks of the river.

CHAPTER LII

*Post of the Ouachita, recently established by the Canadians.
Their occupations. Other inhabitants. Bayous — neither
streams nor brooks. Naturalization of wheat in this region.
Observations on introduction of different items in the Country. Management of English Garden. Lack of conveniences.
This harmful to the well being of the post Anecdotes, Observations on this subject.*

We arrived finally at the post of the Ouachita, 44 or 45 days after
leaving the city. The settlement of the district had been begun
by the Canadians, who followed the Arkansas River down and
followed the prairie south to the Ouachita River (The upper
reaches beyond the Catahoula are no longer called the Black River
but the Ouachita. [*This is, of course, the site of present day Mon-
roe, Louisiana—Tr. note.*] The abundance of game that they
found there, the large number of Indians who used the spot as a
meeting place, the beautiful fields on the shores of a river, navigable in any season, determined some of them to settle there, and
as a matter of fact these original Canadian settlers were still
living there when I arrived.

For twenty-five years the Spanish Government had had a Commandant at the post. The first was a Frenchman named Filiol
who today has settled here. His successor, whom I found in command, is a Spanish officer named Cotard, a man of spirit and
honor and of agreeable company. I received from him a most cordial welcome. [*It is strange that Martin, in his exhaustive listing
of the officers of various posts of the colony never mentions a commandant at Ouachita, although he does mention the presence of a
company of cavalry there.—Tr. note.*] At his insistence I stayed
with him for the entire six weeks of my stay. His young and
beautiful wife, a New Orleanian, presided over his household
in a gracious manner. M. Cotard loves to talk about his country,
but he does not take offense at being contradicted, although he
shows greater spirit at these times. No reading has instructed me
so well in the laws, customs, and government of this country.

The Ouachita Post today has a population of only four hundred and fifty whites with fifty or sixty slaves. The settlements
are mostly on the left bank of the river, where the natural prairies
are to be found and clearing of the forests is not necessary. The
right bank is, for the most part, either hilly or sandy, covered

mostly with pines. The soil there is less suitable for agriculture, because being raised it is promptly leached by the rains after being cleared. The soil on the left bank, however, being flat and covered with a thick layer of humus overlying the reddish subsoil is fertile, and will be inexhaustible for a long time. The lands of the Ex-commandant Filiol, for example, have been cultivated for twenty-five years, without missing a year. They have been sown to corn with which are mixed with pumpkins, melons, beans, and still give harvests as abundant as in the first year.

These settlements are spread out for twenty miles above the post. On the same side of the Ouachita are found the Bayou's communication with the river, circling across the prairie. One called *Bayou de Siard* and the other *Bayou Bartholomew*. The banks of both are thickly settled.

The word *bayou* used so often in the colony, and which I employ familiarly, refers neither to a brook nor a river. It refers to a waterway, which conforms to the particular conditions of the country. When the waters rise, they overflow, and are thrown into long sinuosities, meandering several leagues across the land. These have the appearance of a stream, except that instead of taking water to the river, they carry it away. When the water reaches its zenith, it becomes stagnant, and when the river drops, the water drains back. Several of these bayous resemble rivers, and they are so ramified in some places that the travelers frequently lose their way. One day our host took us on an excursion which lasted all day on one of those bayous, from which we then had to retrace our path. Most of these bayous are filled with large trees especially cypresses. I must remark that these trees carry an enormous load of Spanish Moss, while those near to the running water have little or none. In time of low water, these bayous which were formerly navigable, are dry, or at most show a trickle of water.

With the Canadians settled in that distant region, are found several Spaniards from Mexico, some Irishmen, some Americans coming in via Natchez, and a small number of colonists born in France, some from San Domingo, some from Scioto, and the United States.

The Canadians do little farming, they take the trouble only to grow a little corn to maintain themselves and a little cotton, which their women weave into clothes with which they clothe themselves. Their dominant activity, even today, is hunting. Toward December they disappear into the woods, where they remain until about Easter time. Then they reap the real harvest, and it might be a good one if almost all of them were not gamblers, drunkards and dissipators. This vagabond life in the woods hardly makes them amenable to work and a regular life.

Living outside of the law for a part of the year, they are difficult to govern, and good faith, that virtue of the age of gold, of infancy and of civilization, is hardly to be found among these men so close to nature. Pleasure and violence come to them too easily on their long hunts. Theirs is almost completely the life of savages.

In the cabin which they have constructed, they store their amunition and a little corn. Some stay there as guards, the rest disperse through the woods to hunt deer and bear. They wander alone for days at a time or even weeks, sleeping under trees, stretching out beside the trunk or sleeping in hollow trees if it rains. If they become wet from crossing swamps or streams, they pay no attention. They live on game, which they skin out and hang up on trees to await them while they continue to hunt. Finally they carry their game back to the cabin, where sometimes they have horses to help carry their heavy loads.

What seems so remarkable is, that they do not lose their way in these immense forests, even when they are hunting for the first time. They always find the skins they have pelted and the meat they have cached. I have questioned some of them to see if I could find out how they are able to do this, but they are unbale to tell how.

Those who remain at the cabin dry the meat in strips [*boucanent les viandes*], pelt the skins, drying them and making them pliable, extract the deer tallow from which they make beautiful candles, and melt down the bear oil which is used as a cooking fat throughout the colony, replacing olive oil. One bear yields up to eighty pots of oil, and a pot of oil, which fetches about a piastre in the city, is worth just about half of that in these regions. The bear skins are worth currently about a piastre and a half in these regions, while deer skins, according to their size and weight from one third piastre up to one piastre.

The hunters often form companies and go shares. Sometimes, one of them, a little more thrifty and well off than the others will advance all of the money for ammunition and supplies and hire the others. Their monthly wage varies, according to their hunting skills, from fifteen to thirty piastres. Many of the hunters are in debt for their guns, their powder and their clothes, and in fact have sold the bear skin before having killed the bear. For this reason their returns from hunting are always meagre, for they are forced to buy dearly what is advanced to them, and sell cheap, what they bring back.

And their most unfortunate vice is gambling. Several of these men have lost five or six hundred piastres in one night, and when this happens, they take to the woods again.

The Irish and the Americans are mostly occupied with raising cattle, swine and horses. Two or three of them have already introduced a better strain of horse, an activity much neglected in Louisiana.

The French families, helped by a few Negroes, are especially concerned with agriculture. Along with corn (which is the staple of the men and animals) they raise cotton, which however, did not seem to me to be as pure a white as I have seen elsewhere in Louisiana. Several have tried to grow wheat. They have tried different kinds, some from Mexico, some from the United States and some from the Arkansas River in the neighboring district. This culture is not very successful. The heavy dews during the flowering season seem to abort or blacken the grain. Some have tried dragging a tow rope every morning across the tips of the plants, but this precaution is time consuming and does not seem to completely avert the damage. A certain Norman, who had been a successful truck farmer from Baltimore, noticed in inspecting the field one day some dry spikes which he at first took to be sterile heads, but on breaking them open he found a well formed mature grain, although the rest of the grain in the field was just past the flowering stage. This individual rightly concluded that the precocious grains were better suited to the climate, so he carefully preserved these few seeds, which he sowed the following year, from which he gathered an abundant harvest, from which he gave seed grain to his neighbors. His alertness gave the colony an invaluable discovery.

In these now settled countries, doubtless other crops will come to be acclimated, especially among the fruits. If some kinds of apple or pear fail, doubtless there are others more suitable. Among the grape vines that have already been tried, there are some on which the bud is covered by a cottony coat and others in which the buds are not coated. Obviously these last are destined to grow in climates in which frost and sleet are unknown. In Louisiana where there are sometimes sudden frosts and sleet storms, one should only cultivate the types with the cottony buds.

But quite aside from this important difference, there are species of grapes native to dry coastal lands, while (as we shall see later) there are others destined by nature to grow in damp soil. All of the European varieties of grapes are of the first type, and such vines planted in the low humid soil of Louisiana do not live more than three or four years, because the roots rot. Therefore one should procure plants who like damp soil to grow in Louisiana, and it would not then be necessary to replant vineyards every three years. Even if such vines are not available, one should at least graft the European vines onto the roots of the native vines, and one could get older stems, which could bear more mature and better fruit.

It was not enough to discover at Ouachita a wheat suitable for the climate, it was also necessary to have a mill to grind the grain. For lack of this, the grain rotted in the storehouses, except what was saved for seed. During my stay, the inhabitants were at last preparing to build a mill, and as a consequence several of the farmers were resuming the culture of wheat, for grain brought in from Natchez, cost up to twenty piastres a barrel (weighing 180 to 190 pounds) and was usually sprouted.

M. Danemours, the former French Consul at Baltimore, had retired to the district several years before my visit and had set up a pretty little house. This man, noted for the nicety of his manners and cultivated mind, used several of his Negroes, whom his excessive indulgence had rendered unused to real work, to lay out an English formal garden in his fields. One must admit that the time and the site were ill chosen. There, where the essentials of life are everyone's preoccupation, where an opulent nature provides a varied and imposing scenery, who would think of disfiguring a spacious field with a tiny garden of coldly spaced groups of plants?

What more beautiful Formal Garden, in this immense forest, than this same field itself, regularly divided into squares of corn, cotton, melons and pumpkins? Near cities, when the eye is fatigued by symetrical figures, one should there reproduce deliberate irregularities. For, while, not far from Paris, I took pleasure in walking in rustic groves, here in Louisiana I delighted in strolling along an avenue of sycamores neatly aligned by the same M. Danemours. In these cool shades I had the illusion of being in my native land.

A French *emigré*, the Marquis de Maison Rouge, whom I was told was once the Treasurer of France at Perpignan, had obtained from the Spanish Government a concession of almost two million *arpents* around Ouachita. He wished to take possession of his holdings in a carriage, but the carriage came dismounted, by the same boat that brought him, and when he arrived he found neither roads on which to drive his carriage nor vassals to admire the munificence of their lord. The carriage was sent back the way it came, without ever having rolled over this virgin land.

This Marquis de Maison Rouge had promised to have his huge domain speedily settled, and indeed it would have well repaid the trouble to do it. It stretched for thirty leagues along the river (the Ouachita) containing fine fields, traversed by streams and bayous and bordered by magnificent forests. In addition, the Government provided an ample sum for each family who would undertake to settle there. But M. de Maison Rouge, who loved the arts, brought in clock-makers, jewelers, and other artisans of this type. Crude farmers were not to his taste. Thus, as soon as the King's stipend was exhausted, these artisans moved on, leaving the concession intact, and untilled, to be transmitted upon the death of the Marquis to a New Orleans family named *Bouligny* who have kept it intact on speculation.

Another *emigré*, a Dutchman named Baron de Bastrop, whom I found there, had, some time later, obtained another concession of about fifteen hundred thousand *arpents* farther up along the river toward the Arkansas, including some magnificent prairies. This Dutch baron, too, was to bring in a group of settlers, some Dutch, some German, from a particular region in North Germany, such of them as were subjects of his Catholic Majesty. In order to make some money, he obtained the privilege of trading with the Indians. A New Orleans merchant, named Delisle-Serpi [*Delord-Sarpy.—Tr. note.*], rich but active in trading, had made some *coups* in the trade, and he furnished ample funds. I found this establishment going full blast, vast warehouses and directors, clearing agents of various kinds and two interpreters at a salary of two thousand livres apiece.

In addition, there were arrangements with the military authority, to insure their protection of the enterprise, and, of course, the Baron helped himself to whatever he needed. "What an enormous volume of trade," I said to myself, "it must take to support so many people with the inevitable waste that their maintenance must entail." A month or two later the bankruptcy of the unfortunate Sarpy put an end to my astonishment.

A Basque named Cortes, a clerk in the establishment, received at least part of the loot (if we may compare small matters to large) in much the same way the great Fernando de Cortes repaid the hospitality of Montezuma.

During the three months that the establishment lasted, the Dutch Baron occupied himself, in beginning the construction of, tearing down, and rebuilding, a saw-mill for the future inhabitants of the Ouachita. When the weather permitted he employed twenty to twenty-five workers on this project, at a wage of one piastre a day, paid, of course, from the funds of Delisle-Serpi. At the same time, he took great care that his trading rights on the post were strictly enforced, and because his watchfulness was both effective and far reaching he insured that the inhabitants lacked almost everything and paid dearly for what they got. His blind cupidity prevented him from noticing that he was the principal victim of this policy. If he had generously provided for the provisioning of the district, he would have enticed great numbers of settlers to come there. He could have made an immense fortune overnight, and by the most honorable of means, but far from getting people to come as settlers into these wildernesses, becoming for them a father or at least a protector, he repelled from his concession those who were nearby.

I saw a good and hard-working Canadian named Jean-Pierre, the father of a large family, who had cleared and planted an attractive plantation adjoining the principal settlement, next to the Baron, forced to exchange it for another grant twenty leagues away by water. This honest Canadian wept as he spoke of his plantation, invaded by the insatiable Baron, fallen in ruins and despoiled. That corner of high ground of which I have spoken above occupied by the estimable native of Bordeaux, at Catahoula, was also almost seized by the Baron under the pretext of public utility, and the Bordelais only preserved his holding by the bluntest threats.

However, few men on the surface ever seemed so interested and trustworthy. A sturdy figure, a calm and pleasant face, simple and relaxed in manner, a style of conversation affable, if not brilliant, always obliging, and the best of masters in his own household, his defects were rather vices of the mind than of the heart. Fatally attractive, without much knowledge or ability, he had ruined all who joined him in his projects without especially enriching himself, as in Kenkuti (Kentucky), as in the United States, his every step was marked by disaster. In Louisiana, all of the

Governors and men of substance were captivated by him. He left the Ouachita without having earned a cent and having done more damage than the wickedest of men, and having failed furthermore to establish a single settler on his lands. Note how these large concessions, established to promote the settlement of this fair country, are the greatest obstacle to its prosperity. [*The Bastrop tract, not long after this, became notorious in American history. It was acquired by Aaron Burr, who intended to use it as the staging area for his filibustering expedition against Mexico, New Orleans, or wherever it was.—Tr. note.*]

Coming ashore, I was accosted by a well-dressed, middle-aged man of spiritual appearance, who engaged me in conversation about the news of Europe and finished by inviting me with great insistence to stay at his house just across the way. I accepted and was agreeably surprised to find a house well laid out, both within and without. The orchard and the garden, placed on opposite sides of the house, were planted and tended with great care. I was especially impressed by the barnyard, which in these hot countries it is particularly important to keep clean, especially the chicken houses. If they are not cleaned and aired, the heat causes the generation of poxes which will destroy the flocks. I have seen some of the settlers keep a hundred chicks in a restricted space of which not one survived. But here, the roomy buildings were isolated from each other, well oriented and ventilated, and raised on pillars, with removable planks. They can be cleaned and washed daily. A well-kept field of about fifty arpents stood before the house, circled by the distant forests, towering jaggedly above, and stripped of Spanish moss, that dreary plant which seems everywhere in this colony to tarnish Nature. He told me that this clearing, these buildings, and these plantings were his own work. I then said, "You must have been here for a long time, and you must have a considerable number of workers to do all this work." "No," said he, "it is not quite seven years since I started this house where a Canadian hunter was living in a miserable shack with hardly two or three arpents of cleared land." My astonishment was extreme. He perceived this and then said, "These occupations have not prevented me from cultivating literature with the aid of a selected library. I always take time for composing my poetry, for which I have a passion. I also study botany and medicine, with an eye to being useful, because I am the only doctor here, and I do it for nothing."

"What," I cried, "even here in the wilderness the lyre of Apollo resounds and Nature is studied. How glad I am that I yielded to your entreaties. The evidences of good taste that I see all around me assure me of the excellence of your verses, the product of your carefree leisure, inspired in the solitude of this retreat. These evidences of culture doubtless mean that you must have had a very good education before coming to the colony." "When events brought me to Louisiana," he answered, "my education had hardly begun. I belong to one of the principal families of Montpellier, a family especially distinguished on the bench of the city, and as a matter of fact collaterally related to a very eminent person in France. My older brother, undertaking a voyage to further his education, took me with him. We toured the islands of the Mediterranean and eventually arrived at Martinique, where I lost him. Abandoned thus to myself, I took ship for Louisiana, where my faculty of learning languages enabled me to set up a lucrative business in trading with the Indians. However, I eventually suffered grave losses, so I gathered up the remains of my fortune and retreated here to spend my life in a more peaceful and, I believe, more useful manner." "May I ask, Sir," I said, "the name of the family to whom you belong?" "De Badinsse," he replied. "De Badinsse," I said. "I do not know it."

In the meantime supper had been served, and it was very good. Madame de Badinsse appeared, a short, stout woman, with a pretty daughter, Mademoiselle de Badinsse, as fresh and pretty as one can be at fourteen, and a man who seemed to be some kind of steward or functionary. I cannot say anything about their personalities. No one opened his mouth except M. de Badinsse. This nettled me a little. After rising from the table, the man mentioned above went and got a large book, from which he read us a selection of the poetry of M. de Badinsse, picked out by the author. His poetry consisted of collections of epistles, ballads and epigrams. I observed at once that our poet was familiar with Boileau, among other models. His productions have gaiety and variety, but also carelessness. These were sharp sallies, but I soon discovered that our poet, whom I had assumed would have concerned himself with the beauties of Nature and the happiness of the solitary life, instead wrote mordant satires rising out of his private quarrels. All of his caustic couplets referred to scandals in the district, and these turned out to be serious matters, which had earned the author enemies, punishments and persecutions. He lampooned especially the former Commandant, Filiol, as the most greedy tyrant that ever existed. Among his exaggerations, unfortunately, there was more than a grain of truth. He did not spare the new Commandant, and all of the more disagreeable aspects of the principal families of the district were paraded before us. We spent the whole evening thus, until after midnight, and when I went to bed these depressing recitations of hate, intrigue, spite and crime depressed me so that I passed a bad night.

Next morning the conversation was continued in much the same vein, while waiting for breakfast. We were strolling on the gallery [*Galérie. The wide porch surrounding the house—Tr. note.*] when a man rode up on horseback. His head was wrapped in a handkerchief.

At sight of him M. de Badinsse abruptly left me, to return shortly. The man, who was very large, dismounted and entered the house. Here he related that he was suffering from a toothache that tormented him day and night. "Sit down," said our doctor, "and let's see what the tooth looks like." The man was hardly seated when he cried out. The tooth had been removed so fast that I had not even time to see that M. de Badinsse had a forceps in his hand. We breakfasted. During breakfast, the man whose tooth had been removed talked constantly about the state of health of a lady whom M. de Badinsse had cured of an enormous abscess on the thigh, which he had opened from the pelvis to the knee and cured by treatment thereafter. A discussion of some point of grammar arose, I forget just how, for M. de Badinsse was punctilious in the use of language. He immediately fetched the dictionary and, giving it to me, said, "Look it up and read it." I read the definition aloud. "But it cannot be," he said. "But it is," I said. "Here, read it for yourself." "I cannot read," he replied. "Come now," I said, "You have excellent eyes." "No it it isn't that," he said, "I don't know how to read." "What," I cried in astonishment, "You don't know how?". "No, really I don't. Everyone on the post will tell you that, as well as this gentleman who is with us. Last night you saw how I had my poetry read by a person whom I employ to write at my dictation when I compose, and to read for me in matters of business". Never was anyone as surprised as I. An author, a poet, a doctor who had become all of these things without learning to read. And he had done this in the middle of the wilderness distracted by numerous daily labors, long trips, and great works with impetuous passions in work and play (for our friend was like that). However imperfect his knowledge, the wonder was that he had any at all.

A few days later when I had established a connection with the commandant, I enquired about M. de Badinsse, and I was assured that what he said was true. I also spoke to people about the various things that he had told me about his name, his family and other matters. M. de Badinsse I was informed was extraordinary in many things, but was a liar most extraordinary. When he arrived in the colony his name was Badin [*The name means "prankster" in French. It is easy to see why he would want to change it. —Tr. note.*] a bedraggled little nonentity whose engaging manners attracted attention. His parents were totally obscure. The name *Badinsse* was extrapolated out of Badin, Badine for poetic harmony. A good education, which would have corrected this horrible fault of lying, which would have directed these restless energies towards some higher goal than satire would have doubtless made of this material, a great man.

The secretary of M. de Badinsse, or Badin, who was named Racine was the most patiently passive man who ever existed, for while the impetuous sallies of his master drove away all who came in contact with him, Racine wrote, erased, added, corrected without showing the least emotion, and he believed that in transcribing the thoughts of his great master, he was associating himself with his glory. This Philostratus portrayed for us the humble Damis with Appolonius of Tyanus. The latest fiction of M. de Badinsse was that which he related to a hatter from Paris, several months after my departure, that his property was worth three times its actual value. The hatter, who knew nothing of poetic fiction, although he knew how to read, was such an enemy to learning that he had left Paris because he saw that scholars were occupying high places. Arriving at New Orleans, and finding too much learning there also, he repaired to the Ouachita, to the establishment of M. de Badinsse, and indeed he could not have chosen better.

M. Schol (that was his name) should at least not have scorned the science of correct addition; his complacent and attractive spouse does not seem to have had the same antipathy for instruction, and came out of it much better. M. Schol, a worthy emulator of the Marquis de Maison Rouge, did not, like this last, bring a carriage into the wilderness, but he did bring a great load of sumptuous mahogany furniture, made in Paris by craftsmen. This was even more expensive and troublesome than the carriage and every bit as useless.

CHAPTER LIV

Furs, the Medium of Exchange in the Ouachita: Observations on exchange in kind, More advantageous than those in specie, All countries should encourage exchange in the goods of the country, Types of furs common in the Ouachita, Influence of the Europeans on the manners of the Indians; they have gained rather than lost in this respect. Why the Indians have not been civilized in three centuries. The easy way in which this could be done. Geographical details of the region. Potentiality of the River for commerce. Quarries and mineral springs that are found as one ascends the stream.

A large number of Indians, inhabiting the upper reaches of the Ouachita River, from the Arkansas to the Red River, come to the post of the Ouachita to trade the spoils of their hunting. The usual season for this gathering is in the Spring, which happened to be the time of my visit, and every day they arrived with their families. The abundance of the furs that they brought, combined with those collected by the colonists themselves, means that furs are the commonest commodity in the district, and in fact serve as the medium of exchange. A transaction may be stated in piastres, but it is paid in furs unless the contrary is stipulated.

The Indian trader trades his furs for blankets, gun powder, bullets and cotton cloth, etc. The colonists give the same for linen cloth, shoes, wine, rum and flours. If, instead of these exchanges, they were paid in money, it would be necessary to then purchase the necessary articles. Thus two transactions would be necessary instead of one. But since he who brings the furs expects to gain by the transaction it follows that he who brought money would also expect to gain. The Indians and the colonists would thus get less for their goods in the double operation. But worse would follow because the men who brought money, having in that commodity a rare and precious good, would value it more highly and would expect a higher return, and thus the colonists and the Indians would get still less of the value of their furs. And if the money merchant, secure in the knowledge of the desirability of his commodity, does not trouble himself to go to the ordinary marketplaces of the Indians and colonists, these will have no choice but to seek him out, and to lose thereby, time better spent in hunting or other occupations. Thus there would be fewer furs and less trade on the part of the Indians and colonists, and higher costs all around. And if it should happen that there would not be enough money for all the transactions, the sellers who could not sell, would be burdened with their furs, and could not get the goods they required. They would have to carry back their furs, store them, and care for them until they could get to market again. The money men, seeing this state of affairs, would not hesitate to reduce the price of furs to take advantage of it, which the needs of most of the sellers of the furs would force them to accept. The introduction of money would multiply difficulties, transactions, and anxieties, and diminish the number of furs and their price, because

1. Money would double the number of operations, and

2 Money is a product, that coming from a-far, cannot be produced as readily as the products of the hunt on the one hand and manufacture on the other.

At Ouachita, they very properly let the most common commodity serve as the medium of exchange, and do not attempt the introduction of money. But could not the same be done everywhere in the world? The exchange medium should always be the most common commodity in the region. All other goods would be valued in terms of this one, and would be easily and promptly exchangeable, and at the same time, the medium of exchange, having an intrinsic value, could never be debased. It would give value to the other goods as they would give value to it.

But if, instead of taking as a standard of value, one of your own products, which your labor, your industry would continuous increase in value, if I say, instead of that, you chose as a standard, a metal not found in your country, which being rare in nature, will never be available in sufficient quantity for all the needs of exchange, and which an infinite number of circumstances could make rarer still, you will be forced to give a large quantity of your goods for this metal, or keep them and allow them to deteriorate, if the metal is not available. And the richer you were in goods, the poorer you would actually be, because the standard of exchange would not increase in value in proportion to the value of your goods. If only a million were available in money, and your goods were worth two millions, you could receive in exchange only the million that was available, and if your goods were worth three, you would still receive only the million, and the same for five or more. Thus while you would be rich in goods that are truly wealth, you would actually be poor.

For close to a century, the fur trade has been carried on in this country, and the prices inland have remained exactly the same; so many skins for a blanket, so many for a gun, etc. The greater number of furs available, the more the manufacture of trade objects is stimulated. Thus the more industrious the Indians become, the more the manufacturer is stimulated to industriousness. The well-being of the one, becomes the well-being of the other, and all of them would be upset if money were employed.

Imprudent Europeans! Must you then go to the wildness of the Ouachita to be shown the cause of your miseries? I enter your cellars with their serried rows of piles of filled casks, so numerous as to make even entrance difficult. I hear the sound of mallets, resounding on still more casks, announcing that soon the growing process will release a new flood of wine, to lie in storage beside that which lies here now. "God Be Praised," I cried. "Fortunate people! To live your days among such abundance." But instead of thanksgiving I hear heavyhearted sighs. "We are ruined. We do not have enough money to pay the workers who tend our vines, nor for the trellises which sustain the vines, the casks in which our wine is stored, nor the taxes on the fields or any of our necessities. And money becomes scarcer in proportion as our land becomes more productive, rendering it more necessary."

Further on, I cross spacious fields covered with fattening herds, I see undulating plains of golden grain, farm houses hidden from view by the stacks of sheaves surrounding them. I find, in these farm buildings, men engaged in shoring up their grain bins sagging under the weight of the grain, and everywhere repeating the doleful words, "We have no money, and the abundance of our produce, which requires us to leave it makes it still rarer." And finally, near a great city, I see large factories, besieged by importunate masses of unemployed, asking for work and these same factories are empty and still. "Why are not these men put to work? We do not have the money to pay them", say the owners. "Our warehouses are loaded with cloth of all kinds, for all seasons, ages and conditions, but for lack of consumers with money, we cannot sell them."

"Unfortunates!" "A thousand times unfortunate!" I cried, "Could not these clothes serve those who are increasing their flocks and harvesting the grain and the grapes? And from them could you not procure the produce of the land, necessary to everybody, and your workers, clothed and nourished by your wages, would not the multiplication of their families increase the consumption of your own goods as well as that of the produce of the land?" But once metal has become the sole medium of exchange, all trade is governed by the amount of it available. Above that amount, trade stops, and manufacture in consequence, and population too at the same time. Thus, this metal which regulates agricultural and commercial wealth, imperiously sets limits on population, which according to its abundance, contracts and expands. And an infinite number of circumstances can contribute to the quantity.

If through fear or other motives, money does not circulate, every one suffers, and in large countries money may circulate freely in the center, but slowly and painfully in outlying districts. In that case, the center of the country suffers from the abundance of money, and its failure to circulate further. At the center, this causes a stagnation of trade, and an excess of money, while the lack of money in the provinces causes a state of debility and exhaustion which gradually milks the center of its wealth. It is like a tree whose sap cannot get to the extremities of its branches, and whose crown wilts in consequence.

If, suddenly, the mines, the sources of this fateful metal, were destroyed by subterranean fires; and if, by some extraordinary cause the metal already disseminated among the nations, all social intercourse would be annihilated with it and mankind would disperse once more into the eternal wilderness. "But, No", you say, "In that case, a new medium of exchange would be devised". "Very well. Do presently what you would do then when the scarcity of this medium restricts the growth of your wealth and population". Less severe than the Lawgiver of Sparta, [*Lycurgus—legendary founder of the Constitution of Sparta who according to Plutarch proscribed the use of gold and silver currency.—Tr. note.*] I wouldn't say "Banish it, Proscribe it," but I would say, "Instead of making money more and more indispensible in your affairs, arrange things so as to make it less and less. All of your legislation, your institutions and your regulations should keep in mind the need of lessening the necessity for money, for replacing it with other media of exchange, and above all to favor payment in kind; bills payable in goods rather than in money. This would encourage the proprietors to look to their fields to the greater profit of agriculture.

[*The modern reader is startled by this curious analysis. One especially notices the lack of any mention of paper currency, surely the easiest way out of any shortage of actual currency. The absence or mention of paper money by Robin is the more remarkable when one recalls that inflated paper currency was one of the immediate consequences of the French Revolution, not to mention the American.—Tr. note.]*

If, in the United States, the products of English factories may be found selling more cheaply than in England, it is because (and in addition to the advantages of export bounties) the Americans buy almost always with goods and seldom with money, that dangerous intermediary. I have often compared here sales made in money and in kind and I have always found the sale in kind to be more advantageous to both parties. I may lay it down as a principle that all goods sold for money sell higher than those exchanged for other goods. This important question has many other ramifications which, however, would lead us far from our subject.

The pelts obtained from the Ouachita are principally those of deer, used in Europe as suede. Beavers are also traded as are a few others. Each year the quantity decreases, in proportion as the settlements are extended. Deer meat is here the common meat of the butcher shops. They make a soup from it which is quite good, but the boiled meat is no longer usable. It is more commonly broiled. Bear meat is much better when fresh, I prefer it to pork which it resembles in taste, but is more delicate.

The bears in this region are entirely frugivorous and become astonishingly fat. Individuals have been found from which 80 pots of oil have been rendered. This grease is so fine and delicate, that it remains liquid all summer, although in the winter it congeals a little like olive oil. All of the hunters assert that the bears retire during the winter to the hollows of trees or into the dense cane-brakes, and although the winter is severe enough to really isolate them for only a few days, the bears do not leave their lairs during the winter. They nourish themselves by licking their feet. Some naturalists indeed say that the feet are provided with glands which secrets a milky substance. One would suppose that the immense quantity of liquid fat, which the bear accumulates during the season of fruits, circulates to the glands to be elaborated as secretion. [*This same myth may be found in Pliny (Historia Naturalis, Book 8). It seems to have been widespread in colonial Louisiana. It is found also in Bossu's "Nouveaux voyages aux Indes occidentales, etc."—Tr. note*]

A pig with a thick covering of fat eats much less at that time, showing that the fat is for him also a source of food. The deer also acquires fat during the winter and the rutting time, but as it is in a firm suet not enough of it accumulates to slow down the animal's speed. Its sole defense is flight. Deer hunting is not particularly difficult or onerous. The hunter uses no dogs, but simply walks through the woods. When he sees a deer, he drops back a little and then approaches in such a way as to be masked by the trees. If the deer sees him, he makes several gestures with his hands to fix the deer's attention, and seeming to amuse himself, he gradually raises his gun and takes aim. Often the Indians go out in pairs, one carrying a stuffed deer's head which he raises from behind a tree, and maneuvers in a way that amuses the deer while his companion takes a shot.

The deer of lower Louisiana are much larger than those of upper Louisiana as one can judge from the pelts. Those of the males from lower Louisiana weighing six or seven pounds, while those from Upper Louisiana weigh only three or four.

I will not repeat what so many travelers have already said about the customs of the Indians, but will content myself with a few separate observations, which I consider useful to the study of the history of man.

Many writers have remarked on the change in the customs of Indians brought about by their contact with Europeans. This is fine in some respects, but it has been variously exaggerated according to the beliefs of the writer. The customs of the Indians, like those of all people of the soil, are determined by the means whereby they gain their living. These are the primordial customs of all nations and all conditions. The Indians are principally hunters and other means of survival are only accessory; hunting therefore regulates all their customs.

Before they had firearms, the Indians used to gather in large numbers, and forming long lines of beaters, they drove the animals together and shot them down with arrows; for obviously hunting alone, they could never have brought down large animals like buffalo, bear or elk. These community hunts necessitated preliminary assembling for laying down the duties and deciding the shares of the participants. This necessitated meetings before, during and after the hunt. At the start there were feasts and dances in order to encourage themselves, and if the hunt were successful, there were more solemn and lengthy festivals celebrating the success of those who had distinguished themselves by their skill or courage, interspersed with praises for those who had died on the hunt, then complaints and lamentations and lugubrious chants. Thus communal hunting associated every individual with the general welfare.

With the arrival of fire-arms, far more efficient than arrows, it was possible for a single individual or at best a few hunters to engage in hunting. Thus every hunting affair ceased to be a public occasion, and the great celebrations became less frequent, and no longer involved the same ceremoniousness. The dances and games became obsolescent. Public affairs among the Indians deteriorated. They lived more in single families and small aggregations. They no longer needed to associate themselves into great nations except in time of war, against those who interfered with their hunting. War was thus almost the only bond left to them, but those peoples who were neighbors of the European settlers, no longer fearing destruction by enemy warriors, have almost ceased to exist as nations. They have gradually become dispersed in small bands and families, whose relationship to each other is only casual. At the same time, the use of fire-arms made them dependent upon the Europeans for guns, powder and lead, as well as for iron tools like hatchets and knives, which were far superior to those they had before. These they obtained in exchange for skins which they had formerly used as clothing, but now they accustomed themselves to replacing these with blankets and coarse cloth which were much more convenient. Thus, little by little, they got out of the habit of using skins as clothing. This is the sort of influence that Europeans have had on the Indians.

It has been said that the customs of the Indians have been corrupted by the Europeans, and that we have given them a number of vices. This is not true. The deplorable condition to which the consumption of strong liquor has reduced some of them, has given rise to exaggerated reports. Here is the truth of the matter.

Some Indians living near Europeans, and therefore being practically domesticated, are addicted to drunkenness as are some Europeans. But in distant regions, among the forests, they have no occasion to communicate with the colonists except after the hunt, and this is the only time they are able to obtain intoxicating beverages, but as everyone well knows, the state of frenzy seizes them, and all governments forbid the sale of it to them. The traders have no incentive to get them drunk, because they would thereby endanger their goods and even their persons. It is only at the end of the trading, when the traders are leaving, that they give them a small amount as a present. This is a dangerous time, when the wives of the Indians hide their guns, knives and tomahawks. Thus it is only once or at most twice a year, that the hunters ever have the opportunity to get drunk, and that is hardly enough to cause the degeneration of the race as some writers have maintained. The distant tribes, who having no communications with Europeans, do not have fire-arms, do not have better customs or a more perfect physique than the others.

Furthermore, I believe that as far as morals go they have improved rather than degenerated since their contact with Europeans. Savages are treacherous liars, a usual attribute of weakness. All of the people of the Pacific Ocean, and other regions, when visited for the first time have immediately revealed to the traveler, these characteristics of lying and treachery, which are born of a desire to hide what they are afraid to reveal to another stronger than they. Also, savages all over the world are thieves for the institution of property is only found in advanced nations. All being common in their experience, they do not see why they should not take what they find good. If they are hungry and find meat, hanging from a tree in the woods, they cut off what they need, as they would allow anyone else to cut what he needed from their own. If they find an empty cabin, and are tired they will enter and sleep as readily as if it were their own. The savage, accustomed to using almost always the belongings of others, does not consider that he is doing any real injury to a European if he helps himself to some objects that he feels he wants. He had no idea how much time or labor these objects may have cost the Europeans, and until his ideas are reformed, he sees the European as an eccentric and unobliging person.

During the six weeks I remained at the Ouachita I was domiciled in an isolated cabin, around which a hundred or so Indians slept during the night. During the day, they entered and sat down as often as they wished. I often left them there alone and never did they take or disturb the least object. These Indians were Choctaws, as much robbers in earlier times as any others, but coming yearly as they do to trade their furs, they have, by this contact with Europeans, learned to respect the property of others. This trustworthiness, which has become indispensible to them, has at the same time, made them less likely to lie. Those who stole were chased away. Those who lied caused the Europeans to lose confidence in them and every Indian, fearing to be the victim of lying or thievery of another, found it in his interest to eradicate these vices from among them. Thus relationships with the Europeans improved their morality.

The Indians bring up their children with great indulgence. They do not discipline, and never maltreat them. In this, it must be admitted that they are more humane than we. But these children grow up to live like their fathers by hunting and passing most of their time in inactivity. They therefore do not need to be prepared for making use of skills which are difficult to acquire.

Only the women concern themselves with the details of housework, which indeed, amounts to very little. They dexterously weave light baskets which they ornament with pretty little designs in a sort of mosaic. They carry all of the burdens, which doubtless explains why they are short and stocky and not as well built as the men. The latter, totally occupied with hunting, cannot be burdened with anything that would inconvenience them in hunting. They must be free at all times to follow the game that they run across. It is from this general custom in savage nations that arises the fact that women are left to carry all of the burdens and to care for all of the details of housekeeping.

Those who are most active and diligent at hunting are most esteemed among them. A woman is honored to have such a husband, and as he brings home more meat and furs than others, she is better fed and better clothed as well.

Repeated communications with Europeans, may have modified their customs, but it has certainly not civilized them, that is it has not led them to give up the vagabond life of the hunters to become settled agriculturalists. There does not exist in all of the New World as in some parts of the old, a single people capable of being civilized. At any rate Europeans have not been able to do it in three centuries. [*One is constrained to point out in passing that the Choctaw were settled agriculturalists until violently displaced by the white man.—Tr. note.*]

Zealous missionaries have fanned out among the nations, have passed their entire lives among them in instructing and reforming them. They have given themselves up with a heroic constancy to the most painful of labors. They have withstood all privations, have braved a thousand kinds of dangers, and have combined the greatest ability with the highest virtue. It must be said that the annals of the world have nothing comparable.

I do not know if the founders of Christianity required for their conversions even more constancy, more labor or more ability, but in any case, these missionaries have not succeeded even with the aid of the civil authority. They have formed a few congregations of Indians, but these have been temporary. They have returned to their former customs as soon as they were free to do so. What has been the cause? Does it lie in the mind of the savage? But these people have a civil organization comparable to ours. They are capable of the same affections, the same passions. If under these circumstances, not a single one has been civilized, the fault must lie in the methods that have been employed.

Is it possible that the Christian Religion, which has served as the basis of civilization, is not suited to these people? It is true that their ideas are few and simple, unmixed with abstractions, and interlocking so that they do not conflict. All of them, whatever is said of them, have the idea of a Supreme Being, which they call the Great Spirit, and many of them surround him with inferior intelligences, who together rule the world. This, together with a few notions of the immortality of the soul, is all their religion. They have no cult. Would one expect a wandering people who live in huts roofed with leaves, who leave no trace of their passing once they have moved on, to have a cult? Does not this presuppose temples, rites, priests and the facilities for gathering together at specific places and times? Under these circumstances how could one expect them to adopt these mysterious dogmas contrary to their clear if limited ideas?

The European pagans, steeped in their bizarre mythology, groaning under the vilest despotism, were susceptible to any dogma, no matter how contrary to their former belief. These rigorous moral obligations, which have arisen from such varied customs, how could they be suitable for people whose obligations are few, and who cannot conceive of others? In a state of civilization, when individuals are in close contact, when people require to aid each other more, and are able to damage each other more, one must have a severe morality; but this same morality may be harmful, to men living widely separated, almost always isolated, indeed having, strictly speaking, only two kinds of contact, that associated with hunting and with war. Regular prayers, daily devotions, abstinence, sacrifices, chantings, these are things easily required of sedentary people, sheltered in permanent houses, and provided with all necessities, but they are impracticable to men who continually wander and live from day to day.

How for example, could we require abstinence from meat of a people who derive their daily nourishment from it, and do not know how to procure anything else? How would you establish fast days among people who often have famines, which take off great numbers, if a day of fast coincides with a day on which they happen to acquire the most to eat? How can one ask them to rejoice when hunting has been bad, and weep when after a long run of bad luck they have killed a lot of game? How could you make a crime of their nudity, when they have no clothes to cover themselves with and when clothes would be an embarrassment for them? How to persuade them to forgive their enemies instead of massacreing them, when they have no chains to bind or prisons in which to keep them? If they were to set their enemies at liberty, they would soon return again to hunt on their lands and thus to deprive them again of the means of sustenance. For the Indians, morality dictates the destruction of all enemies in order to preserve themselves and their families.

In running through the dogmas of Christianity, it is easy to see that they are unsuitable for the culture of the Indians. If one wishes to impose the yoke of this religion on them, they must first be prepared for civilization, and be lead to civilization by means of a religion which is only suited for people already civilized.

How is this to be done? First, one should not begin by imposing the more painful obligations of society upon them without letting them sample its advantages. Their customs should not be destroyed, but they should be permitted to be mixed with those which lead to civilization. The Indians should not be subjected to our precepts but to encouraging examples. Appeal should not be to their minds, but to their imaginations. They should be more subjected to the appeal of pleasure than to the reason of cold necessities. Their senses should be seduced in order to reach their souls. If I am suggesting a different method from that of the missionaries, neither would I follow that used by the Americans, who have established commissioners among the Indians, dispensing agricultural instruments, in order to show them how to mechanically cultivate the earth.

The Indians have a passion for grand assemblies, dances and chants and these are the principal means I would employ. In Spring, when the earth begins to bring forth its fruits, decorated ploughs would be brought forth before a most solemn assembly, and songs would be sung describing the riches that the ploughs could produce. Rewards (which would be publicly displayed) would be promised to the first of the multitude that would learn how to use them. When the crops have covered the fields, another assembly would be called, more dances, more songs, and more rewards would be produced for those who had labored most earnestly in plowing and fencing their fields. At harvest time, even more colorful ceremonies would be held, with still greater rewards, more majestic hymns, banquets even more sumptuous. Thus at every season appropriate festivities would be held celebrating the glory of agriculture and its practitioners. The self-confidence arising from these festivities, linked with all these people hold dear and most agreeable, would found an empire that nothing could shake. Religious ideas would be introduced automatically, as part of the praises of the gifts of the country and the marvels of Nature. The strongest human idea, that of the existence of God, could only be conceived in gratitude. The idea of the beneficence of Nature would be naturally suggested to those who were conscious of benefits. Little by little, ideas of religion and morality would develop and give a more up-lifting character to those gatherings. Thus would commence one of those cults necessary to all nations that become civilized. In vain your celebrations with secular solemnity, in vain those embellished with the marvels of Art. They will always be strange to the majority. They may amuse and astonish, but never elicit genuine emotion. Only those celebrations containing religious ideas will be taken to heart by all classes, all ages, both sexes. Divinity, that ultimate thought of mortals, which appears as a far-off vision, attracts the attention of everyone, and holds everyone's interest, like far off perspectives vanishing into the distances. Happy those people, who have never separated pleasure from their religion. Once they have discovered pleasure apart from religion, these pleasures become vicious or else their religion itself becomes vicious.

That the Indians are disposed to receive instructions from Nature in their assemblies, is shown by the fact that there they become eloquent orators, producing masterpieces of oration worthy of our greatest masters, abounding in images taken from their environment, that is from nature, the forests, the prairies, waters, fire, the stars; indeed these images of nature habitually animate and lend color to their speech. Among us, however, the poet, the orator, the historian, the scholar must clothe his ideas in reference to mythology, history, liberal and mechanical arts, the most abstract science and foreign languages, and moreover languages that have been dead for centuries, so that, with us, in order to even begin to speak well one must know all of these things or at least have some notion of them. The impromptu couplet or even the most casual conversation is necessarily shot through with this scholarly mixture. Thus poetry, whose aim has always been to popularize ideas, among modern people is a mysterious science reserved to a few initiates. There can be no more poets, because there is truly no longer any poetry. A popular Homer today would not dare to recite his Iliad or his Odyssey among ordinary people.

The post of the Ouachita, located at thirty three degrees, thirty minutes latitude, is not located near any high mountains. The land on the left bank of the river is flat, consisting of prairies interspersed with woods, stretching to the river and Bayou Boeufs. This land is periodically flooded. On the other side are found sandy hills containing sandstone, obviously formed in seas, with here and there some pretty cypress swamps. As one ascends the Bayou Bartholomew, the prairie becomes more extensive and stretches all the way to the Arkansas River. One must go at least sixty leagues to the north before finding any real mountains. One of the largest of these is called by the hunters "The Sundial." Its cliffs brilliantly reflect the sun. These cliffs are composed of gypsum of which an excellent plaster could be made. Also, in the bed of the upper river there are slate quarries and I was shown a piece of crystal very pure, which I tried out as a flint. At more than a hundred leagues there are hot springs so hot that one can cook meat in them. Already they are being successfully used for various diseases. The river, one of the prettiest in Louisiana, is navigable the year round, and offers an opportunity for future speculation.

The upper reaches of the Ouachita are close to the Arkansas, and also the Red, so that it serves as a point of communication between the two. Already the journey across by land is being frequently made.

CHAPTER LV

The American Commandant takes possession of the Ouachita post during the author's stay. He leaves a few days later for New Orleans. Changes which have occurred in the city. Anecdotes. The Americans wish to introduce the English Language in Louisiana. Inconvenience and complaints which result. The author is solicited to submit a memorandum on the subject.

The American Commandant arrived during my stay with about twenty soldiers, and he was in such a hurry to take possession (although he was already late) that he could hardly wait until the next morning. He was a young man of twenty-five to twenty-seven years, a lieutenant or second lieutenant, a native of some small village in the United States. His education and abilities were very limited, and yet he was dispatched to this distant post, and provided with the extensive powers of the Spanish Commandants to govern the heads of families of whom some were venerable gray-beards, including veterans of military service. I was much surprised at this choice, having previously had an impression that the United States Government was more prudent than this. What astonished me even more was the fact that he knew not one word of French and neither did any of his troops.

After the Spanish Commandant, M. Cotard, had surrendered the post, he prepared to depart. He loaded his artillery and other Spanish Government property and made ready. He cordially entreated me to travel back with him, but I was in a hurry so I left before he did.

I arrived in the city after an absence of more than four months. Things had considerably changed. The city looked cleaner. The streets had been raised. The ditches cleaned, and drainage improved. Shops had increased in numbers. They were being constructed everywhere. Anglo-Americans were arriving daily.

A single newspaper entitled the *Moniteur de la Louisianne* edited by a former Comedian of the Cape named Fontaine, who had also become a printer, came out once or twice a week and had not been able to obtain more than eighty subscribers in all the colony. But now other journals in both French and English were beginning to appear.

I received among others, the prospectus of *"Le Telegraph"* whose editor, named Beleurgey, promised marvels. There is nothing astonishing in that, but the manner in which he advanced his claims is extremely curious. After a pompous declaration, with which I will not regale the reader, he adds. "A printer for twenty-five years, having lived in the Antilles for five years, and in the United States for seven years. These facts will I believe attest to those who honor me with their subscriptions, that I am incompetent to discuss the laws of the locality *(inhabile à traiter des lois de localité)"*.

These credentials bore so much weight with the Louisianians' mind, that the plodding editor of the *Moniteur* could foresee the time when all of his subscribers would abandon him.

The news that banks were to be established in Louisiana struck terror in the hearts of people who could not conceive that bits of paper could have the same value as piastres, stamped with the Mexican mint mark.

I was witness by chance to a no less strange fright. It had been proposed to a prominent merchant, that he put his name to a list of those upholding the laws, which was to be printed, "God preserve me," he cried with terror, "from ever finding my name on any list".

However, the French character occasionally shines through these shadows. A militia was organized, and it appeared that there were more officers than soldiers. Among these was a former *alcalde* (judge) named Merieux. "We know too well," declared the troops", that you did not always keep your balances. Return to the ranks to learn better how to do so". A second named Charpin, presented himself wearing the epaulettes of the *Ancient Regime*. "What! You display these epaulettes that but a short time ago would have cost you your head! The last of Frenchmen to the tail end of the file."

The American Government had been installed in the meantime, and foreigners, ignorant of the language, the laws, the customs of the people had been appointed to all official positions. Louisianians had the greatest difficulty now in communicating with the administrators. They required interpreters for everything, even in the courts of law which thus became even more costly. They saw how, through the intervention of these expensive interpreters their ideas, their motives, and their cases were poorly presented. They complained and agitated not so much because of the future ills, that the situation was sure to create, but because of the present annoyances, heavy customs duties, and the prohibition of the importation of Negroes added to their discontent.

Several persons solicited me to write on this subject, so weighty and so universally absorbing, but I had been back in the city only a few days and was preparing to leave once more. The press of business and the preparation for new travel, hardly left me time to prepare a brief on these points upon which I had not sufficiently meditated. However, without wishing it, my reflexion stimulated my thoughts. I saw, by what was taking place before my eyes, that a strange metamorphosis was occurring in the colony. A large number of discontented Louisianians had already formed the project of migrating to other regions under Spanish Dominion and there was the prospect that an abandoned Louisiana would metamorphose into an Anglo-Saxon-American colony, an event which would deprive France of the advantages promised to her at the cession. Her commercial outlets would be closed, as I saw that the Anglo-Americans traded exclusively in English goods, whereas the French availed themselves of both French and English merchandise. Moreover, the Anglo-Americans already seemed likely to extend their influence even farther than the limits of the colony, and to open up still further markets for English goods.

The destruction of the French language in Louisiana would thus not only be a calamity for French Louisianians, but a scarcely lesser one for France itself. Fired by these reflections, I delayed my departure and began to write on a question that the publicists have overlooked, and which circumstances have rendered so important. I made my points briefly and clearly, in a manner that seemed to me suited to the place and time. The present state of affairs has in no way lessened the interest of the subject, rather it has increased. One may judge for himself. Here is the memorandum as I wrote it.

CHAPTER LVI

Importance of the French Language for Louisiana; its retention by the Spanish Government. The right of Louisianians to keep their language founded on the Federal Constitution and the treaty of cession to the United States. Advantages for them, and the danger of depriving them of it. Memorandum on the Question: Should the French Language continue to be the language of the Louisiana Colony?

The right of preserving its original language is a matter of interest to the entire colony; all of its families and all of its individuals. It is related to individual prosperity as well as public welfare. It relates also, essentially to the integrity of the principles upon which the United States were founded, and at the same time is of interest to several other nations, especially France, a party to an agreement with the United States. No other matter is of greater potential importance to the future of the United States and that of this immense continent and indeed perhaps, to that of the whole world. I cannot, in the discussion that follows, take up all of the ramifications of this vast subject, but will content myself with certain of the principal matters, particularly those that relate to the immediate interests of Louisiana and the United States. Perhaps this brief argument will contribute to the dissipation of errors and put a stop to wrong-headed measures whose consequences will be deplorable.

The French language is the original language of Louisiana. Founded by the French and under the French government it had no other language. When in 1762, through the misfortunes of war, and still more through the profligacy of that weak monarch, Louis XV, Louisiana passed under Spanish Dominion, it was with the assurance that the colony would be governed according to the laws, forms and usages of the colony, and that the inhabitants would be protected in the possession of their property.

Too well known is the reproach to monarchs that they pay no attention to those treaties which bind their subjects to them, but it must be admitted that it is to the credit of the King of Spain that his paternal care did not diminish during the forty years that he possessed the colony. He retained and respected the laws, forms and usages of the colony in a manner exceeding expectations. Liberty of conscience, so trammelled by the powerful Inquisition in Spain, was freely respected in Louisiana, and the odious attempts of a few priests to establish the Inquisitorial regime here, in order to strengthen the priestly power, were stringently repressed by the government. The customs continued to be French and the French language remained the dominant language of the country. The clergymen, although paid by the king of Spain, taught only French. The French language was so much a part of the colony's official affairs, that the inhabitants did not have to accustom themselves to Spanish, nor teach it to their children. The Spanish language was scarcely used except in matters that had to be referred to the government at Havana, or to the Court of Spain, and the commandants of the inland posts made no use of any other language than French, indeed several of them were ignorant of Spanish altogether. In conserving foreign usages in Louisiana, the Spanish monarch displayed a paternal affection, no less than when he supplemented from his own purse the meagre return from the customs duties (sole source of public revenue in Louisiana) for public expenditure. The colonists, today, speaking among themselves, recall his benefactions, and transmit the memory of them to their children. But, whatever might have been the tribulation to which Spain might have subjected Louisiana, in whatever state of subjection, she might have been reduced (and I repeat that the colonists' well-being was indeed preserved), Louisiana would have recovered her rights when returned to the government of France. The colony, returned to France, re-became what it was under Louis XV, and reentered into the possession of her laws, forms and usages. More than this, from the moment that the colony re-became French, its citizens acquired all of the rights of France in their entirety, and from being French, even if only for a few days, all French rights became common to it, in all their fullness and freedom, as much so as if the colony had remained French for centuries. It was a French colony that France ceded to the United States, not a Spanish one. The mother language of France is the only language of its government, that is to say, it is the language proper to France. It is the language that should be maintained as proper to Louisiana. It is in this state of reintegration that Louisiana was ceded to a United America. Under the following conditions:

"The inhabitants of the ceded territory will be incorporated into the Union of the United States, as soon as possible, in conformity with the principles of the Federal constitution, to enjoy all of the rights, advantages, and immunities of the citizens of the United States and at the same time, they will be maintained and protected in the free exercise of their liberty, customs and religion."

In the language of diplomacy, it is seen that Louisiana was not a conquest, abandoned to the Victors, nor yet purchased subjects, but a territory ceded, in order that its inhabitants;

1. could enjoy all the advantages and immunities of citizens of the United States, and

2. to be still maintained and protected in the free exercise of their liberties and customs.

1. Could Louisiana participate in all of the advantages and immunities of citizens of the United States, if they were governed in a language that was foreign to them? A new language would be an instrument that they could only use with difficulty in understanding and being understood. They could not defend themselves before the bar in civil, administrative, or criminal procedures, with the same ability as an adversary, who possessed over them the advantages of the use of the official language. They would not be able to fill the different functions of magistrate, or political office. Thus, in losing the legal use of their mother tongue, Louisianians would not be participants of all of the advantages and immunities of citizens of the United States. They would, by this fact, be excluded from political functions and judicial office and at the same time would be at a disadvantage in defending their own interests. They would fall into a state of perpetual dependence, nullity and degradation. 2. In losing the legal and political use of their maternal language, Louisianians would no longer be upheld in the exercise of their liberties and customs. Is there a liberty more dear, or a usage more sacred than that of speaking the language in which one best enunciates his thoughts, best expresses his sentiments, best develops his ideas, best defends his rights and proclaims his needs? If a man who after long labor, has perfected himself in some useful art, has he the right to protection in the free practice of that art, in order to obtain the benefits resulting therefrom? With much more reason, the majority of citizens of a country who have diligently practiced a language, who have spoken it since infancy, and who have made of it an object of study and perfection, with much more reason, I say, this majority of the citizens has the right to the free exercise of this language, and to all of the advantages springing therefrom. And when, in addition to the possession of this right, a succession of clauses in an agreement guarantees the respect of this right

by the power with whom the people are associated, they cannot be deprived of it without violation both of eternal justice and the sacred faith of treaties.

But these clauses, founded as they are, on sacred agreements to the improscribable rights of the colonists to be "participants to all of the advantages and immunities of citizens of the United States . . . to be maintained in the free exercise of their liberties and customs," have suffered damaging attrition when in the capital of the colony, and in all of the posts dependent on it, persons are to be found possessing the double power of civil and military authority without the least knowledge of the language of the Louisianians. From this time on Louisianians will no longer have the full exercise of their rights, as they cannot communicate directly with the administrators. They cannot understand them or make themselves understood. They cannot communicate their purposes or protests to the administrators in their own language, nor transmit information to them about local conditions, so far from the other states, so different in climate, topography, needs and commercial relations. The humiliating isolation from their administrators, to which the Louisianians are now reduced, must result in, and does result in injustice, errors and finally in a lack of the means for enlightening the legislature and the government about matters of interest to it. Already laws have been formulated and taxes enacted, which probably would have been mitigated or delayed in application. It is from this lack of communication that the dangerous and painful lethargy in all parts of the colony arises. To think that France, that nation so grand and terrible, sublime even in its errors, whose power shakes the universe, should have entered into an agreement to despoil Frenchmen of their most glorious possession, to deliver them into a degrading nonentity. And you, free children of the new World will you violate the rights of those who give you strength, of those to whom you owe your political existence? These are the same French who on the ramparts of Yorktown, conquered and ratified your independence with their blood. You blighted your virginal glory, and desecrated that immortal charter that you have solemnly declared to emanate from heaven. [*The Declaration of Independence, of course.—Tr. note*] and which you have ratified again with new agreements.

Must one avow that the language spoken in the various states of the Union has become *the* language of all the states. No specific law establishes any such privileged position of one language over another, and if no man, or no people can enforce a retroactive effect of a law, how much less can a non-existent law be enforced? And even if such a law existed, it could not affect Louisianians, because the act of retrocession assures them that they will be ". . . maintained and protected in the free exercise of their liberties and customs", and these liberties and customs are independent even of the Constitution. They cannot be confounded with matter subject to amendment in the Constitution. Anteceding this, these rights are detached from it, and are absolutely independent of the Constitutional Act. Consequently the Constitution can neither nullify, alter nor modify them. The political and legal use of French in Louisiana cannot be altered by any consideration brought forward in the name of the Constitution.

The Federated States have conserved in their various laws, differing customs and opinions, often opposite to each other, as in religious preference, or in the status of colored people; why then should not Louisiana, imperiously called upon to be incorporated into the United States as soon as possible, conserve a difference in language? This does not make legal in one place an act that is criminal in another [*I suspect he refers to slavery— Tr. note.*] and in no way destroys the agreement of principle between the states. Has not a dangerous attack upon the federating act already been made in the matter? If, under the pretext of general utility, the rights of Louisianians may be violated, does not this open the dangerous precedent that the rights of any state or any individual may be similarly violated and thus to destroy the Federal Constitution?

Citizens of the United States! When in the impending future you invite the Canadians to throw off the yoke of England to make common cause with you, will you not take pains to make them realize the advantage of retaining in your confederation, their opinions, their laws, their customs and particular ways? Will you not cite to them the example of Holland and Switzerland? Will you then think of despoiling them of their mother tongue? Do not Louisianians have the right to the same advantages? Will not the same consideration of policy apply? Is it not consistent with the appeal that you are presently making to the parliament of England, its people and its king? Do you not damage your case in pressing the rights in that question while depriving Louisianians of the right to express themselves in their own tongue?

The general welfare of all the federated states urgently demand the uniformity of Language, perhaps you say. The General

Welfare, a phrase so often profaned to cover injustices and to despoil people of their rights. The general welfare can never authorize an injustice and a people, even more than an individual, must be severely just. Individuals have everything to fear when their governments violate justice in the name of the General Welfare. [*Remember that Robin had lived through the French Revolution and had firsthand experience of the excesses of the Committee of Public Safety committed in the name of* LE BIEN PUBLIQUE—*Tr. note.*]

Their rights, their properties, and their persons will be endangered by the demands of the General Welfare. Such is the history of all the people of the earth. And even if the General Welfare of all of the United States demanded such a uniformity of language, Louisianians were not incorporated into the United States in order to be sacrificed to the general welfare of the other states. They were admitted to the incorporation of the federal states with the express condition that they would be "maintained and protected in the free exercise of their liberties and customs." And whatever may be the inconvenience of their condition for the other states, by signing the contract of accession of Louisiana they have committed themselves to put up with the inconvenience. *Qui habet commodum, habet incommodum!**

But the admission of the French language into one of the American States, far from being an evil, would be a benefit, as one may convince himself.

The French language is the language of one of the most populous nations in the world. It is the language of an active and en-

---

*What has passed since the writing of this memorandum proves that two languages are not incompatible with the American Constitution, for the United States has introduced both languages into the courts in Louisiana so that two parties can plead there, one in French and the other in English, and the same thing takes place in the legislature at New Orleans. The orators speak either English or French as it pleases them. Moreover, the individual states are the elements of the federated body. If the individual fourteen states may one day admit various languages, the Federal Union which only exists by reason of the participation of the individual states must accept what they bring to it. Thus the amalgam brings with it the obligation to admit different languages according to the needs of the individual states. But if the Union is obliged to accept several languages through the needs of the several states, it is a consequence of the basic principle that every man has the right to the usage of his native tongue. That being so, the Union has no right to introduce a new language into Louisiana to compete with that of the Louisianians, because that competition would be dangerous to that spoken by Louisianians.

terprising people, who have an adventurous spirit and who have been stimulated by the occurrence of their revolution to emigration to distant lands. Louisiana, whose climate approaches that of France, inhabited by Frenchmen with French manners and language would be the country of preference for these European French. They would quickly populate the colony and would enrich it with their fortunes, their industry and their labor. The French language is known in all of the civilized nations of Europe, and it is spoken at the courts of all sovereigns, and is a part of the education of all cultivated persons. If, in one of the States of the Union, that language were official, that state would collect a host of non-English settlers, who for any of a thousand reasons had left their homes. And what region requires settlers? Is it not Louisiana, whose extent is perhaps greater than all of the other United States? For a long time, for too long, these far-flung regions will remain a wilderness if the United States alters its political tolerance in this matter.

But in addition, would the United States be insensible to the glory of combining in its states the two languages of the Universe, the two richest in the production of genius? Is there any region of the arts and sciences not covered by the French language, or any region of the human mind? Has not Natural History been enriched by the work of Raumer (Réaumur) Buffon and Lacèpède? Chemistry, which is related to all of human arts and needs, had made and is still making such rapid progress that Lavoisier, Fourcroy, Chaptal and Buisson had to create in the French language a new idiom in which to transmit their discoveries, as their new ideas necessitated new symbols.

Have not the masterpieces of French poetry, in all its branches, but especially in dramatic art, inspired in men the love of humanity, the heroism of virtue and the enthusiasm for liberty? Athens and Rome produced nothing more perfect. Its eloquence, both sacred and profane, give place to the greatest of models. In Philosophy, among the multitude of illustrious writers, the names of Montesquieu, Rousseau, and Mably will be venerated everywhere that the dignity of man is recognized. That immortal work, the essay of *The Wealth of Nations*, by the Englishman Schmith [Adam Smith], would not exist except for the writings of the French economists. They were, for Schmith, what the writings of Descartes were for Newton. Every day Medicine adds to its powers, Agriculture increases its experience. The liberal and manual arts are perfected by a multitude of inventions. Thus everything that could contribute to happiness and prosperity would, through the currency of both languages, illuminate and enlighten a united America. Such a meeting of languages would be the source of happiness and glory for the United States. A part of the richness and beauty of the English language is due to the communication it has had with French. The languages are twin sisters who, each provided with her own riches, would reach new heights of brilliance in their mixture on the free soil of the Federal Union.

Languages never perfect nor retain their greatness except through mutual communications. A good education is one which keeps two languages abreast of each other, especially two living languages. The Romans, those masters of the world, descended from the capital, to go to the gate of Athens in order to practice Greek. Their manners were softened by this, and they acquired there a taste for good philosophy and letters. Cicero owes to them his immortal orations and the attractive amiability of his philosophical writings. Livy and Tacitus, guided by Herodotus and Thucydides, made known to future races, both the benefits of liberty and the evils and the degradation of men under tyranny.

Without this communication of the Romans with the Greek language, their conquerors, having remained barbarians, would have covered the earth with ruins and all nations plunged into darkness which would be with us yet. America would not have been discovered; you numerous inhabitants of the Federal States would not exist. The eternal gloom of nothingness would shroud you still. Do not then imitate lazy tyranny and stupid ignorance, which, in attempting to depress everything to its inflexible level, destroys everything. Children of Nature, learn to love its rich variety, and since Man has so variously modulated languages, learn to enjoy these fertile modulations. Let the Northern and Southern states of the Union lend each other mutual aid in exchanging members of families in order to perfect themselves in each other's languages. Let it never be necessary to send these dear children, at such great expense, to Europe, from where too often they bring back more vices and expensive tastes than useful knowledge, and where almost always they lose the sacred love of country.

Jefferson, for whom the gates of immortality are open, whom history paints in inexorable faithfulness, will you live too long for your glory? Will those Frenchmen, enthusiastic admirers of your writings, be wounded in their dearest places by your own hand? and must their complaints, repeated from one end of the United States to the other, spill over into the legislation, or more unfortunately still, must the Mother Country, France, visibly moved by the cries of her children, raise in their interest, that imposing voice which is not heard in vain. Even if France, guided by her irresistable love of peace, restricted herself to obtaining from her ally, Spain, a portion of the immense and rolling domain which separates Louisiana from Mexico, for the discontented Louisianians, what a calamity that would be for the United States! The Louisiana French, swarming to the fortunate region whose immense prairies are covered with bands of horses and cattle—[*buffalo—Tr. note.*] so numerous that they block the pathway of the astonished traveler, would take with them a great number of Anglo-American families. Louisiana, thus suddenly deserted, (and other states depopulated as well) it would take centuries to repair these losses. During this time, these despised Frenchmen, whose national character was to have been destroyed, prosperous in their new land, more fertile than those of the United States, would transmit to their descendants, the memory of the injuries they had received and would multiply into a powerful rival nation, restricting the limits of the United States, halting its population growth, destroying a portion of its commercial relations, and damaging its industry in every way.

These, Jefferson, are the evils without remedy for which you would be accountable to posterity. It is black jealousy, that passion of narrow minds that caused you to attempt to erase from Louisiana the traces of the French that founded it, whose victory gave to the United States independence that they would not otherwise have achieved? However, if involuntary errors and unintentional offenses are the cause of these nascent evils, then Jefferson, and the legislature should immediately proclaim that Louisiana is a colony, "incorporated into the United States, 1. to enjoy all of the rights, advantages and immunities of citizens of the United States. and, 2. to be maintained and protected in the free exercise of their liberties and customs." Louisianians could only enjoy the fullness of that double right by retaining their native language. Even if this right is contrary to the Federal Constitution it must be preserved in Louisiana because it procedes from an agreement, inserted into the treaty of cession, which takes precedence over the Constitution's provisions. This is an additional article in the form of an amendment which removes this matter from the purview of the Constitution and renders it totally independent thereof.

But this prerogative of Louisianians of retaining in their native language the free exercise of their liberties and customs, independently of the Federal Constitution, has the great advantage that it poses no threat to the Constitution and is not discordant with it, as are some of the principles of certain of the states, in regard to religion, laws and especially slavery. This prerogative is for Louisiana a most sacred right which no consideration may attenuate. When at the same time, political expediency, prosperity and glory for the United States are tied to the maintenance of this prerogative of the Louisianians to retain their native tongue, every state of the Union, every political entity of the country should be impelled to uphold this useful prerogative. If these principles are recognized and proclaimed in all the United States, assuring the Louisianians of the complete freedom of administrative communication, they will be bound to the Union with indestructible ties. They will come to regard their new country as a true Mother-land since she will have acted as a good mother in assuring to Louisiana the same affection she displays toward her other children.

There should not be in this great family of states, any jealousies or quarrels. They should all have the same rights, the same interests and instead of that gloomy Roman principle that holds that a central government can only rule by dividing, we shall see a nation in which the stimulus of friendly competition will certainly tend to reunite the states for their common good.

CHAPTER LVII

What the Louisianians should do to conserve their native language; why they have not done so. Unhappy results of this for Louisianians. The interest of France gravely compromised; Contempt and scorn with which the Louisiana delegation to congress was received. Proof that Louisianians could retain the use of their language by what the author did at Atakapas. Other developments in the oppression of Louisiana.

My ever faithful pen had written in the foregoing memorandum nothing that I did not strongly believe. I believed, therefore, that I ought to show it to as large a number of people that I knew as possible to do with it what they would. Several of them asked me to lend it to them to read before their various societies, a request which I granted with pleasure, in the meantime hastening my preparations for departure to the Interior. The memorandum was read in this manner at the home of M. le Marquis Casa-Calvo, at a crowded gathering which included Don Andrè, the Secretary General. Both of these gentlemen made flattering remarks to me about it, and told me they would adopt my principles and work toward implementing them, insofar as their obligations and position permitted them to do so. I wanted to have it printed, in order that it might be circulated during my absence, but this would have cost me five or six hundred francs. This exhorbitant price was beyond my means [*Yet according to Robin's own statement, he paid a 500 franc bribe to the Spanish authorities upon his arrival at New Orleans in order to have his baggage unloaded.—Tr. note.*] I applied, among others, to the Editor of the *Moniteur*, M. Fontaine. He did not even dare to print excerpts of my memorandum in his journal, although I was willing to pay for it, unless I would agree to apply myself to the Governor for permission. A strange development, considering the principles of the American Constitution!

A considerable number of citizens had, in the meantime, formed a committee to draft a petition to Congress concerning the various grievances of Louisiana. M. Boré, the President of the committee, having learned of my memorandum, had several times tried to see me, but found me out. Finally he wrote me, on the 28th of June:

"Be assured that I esteem your memorandum highly. Your presentation of the facts concerning our rights to retain the use of our mother tongue, seems to me especially helpful for the attempt we are making in this area. Would you be kind enough to give me permission to abstract this material, to use for the benefit of my compatriots in the light that you furnish on this subject. I should esteem it a pleasure to make your acquaintance. If time is pressing I can send my carriage for you to visit me at home or if it would be an easier arrangement for you my house is on your way out of town. I would much esteem the privilege of your acquaintance even for a short time. I shall visit you in person before your departure to repeat my invitation. Awaiting in the hope of a favorable reply, I remain yours, etc."

I yielded to this pressing invitation. Quite apart from the desire to respond to so flattering an invitation, I was anxious to advise M. Boré as President of the Committee of Louisianians on several considerations in proceeding in the presentation of the proposed petition, upon which I considered would depend the success of the project. M. Boré had been a musketeer, and his wife, raised in Parisian society, had preserved the gracious manner of living, so I received a warm welcome. The extensive gardens of M. Boré, which are the best in the colony, include magnificent avenues of orange trees, intelligently placed so as to give a cooling shade at all time of the day. There are full size lemon trees, protected during the winter by a wooden framework carefully covered during the cold. It was in these shady avenues, where we discussed during part of the day, the subject of our interview.

The Congress to whom your petition is addressed, I told him, is composed of delegates who have different and even opposed interests and manners. Those of the north-eastern states lean toward democratic principles, are better educated, and are more active and vigorous. They therefore display more ability and energy in the Congress and are more influential. Those of the South-western provinces, mostly large land holders, living in isolation among their slaves, do not highly value education, and really do not require it. They have a more aristocratic tendency. That is to say, the ideas of government held by the two groups hardly coincide. Their interests are completely opposed. Whereas the first regard slavery as a crime, the second regard it as a necessity. The first bend their efforts to destroy it, while the second labor in its defense. At the same time, the first attentively watch out for the interest of democratic liberty, and are alert to anything that might be harmful to it, while the second are indifferent to this consideration, or are even disposed to reduce the popular power. Since the Democratic party has the greater influence in the Congress, the patent strategy of the Louisianians should be to gain their sympathy.

Some of the complaints of the Louisianians conform to the principles of this party but others do not. If you present a petition which simply lists everyone's complaints, the requests which displease the democratic majority, will nullify other matters, which presented alone, might interest them. The same consideration would apply to the aristocratic party. If all of these remonstrances are recorded in a single petition, they will cause the opposition of both parties. Therefore, it is of prime importance to isolate your grievances, to present them successively, and to begin with those most appealing to democratic principles, whose successful outcome, will form a solid base for the acceptance of the others.

That question is the retention of your native language, which if you obtain it, will give you the means of obtaining everything else you desire, since it will give you the right to be governed by leaders of your choice. If you do not obtain it, all other gains that you may obtain will be illusory. Further, its attainment will be a first breach in the Federal Constitution. But if, instead of this grand object whose consequences should stir the feelings of every man of Congress, even stilling their excessive affection for the English language and all things English, if instead of this grand and decisive object, you begin by asking for the introduction of Negroes, you will antagonize both parties at once. As you know, the party of the Northeast is democratic and the party of the Southeast (sic) is aristocratic.

In the last named states the price of Negroes is two or three times what it is in Louisiana. The delegates of these states have an interest in the introduction of additional Negroes in Louisiana, for many of their inhabitants are planning to emigrate to Louisiana, bringing their Negroes with them, and doubling or tripling their fortunes in the process. And the more of the inhabitants that leave those states with their Negroes, the higher will the price rise in those same states.

Above all, if you are to succeed in your demands, Louisiana must display a distinctive character, and this must be created if it does not yet exist. Such a character can only spring from a subject that vitally interests all Louisianians, that will rally everyone to the same cause whatever may be their profession, their age or even their sex. This universal cause is the necessity for conserving the mother tongue, an issue that appeals to everyone, even the children, in a country where paternity impresses so impelling a feeling.

But this need for all Louisianians to retain their mother tongue, the dangers that they run in losing it, and the unfortunate consequences for them and their descendants in doing so, are poorly known to Louisianians because of the ignorance and isolation in which they live. You should begin, therefore, by instructing them, using for this purpose, the newspapers and all of the means of communication. In illuminating this question, in warning the citizens of the danger that they run, you will soon rouse them. If all simultaneously declare, across these far-flung wildernesses, their wish and their will, and all show themselves ready to sacrifice everything to obtain justice, the United States, spectators to this great movement, disturbed by the prospect of its consequences, will not dare to refuse justice in this matter, and especially not when a large number of them see that the refusal would be the first step in the losing of their own liberty.

The acquisition of Louisiana by the United States, executed by Jefferson, has found numerous critics among Americans, who have already formed a powerful opposition party in Congress. This opposition party will feed on resistance by Louisianians. The government, therefore, will be all the more afraid to antagonize them. France herself will not be indifferent to this state of things. She has guarantees of the conditions of cession and has the greatest interest in seeing that they are fulfilled. These matters affect her commerce, her glory and that maternal sense that affects great nations, as well as simple families. France will intervene all the more when Louisiana shows herself worthy of it.

But if, instead of spreading word of the matter publicly, you limit yourself to considering the interests of all of the colony by an assembly composed entirely of great land owners, and subsequently you content yourself with sending envoys to obtain signatures for your privately-considered petition, without having aroused and instructed the signatories, you will not have aroused much interest in the matter. They will have signed obligingly, without real knowledge, as they might have signed an opposite petition if it had been presented to them. A failure will not affect them much. The United States will see in it, only the work of a *clique*, as its government will take pains to assure everybody. The two parties in Congress will look upon it coldly, and neither of them will any longer see in Louisiana a French colony to be incorporated into the United States, but a purchased territory to be colonized at their pleasure by Anglo-Saxons.

These arguments, which I expounded at length and with some vehemence to M. Boré, were not able to alter his opinions. He is a great landowner, and sugar maker, like the small number of other great land-owners, who feel that it is necessary, above all, to obtain the importation of more Negroes. Everything else yielded to this consideration and everything was, in effect, sacrificed to this object. The petition, drawn up *in camera,* circulated at great expense in all of the cantons to obtain the signatures of isolated inhabitants, carried to Congress at great cost by three delegates, Mm. Destréan, Sauvé and Derbigny, met the fate that was not difficult to foresee. The delegates had to contend with only too just accusations. They were coldly received, listened to with disdain, and sent away covered with humiliation, having obtained only illusory satisfaction.

In the account that they gave of their mission they stated: "The Obstacles that we *(see the Moniteur de La Louisianne No. 513, 25 May 1805, and other public papers)* had to combat here ascertaining the will of the people, pursued us to Washington. We found well established there the most unfavorable prejudice, namely that we were bringing the demands of only a portion of Louisianians, and we heard on all sides, perjorative rumors about both the petition and the petitioners. We presented our petition when we believed we had prepared ourselves to secure it a favorable hearing. It was sent to a committee, already established to consider the amelioration of the Government of Louisiana, and from that moment we passed into the state of anxiety in which we have remained throughout the session of Congress.

"The communication that the committee showed itself willing to establish with us, was limited to a single interview. Days, weeks went by without the committee's seeming to think of us. In vain, did we seek the attention of the members charged with our business, by our assiduous presence at the meetings of Congress, and by frequent visits to the members. The interests of Louisiana seemed to fall into a sort of Limbo, which argued very early for the result we were to expect . . .

"Our anxiety grew as time passed, and finally reached the point where we yielded to those who urged us to ask the Senate to speed up the process of rendering a decision in our case, at the same time drawing attention to it of both of the houses. A few days later.

the committee named to examine the affair held a meeting with us . . . Things remained at this point for several weeks.

"In this simple relation of facts, it will be all too easily seen by all who cherish the principles of justice, that we never expected to be treated in this arbitrary manner in the sanctuary of Liberty.

"In sum, during the time when the Congress was hardly occupied with matters worthy of its attention, when the Louisiana business was the only important matter upon which it had to deliberate, we saw weeks and months go by during which we were granted only a small amount of time, so precious to us, to discuss our course. We waited during the entire session, at the seat of the government for some decision, while we listened daily to the long and opinionated debates upon matters of little consequence. We saw rejected, with no regard for our situation, all of the requests for permission to import Africans for our plantations, in spite of the fact that we had demonstrated that this country cannot exist without their help. We saw our cause, that of an entire province, fall into a sort of oblivion, while the trial of a single individual occupied both branches of the legislature, for an entire month. We saw decisions favorable to a great number, paralyzed by the ill will of a few. Finally, after the session had ended, we saw created in haste a government, against which we have protested, without cease, which we have shown to be in no way suitable in our situation.

"You are regarded today not as vassals but as equals. There has fixed for your entry into the union, an arbitrary term of years, which is however not irrevocable."

The result of this ill considered and inconsequent attempt shows also, the hateful s c o r n that the Americans have for the French national character, and that in their impatience to destroy it, they will sacrifice, their own interests, justice, and the obligations that they owe both to France and to the faith of great treaties. [Governor William Claiborne named the following: Daniel Clark, Edward Livingston, Evan Jones, Etienne de Boré and James Pitot as persons known to him out of about twenty who had organized the petition (See his official letter Vol. I). The object of the petition was the immediate entry of Louisiana into the Union as a State, and the further object of this, was to open up the region for the importation of more slaves. The question of language was secondary. The whole question of Statehood for Louisiana, was therefore, tied up with the fateful question of the extension of Slavery into new states, and as is well known, no real agreement *was reached on this matter until the Missouri Compromise of 1820. Robin's idea that delay on the matter of statehood was taken out of malevolence to the French inhabitants was nonsense, as a glance at the mixed English and French names listed easily shows. —Tr. note.]*

What a difference if all Louisiana, properly instructed and fired with zeal, had claimed the right of *retaining their mother tongue!* This single consideration would have prevented the precipitous formation of this government so contrary to the customs and interests of Louisianians. It would have prevented the monstrous establishment of those quantities of bizarre laws, unknown and unknowable to Louisianians. They would not have been abandoned to venal and ignorant magistrates, stained with every vice. All of Louisiana would not have been, from one end to the other, covered with the black vapors of terror, and clouds of jack-leg lawyers would not have dispersed through the land like reincarnated harpies corrupting everything with their fetid breath, and feasting on the blood and flesh of the cowed inhabitants.*

---

*I do not exaggerate. Throughout Louisiana, particularly in isolated regions, one finds the most appalling vexations. Ignorant farmers have been persecuted, judged, arrested and imprisoned without being able to defend themselves, and this has happened even at New Orleans where one would expect abuses to be less flagrant. Here is an extract of an article published in the Moniteur, August 23, 1804, by M. Mahi-Dermontils. [*So it seems, M. Fontaine was not so pusillanimous after all.—Tr. note.*]

". . . The tribunals were established on the principle that they would be conducted in the predominant idiom of the district, and this was the only one in which matters of interest to the citizens were discussed. Soon a swarm of lawyers, foreigners in the country arrived, speaking a foreign idiom, and from that time on we have experienced a living Tower of Babel, a confusion scarcely paralleled anywhere. The case of one party may be pleaded in French, the case of the other in English. The judges, for the most part, do not speak the first, and the others don't understand the second. The lawyers speak either one or the other. No matter, they plead anyway, and the judges decide.

"I was myself witness to an incident in which M. Duncan, an American lawyer, in a case argued on appeal, got the judges to sign an entirely different judgment from the one they had just pronounced, by setting it before them in English, which they did not understand. This cacaphony, this confusion has caused the honest judges to resign, and they have been replaced by Americans, and since then, the remaining judges have not wished to preside. The resignation of some, and the effective retirement of the rest, has given rise to new incongruities. The vacant seats have been replaced by foreigners, newly arrived, who do not know the language of the country . . . From this time on, the most flagrant abuses

Here is the proof that the will to retain the **French language,** and that alone, would have been enough to prevent those calamities and to preserve to the colony its national character, in accordance with the intent of the treaty. I must again, break the chronological sequence of events and take up matters at another time. I was then in the Atakapas, whither I had extended my travels, and I had bought a house with some land, since I was unable to obtain lodging in any other way. Atakapas was at this time, formed into a county, and provided with a criminal court. I was named a member of the first Grand Jury called. We had to deliberate on several grave crimes, punishable by severe penalties. The Jury, it is true, had been established by law, but the new code did not yet establish the penalties for the crimes which had been committed prior to its existence, whether they should be inflicted according to the French code, the Spanish code, or the American, or even the English code, and there did not even exist, a mechanism for promulgation of laws, so that we did not know when laws of either the Congress or the legislative body at New Orleans, should go into effect.

After having taken the oath, we retired to a special chamber and were advised of the various crimes that should be submitted for our deliberation. An individual, unknown to us, appeared, with an English law code in his hand, and began to read from this gazette, explaining in an unintelligible French what was written there. He read us these long columns of crimes and their penalties, including among others, the penalties for rape, sodomy, bestiality, cutting or cuting off an ear, cutting or mutilating a tongue,

---

have occurred without restraint. The most obvious partiality is manifested in the judgments. In a case between a Louisianian and a foreigner, the former may be assured that his interest will be sacrificed to the avarice and cupidity of his adversary, and the latter that the balance will always be weighted in his favor.

". . . Fretté, a Louisianian, had obtained a judgment against an Englishman named Patrick Morgan, who had appealed the case to the Superior Tribunal of Governor Claiborne. Notwithstanding these two defeats, both in the trial and appeal courts, the case was brought again in civil court, on a day when two judges out of the three, were Americans. The Louisianian, Fretté, lost his case. The mulatress, Marie-Ann Chalemberg, sued young Delisle-Duparc in civil court claiming of him the payment of two hundred piastres which she claimed he owed her. The mulatress, who was represented by an American lawyer, had no titles to credibility. In vain, I insisted that she should justify her demand. All my efforts were useless. My client was ordered to pay the sum she demanded, on her word alone.

gouging an eye, cutting off a tip of a nose, mutilation of various members, and scarring the face. Each crime had its respective fine in piastres to be paid, and prison sentence. This hair-raising anthropophagous code, had fifty odd articles. Finally, the interpreter retired, leaving us his code, which had no more official character than he did.

I asked my honorable colleagues, "Are we then twenty-five butchers, who are to slaughter these victims presented to us, in the way we are told to do it? We do not even know by what legal right we are assembled, and we know even less what we are supposed to do. The accused will have no means of defending themselves before this court. They will not find a single lawyer familiar with the French language to defend them or to present their case to us. They will have to defend them, only those young foreigners, who know no French, and who will be neither able to understand their clients, nor enlighten us, since we know no English. These facts prohibit us from pronouncing on the life and honor of our fellow citizens, and for my part, I declare myself incompetent to do so."

This opinion was unanimously approved, and I then proposed the following resolution which was unanimously adopted.

The members of the First Grand Jury of the County of the Atakapas.

Whereas the criminal law of the United States is unknown to the members of the Grand Jury, or even to the population of the county of the Atakapas at large, and at this moment it is impossible to inform ourselves about them as there is no translation of them in our language, and the English language, in which they are written, is unknown to most of us, and whereas in this state of things, the members of the jury find it impossible to enlighten their consciences in regard to the crimes referred to them as members of the Grand Jury, it would be contemptibly presumptuous of us to administer these laws and possibly even a violation of them.

The members of the Grand Jury considering further that the accused, their fellow citizens, are in the same state of invincible ignorance, that these laws are for them, as though they did not exist, that to attempt to apply them would be in effect to enforce retroactive laws, a course of which sound morality in legislation among all people disapproves, and which would be contrary to the constitution of the United States, which holds laws may never have a retroactive effect, Therefore, these impelling motives lead us, the members of the first Grand Jury of the County of the Atakapas to unanimously declare that we are obliged to abstain from judging crimes according to these laws and an account of this painful situation in which the members of the Grand Jury find themselves, we ask the chief Magistrate of the Court to forward this resolution, dictated by conscience, to the Governor, and the Legislative body.

After this resolution was signed by all of the jurymen, we presented it to the presiding judge. I read it to him in open court. He responded publicly, that he likewise shared in this painful situation, that he approved the wisdom of the resolution, and that he would forward it immediately to the higher authorities. Court was adjourned, and was not convened again until six months later.

Notwithstanding, the juries of the eleven other counties, even that of New Orleans, where one would have expected to find at least a few reasonable people, judged condemned and besmirched reputations, in accordance with laws of which they had not the least idea.

I employed here, as the principal means of protest the simple notion of the necessity of translation of the laws into French. From this would follow the necessity of pleading and instructing the jury solely in that language. If in addition, I had, at great expense, dispatched couriers to the other counties, to spread my resolution, and at the same time had published it in the newspapers, where its effect would have been strengthened by interested comment, I could have brought about the revolution single handed. By this simple means, all of Louisiana could have retained its native language, by suspending the courts and bringing the government to a standstill. This would have assured to France, forever, a state, included in the American federation to be sure, but a state, which, by retaining its French character, would never cease to feed the commerce of France.

And if the deputies above, had then presented themselves to Congress, strengthened by the will of the Louisianians thus strongly proclaimed, would that haughty Congress have dared to scorn those delegates and to send them away having scarcely listened to them, and refused them everything that they asked?

CHAPTER LVIII

Departure of the Author for the Atakapas. Difficulties of the Route. Extraordinary region: Geographical details of the Teche river. The edges of the Forest bordering it, and the Prairies through which it runs. The Beauty of this country giving one the idea of the country between here and Mexico. Origin of the Soil of the Atakapas. Deposited by the Red River which at that time ran to the sea. Proofs.

A few days after my interview with the president of the Assembly of Louisiana, I left New Orleans, for the Atakapas, where I intended to stay for some time. The western part of Louisiana is little known to travelers. I ascended the river, with six oarsmen and a captain, on a boat that I had bought. The first place from which one may reach the Atakapas is Bayou Lafourche, a western branch of the river found about twenty-five leagues above New Orleans. [*Present site at Donaldsonville.—Tr. note.*] This branch communicates, by various ramifications with the Atchafalaya, or *Grande Riviere* which in turn communicates with the Teche, the first river of the Atakapas. But the entrance of the LaFourche is daily obstructed by large amounts of driftwood, which push into it, so that the entrance is only passable for a short time from February to July, when the river is high, and the river was already too low when I arrived there. The inhabitants of this district, whose population has risen to more than 1,200 individuals, and those of Atakapas and Opelousas much more numerous, although vitally interested in the removal of this obstruction to a waterway they need badly, have only made feeble, and so far, unproductive efforts to open it, and the need is growing. I had to ascend another ten leagues to the entrance of Bayou Plaquemine.

Bayou Plaquemine, another arm of the river, which then is seen to communicate by various ramifications with the Atchafalaya, is itself blocked at its entrance by enormous floating logs which have been allowed to accumulate there through negligence. As the bayou is aligned with the current of the river which turns at that point, it follows that continual care is necessary to see that new encumbrances do not accumulate. Since the rapid current naturally pushes logs into the bayou's mouth, in order to reduce the expensive care, a little canal has been built lower down, whose entrance is less in line with the river's current. The canal opens into the bayou and is about two hundred paces long. But it is still not oblique enough to the current and still is subject to blocking by driftwood as scouring action of the current enlarges it. It should have been dug further downstream, at a more oblique angle with the river. I had the misfortune to arrive two or three hours after the current had dropped, for the canal is quite shallow. I therefore, had to unload the boat to put it, empty, over the piled up driftwood in the entrance, by sliding, with the aid of a great number of people, and a block and tackle, at the grave risk of puncturing it. The unloaded objects had to be carried in carts to the boat. This took several days and cost a great deal of trouble and expense.

Bayou Plaquemine, narrow and winding, receives water only from the river. At the entrance, and until the waters drop to the level of the lake, into which the bayou disgorges, the current is frightenly swift, so that it often happens that long boats, that are not able to turn quickly enough, in the tortuous channel, are wrecked. After a few leagues, the current slackens until finally it is imperceptible. The bayou breaks up into innumerable channels, as it flows along, in which one is easily lost if he is not familiar with them. Sometimes, the channel enlarges into lakes, sometimes it narrows suddenly and one finds oneself in shadowy avenues, overhung with enormous trees, impenetrable by the rays of the sun, interlaced with dense vines, and l o a d e d with grayish streamers of Spanish moss, barely leaving room for the passage of the boat. One imagines himself crossing the shadowy Styx with Acheron. Alligators in swarms, surround the travelers or are seen sleeping everywhere on the shell beaches. Mixed with the deep-throated bugling of giant frogs* and the sharp cries of black commorants [*the anhinga or snake bird—Tr. note*] and the melancholy love note of the owls.

After long sinuosities which form innumerable islands, among which the inexperienced traveler would require the thread of Ariadne in order not to wander forever, the river opens suddenly into a magnificent lake of several leagues extent. The sudden light surprises the traveler and the beauty of the water, set about with tall trees, forms an enchanting sight.

These tall trees are cypresses. Stretching away from us as far as the eye can see, each cindery column, based upon a broad, deeply

---

*The species of frog called the roarer [*La mugissante*] imitates the bellowing of a bull so exactly that it can be mistaken for one. [*It is surprising that Robin did not pick up the melifluous, onomatopoeic Creole name for the bull frog,* OUAOUARON—*Tr. note.*]

furrowed cone, crowned with branches which hardly bend down at all. These columns seem to form the portico, and one fancies that he is before the immense palace of the God of the Waters. The mysterious lair of Old Proteus of the thousand forms, declaiming his prophecy, and the dark retreats of the sporting Nereids, while the tritons sound their conch shells.

From this lake, called Lake Natchez, one enters still more winding and complex channels, which traverse the extremity of a much larger lake, called Grand Lake, and entering the shadowy and narrow channels once more, one comes finally to the Atchafalaya, which communicates lower down with the Teche by v a r i o u s branches. But further up the river, a side bayou comes to within less than two leagues of the Teche, opposite the chief settlement of the district, and one can cut twenty or thirty leagues off the distance, if he were to make this crossing by land. A canal dug across this short space, through this level and settled region would cost the inhabitants only several days work of their Negroes, and everyone who has to have necessary supplies shipped every year, must lose more each trip by this long detour than the total cost of such a canal.

The Teche runs parallel to the Atchafalaya from North to South, communicates with it by various branches, and finally empties into the Atchafalaya, not far from the sea. Thus it may be considered one of the bayous of the large river, receiving its waters in flood time, and in fact, rising and falling with the rise and fall of the main river. As it runs through the prairies of the Atakapas it receives also the water that filters through the soil. The current of this extremely tortuous river is so slow that it is imperceptible. The water rises with the slightest tide, or even when the wind is from the south. The great depth of the river in its narrow, well banked channel would make it highly useful as a waterway, if it were cleared of the tree trunks that obstruct it everywhere. The negligent inhabitants let them lie there, or even fell new ones across the stream in the course of clearing. The bayou must be navigated like a canal. The boat must be dragged by hand.

The water is cloudy, the color of dishwater, and the stagnant reaches are covered with slime, but this does not render it un-healthy. No one drinks anything else.

At the lower end of the bayou the banks are nothing but trem-bling prairies, but they become more solid as one ascends. At first there is only a narrow crest of dry ground, but this gradually en-

larges as one proceeds upstream. Toward the upper end, the banks
of the river are wooded, and behind this curtain of forest, about
two hundred paces wide, spacious prairies stretch out, as far as
the eye can see, broken here and there by patches of woods, forming a most agreeable landscape. Patches of swamps, little lakes
and winding creeks are also met with from time to time. Almost
all of the houses here are found between the strip of woods and
the prairie, not along the river, and this gives them a more airy
and cheery aspect. No region on earth offers to civilized man more
opportunity for happy hours. Herds wandering at large multiply
without requiring any other trouble to their owners beyond that
of reassembling them in the spring to mark them so that they can
be recognized. The prairie land is already cleared and awaits only
the plow or the spade. The landowner may easily house himself.
It takes only a few days to build a cabin. It takes only a few morn-
ings' work to place this prodigious land into production sufficiently
to support a family. These prairies are well stocked with game
and, especially during the winter, they are covered with ducks and
geese, so the inhabitant has his choice of birds as if they were in
his own poultry yard.

As one ascends further up the Teche, towards the Opelousas
district contiguous with the Atakapas on the north, the terrain is
higher and becomes slightly hilly and is cut by deep ravines, and,
in addition, the patches of woods among the prairies are thicker
and more numerous, giving to the country a more varied and pic-
turesque aspect.

This description of prairies stretching out to either side of the
Teche, bordered by a strip of woods which shade its banks, would
do as well for all the other streams which parallel it to empty into
the sea between the Teche and the Rio Brazos, a stretch of about
two hundred leagues. Each of these rivers in the same way is bordered by a strip of woodland beyond which lie the open prairies.
The only differences are that the rivers are almost all larger and
more navigable, that the prairies are broader and more spacious,
stretching up to twenty-five leagues in extent, that the winters,
which are mild in the Atakapas, appear to be even more so to the
west, and, finally, that these countries are as yet uninhabited and
are covered with innumerable herds of cattle [buffalo] and wild
horses, as well as all kinds of game.

Further north one enters regions still unknown, where there
are Indian nations who still have so little contact with Europeans

that they use only arrows, with whom one could establish the richest fur trade in the universe.

Northwest of Opelousas, the terrain becomes higher little by little. No longer does one find prairies, but sandy hillocks covered with pines and oaks. This area was not deposited by the river but was rather laid down by the sea.

All of these prairies are covered to a depth of ten or twelve inches by humus, below which is a compact, fine-grained red earth, from fifteen to twenty feet thick, which overlies the same sand which makes up the hills above Opelousas. This shows that the red soil has been laid down by the rivers on top of the sea sand. This red soil is of the same type as that deposited by the thick waters of the Red River, and must therefore represent the deposits of that river [*Of course it means nothing of the sort. The red laterite soil is the typical soil of high rainfall areas, and the color results from the leaching out of organic material by the percolation of surface water.—Tr. note.*], which at that time had its mouth not in the Mississippi but directly into the sea, for the banks of the river on the opposite side show a uniformly greyish soil, much less compacted. I first formulated these ideas upon inspection of the soil of the area, but any doubts of their correctness were removed when after questioning several old inhabitants of the district I learned that the Indians had told them that they had often seen the land flooded by the Red River, and only sixteen or seventeen years ago (1788-1789) exceptionally high water in the Red River had raised water in Bayou Boeuf and other streams, thus it had flooded the prairies of the Atakapas, covering them so deep that boats could be used in getting about.

Floods of the Red River on the prairies of the Atakapas have become rarer because: 1] the vegetable humus has raised them more than a foot, and 2] the more frequent navigation of that river, since it has become settled, has resulted in a cleaning and widening of its bed.

It is easy to see how these muddy waters, depositing their silt at the river's mouth, would obstruct the former bed as the deposits increased and would become even more sinuous, by reason of this enforced detour, until, finally, it would meet the Mississippi, which would be doing the same thing, whereupon the two great streams would be finally united forever.

CHAPTER LXII

The Recentness of the Establishment of the Atakapas. The Cause. Atakapas means man eater. First French who landed in the region, Adventures of Belle-Isle, a slave among the Indians, First colonists established there, Advantages of this Establishment, why it has not prospered as it should. Multiplication of herds without care. Principal resource of the country. Remarks on the cause of epizootics. Singular anatomy of a heifer. Acadians established here, retaining their customs. The harmfulness of burning the prairies.

The beautiful regions of the Atakapas and Opelousas, even though they are close to New Orleans, and lying along the Atchafalaya, and easily reached through the waterway of the river, are the most recent settlements of the colony. Only the vigorous Canadians have penetrated here. Doubtless because only they are unafraid to risk the trackless windings of the waterways which lead here and are likewise unintimidated by the ferocity of the native inhabitants, who are called "Atakapas," which means "man-eater."

And now a deplorable event occurred which strengthened still more the fear of these Indians among the Louisianians. About 1720 a ship of the company of the West Indies missed Balise (at the mouth of the river) and was carried by the currents to the west to the Bay of Saint Bernard [Atchafalaya Bay] to the vicinity of the peninsula called today Belle-Isle. Five officers went with the longboat that put ashore to look for water, in order to hunt. The longboat made several trips back and forth, but having waited in vain for the officers, after a time, returned finally to the ship. The captain had the barbarity to weigh anchor and abandon the five officers. They wandered for a long time on those wild and marshy coasts, in the greatest trepidation of meeting the Indians, whose anthropophagic reputation they already knew. Four of these unfortunates eventually died of hunger. The fifth, named Belle-Isle, who survived them, buried them with his own hands in order to keep the cadavers from being eaten by wild animals.

Belle-Isle wandered for several days, sharing what he found to eat with his dog, but the animal was wounded by a wildcat, and his master was obliged to kill him, and afterwards to eat him. At length, almost ready to die of hunger, he came across traces of human beings and followed them to a river, where he found a pirogue. Using this, he crossed the river to the other bank, where he found himself among a group of Indians who were engaged in stripping and drying fish and meat. His thinness frightened them, but they despoiled him of his clothes, which they divided. They at first gave him human meat to eat, but when he refused this horrible meal, they offered him fish. The savages, having decided that he had not come to harm them, but rather as a guest requesting hospitality, did not treat him as an enemy. He was made the slave of a widow. His regular occupation was carrying the bodies of the enemies destined to be eaten. He was soon adopted by the widow and taken into the tribe. He went with them in war, where he distinguished himself, but he was never able to get used to eating human flesh, although he observed this odious spectacle daily. Two years went by in this way, when finally a deputation of some of the Indians, who lived near the post of Natchitoches, arrived at the encampment, and by this means he was able to send news of his plight to the commandant of that post (M. de Saint-Denis), who took measures to deliver him. Back among his people, Belle-Isle, by his narrative, still further discouraged settlers in the region, and even today Louisianians speak of the bay of St. Bernard with horror.

However, the Atakapas Indians gradually became accustomed to going to New Orleans to exchange their furs, and traders there, conversely, began to go among them, and these reciprocal relations softened the customs of the Atakapas. Some of the colonists finally dared to go and settle on these spacious prairies. One of the first who went there about fifty years ago was named Masse, a scion of a rich family of Grenoble. This individual brought with him twenty Negroes, and it might be said he was rather the father than the master of them. He hardly gleaned enough from their labors to live on. His dwelling was a simple cabin, open to the air. He slept on a bearskin, stretched on boards. He was dressed from head to foot in buckskin.* His only eating utensils were a knife and a horn spoon hung at his belt. He lived thus for twenty years in the wilderness, offering hospitality to all who asked for it for as long as they wished. However, the number of parasites living on him was never large; his austerities drove them away. His Negroes, whom he made content, and who had gotten out of the habit of work, were freed on his death, and they form today, at the lower

---

*The Indians dress their skins with the brains of animals of all sorts. For this purpose, they carefully dry and keep the brains of all animals that they kill. The operation is swift and easy.

end of the Teche, a little community, as indolent as in the time of their master.

Two of his compatriots, poor natives of Dauphiné, whom he took in for several years, profited so well from his hospitality that they laid the foundation of their fortunes there, and today are the principal inhabitants of the district. One is named Sorel and the other Bérard. The fortune of the former is estimated at more than two hundred thousand piastres (more than a million livres). M. Sorel has so taken to heart the lessons in frugality he learned from the good Masse that he serves only water to travelers. Large bowls of milk cover his long and narrow table, and the other dishes are so scanty that not all of the guests are even permitted to see them.

The same severe economy reigns in the construction of his house. It is low, in order to be protected from the wind, solid doors and shutters, the same all amply provided with bolts and locks (all, however, made of wood). There is not to be found in that economical office a single piece of iron, not even a nail. However, we must except from our description as being without metal a little outhouse, where I am told there are numerous casks circled with thick bands of iron.

As for his compatriot, M. Bérard, things are entirely different. He is a friend of joy and good cheer, and one is always splendidly treated there. Also, God has made him the father of a numerous posterity. It was the acquisition of a few cows that laid the foundation of the fortune of these two individuals, like that of most of the inhabitants of the district. These cows, abandoned to themselves, have multiplied so that, after forty years, they form herds of several thousand, notwithstanding those that have been consumed locally and those that are annually sold in the city to those inhabitants along the river who cannot, or rather, do not know how to raise their own.

These first establishments of Louisiana colonists were made, as we have seen without the aid of the government, who at that time knew nothing of the nature, the extent or the resources of that country. It was only about the time that the colony was ceded to the Spanish (1765-1770) that a commandant, that is to say, someone representing the Government was appointed. This first governor was named *Fusilier*, and his widow and children still live in the colony.

What has most contributed to the importance of this post was the establishment here of the Acadians at great expense by the

— 190 —

Spanish government. These unfortunate victims of their patriotism had been taken to San Domingo, where their population might have saved that island for France at the time, if so many of them had not perished of neglect. They have found a more favorable climate on the soil of Louisiana, where their originally small numbers have considerably multiplied, both on the River and here at the Atakapas. Among them are some who have become extremely rich, who have amassed herds of several thousand head of cattle. A great number of these people it is true simply vegetate in these beautiful regions. The difficulty of navigation, subject to expensive portages across land, at certain times of the year, and the all too common obstacles to commerce under the Spanish regime, which prevented the settlers from exporting their produce and importing necessary goods, caused some of them to decline into indolence. Rich and poor (if one can speak of poor, where one has the means to satisfy all of his ordinary wants), they have, both here and along the River retained their customs, these being much like those of our farmers in France. Through observation I cannot repeat too often, to point out how important it is, in founding colonies, to provide good stock as colonists.

These Acadians work their land themselves. The women and children go into the fields to pick corn and cotton, they take care of the barnyard, milk the cows, and spin the cotton into thread of which they make coarse muslin shirts, fine cloth, mosquito nets, and that multi-colored striped cotton cloth so agreeable to the eye, resembling very much our *siamoises,* out of which they make skirts and blouses, and for the men, pants and jackets.

The families descended from French officers or merchants, live quite differently. They live in indolent ease, even those with little money. They use a portion of their slaves as indoor servants, in an attempt to recapture a sense of the easy and sumptuous life. Several have fallen into this decadence. The Acadians, simpler and more economical, are prospering and will become, in consequence, more useful to the colony and the mother country.

The Acadians like to live to themselves and they have the good sense to have little to do with the families who are pretentious. These latter, however, seek out the acquaintance of the Acadians, and like very much to be a part of the joyful celebration of their balls.

All of the inhabitants have received free grants of land from the Spanish Government, which their descendants have subdivided. These grants are always of forty arpents deep by a varying width, often thirty arpents. Thus, as in the rest of Louisiana, when a reference is made to one arpent of frontage, it means a total area of forty arpents, ten arpents of frontage means four hundred of total area, and so forth. [*The front was, of course, along a river, the principal avenues of commerce in Louisiana, the uniform depth being the average of available land. Beyond that the land sinks into swamp.—Tr. note.*]

All of the domestic animals of Europe do marvellously in this country. The climate is much better for poultry than that of France. The inhabitants raise chickens almost all winter long. From February or March on, numerous clutches of eggs are set. The sustained warm weather of the country, the vast area of ground for scratching, many little insects, seeds and soft grasses, all of these make the chicks thrive.

Turkeys should do even better here, as they are natives of this country, and indeed the woods are full of them. The same is true of ducks and geese which are little raised here, because in the winter time, the rivers, lakes, marshes and prairies are covered with them. In a few hours one can obtain enough for a whole week.

Pigs multiply here in an astonishing manner. The settlers do not bother to shelter or feed them. They don't even know how many they own. The sows farrow in the woods and undergrowth. In order to get them used to coming to houses, and to tame them a few ears of corn are put out for them from time to time. Wolves and tigers [*presumably the panther or mountain lion, but possibly a reference to the bob cat which however, elsewhere Robin calls* CHAT-TIGRE. *The wolf is the red wolf* (CANIS NIGER) *a closer relative to the coyote than to the true wolf or timber wolf* (CANIS LUPUS)—*Tr. note.*] which no one takes the trouble to hunt down, destroy many pigs, both here and in other districts of Louisiana. Sheep do equally well all year round. They remain outdoors, so that it is not necessary to feed them over the winter. They become fat and develop a good configuration, but it must be admitted that their meat does not taste as good as that of the sheep of France. Wool is not put to use. It is thrown away. No one spins it, for wool is little used here. Mattresses are of cotton or Spanish moss. When this moss is dried, it loses its exterior pellicle, leaving behind only a fine black filament resembling horsehair, for which indeed it can easily be mistaken. With the sheep is raised also a small type of goat. The strain of cow that is raised here is a good one. They are remarkable for the beauty of their horns. Their coats are red, brown, white, but few of them are black. The steers, raised from them are also large and strong. According to the seasons, these animals browse in the woods, the fields, or the canebrakes. The care given these beasts consists only in gathering them together at one time or another in an enclosure called a *coraille* [*Spanish Corral—Tr. note.*] in order to accustom them to man, to tame them or as they call it so often there, *adoucir*. Little by little, the cows become accustomed to being touched and milked, the oxen submit to the yoke. The calves require only to be fastened up for a few days and prevented from eating. The calves are those of the cows that one desires to milk. Their mothers come to them every morning to give them milk. These herds multiply without difficulty, often to the extent that not even their numbers are known. I have known settlers in remote regions who saw their animals only once in two or three years, as they wandered in these woods and immense pasturages. During the winter, when the grass is dry, and the vegetation dormant, the cattle appear at the farmhouses. When they have been tamed, a few ears of corn and some salt will suffice to keep them in this habit.

A small number of the inhabitants, less indolent than the rest, cut several wagon loads of hay which they store in their enclosure, and with this and corn shucks, they maintain a few beasts throughout the winter.

It must be admitted, however, that, while the winters are not rigorous, and the cold very brief, the cattle suffer from it a good deal, particularly in certain districts. These vast prairies are covered by tall grasses most of which do well in cool places. The first frosts dry out their tall stems, and stop their growth, so that animals browsing on them fare pretty poorly, and they become even less nourishing after they have been washed by the rains.

This type of couch-grass which is abundant in their enclosures is fine, tall, and tufted. The cattle like it very much, but it loses its quality with the first light frost. It is in the cotton harvest time that this hay must be mowed. This is the time of the year when work is most pressing and when indolence has most excuse for not providing this winter nourishment. The animals abandoned to themselves suffer considerably, and when even the transitory frosts of this region render the vegetation dormant for a long time, the cattle become frightfully thin and many of them perish. The sudden change from cold to hot, or torrid days with chill nights is still more inimical to them. The calves are less hardy than the adults and it is easily noticed that a rigorous winter will destroy many of them.

In the district where cane is found, vegetation reaches a height of 15 to 20 feet and is so dense that it can only be penetrated with an ax. This vegetation serves as a shelter to the animals against the bitter winds of the north. The animals obtain nourishment from the still green leaves, which they like very much, and from the seed, which the Indians themselves carefully harvest.

One abuse, that of the inhabitants setting fire to the prairie and the pine woods, is extremely damaging to the herds and to the countryside in general. These tall dry grasses would be at least food of some sort for the herds. It would serve to shelter them from the cold. It would serve as bedding to keep the animals from lying down on the damp ground. The new grass which sprouts early in the year would itself be protected by the old from the effect of the first frost and this would afford the animals a source of early green food. This dry grass would serve as a manure for the new plants and would, in the long run, tend to raise the ground and contribute to drying of the soil.

In the pine wood the big trees are resistant to the annual burning but the young ones suffer a great deal and the sandy soil is also deprived of the necessary compost which would encourage the growth of grass.

It is generally estimated that the annual produce of a herd is 25% in value, that is to say, the herd doubles in 4 years. However, the more numerous the herd, the less productive it is annually in proportion. Too many animals together in one place are harmful to each other in the circumstances referred to above. They are more likely to communicate to each other contagious diseases. In the early times these epizootics were unknown, but very soon the inhabitants will be reduced to having no larger herds than could have been supported on their own lands and they will gain from this and the country still more. Those who have herds will be a little more careful of them and they will produce more milk and more calves. The steers will be stronger and fatter and whereas they now weigh no more than 5 or 6 hundred pounds, they will double in weight and price.

An important observation which I have often repeated is that I have never seen the liver of a cow, horse or pig in this country that was not diseased. The animals abandoned to themselves tend thus to degenerate not in the exterior form which is as large and proper as those in Europe, but this degeneration is in their internal structure and this disposes them to the ravages of destructive epizootics. In this connection I have observed in France itself that the animals who are abandoned in pasture without being fed hay tend to the same alteration of the blood. One must conclude that these animals under the civilized management of man tend to improve rather than degenerate as is believed by naturalists. One should not be surprised, therefore of the care with which the ancients consulted the entrails of beasts as oracles, or of the precepts of Moses or other law-givers on this subject. A healthy animal was a fortunate object; a good omen of health and a subject for public rejoicing. It was the basis therefore, of proof of prosperity for the herds, and health for the men who derived their nourishment from them. The contrary indicated affliction and a presaged mortality and pestilence. To prevent these disasters it was necessary to have recourse to sprinkling, fumigation and fasting. Superstition born of the ignorance of causes was gradually mingled with this along with other useless practices, and little by little, the grain of truth in the matter was lost to view.

When I was in the Atakapas a resident of my neighborhood killed a heifer who showed the character of both sexes in an extraordinary conformation. This heifer had a stronger neck and shoulders than the usual animal of its sex. It was livelier, more restless, and it had already gone past by about two years the time when one would have expected gestation. The Negroes on the plantation had noticed it and especially been struck by the fact that she ejected urine in the air like a jet of water pushed by a piston. They reported this several times to their master and believed that she was bewitched. The master, thereupon, ordered her killed. We found testicles adherent to the thighs below the vagina and a phallus recurving in the opposite direction whose extremity ended in the opening of the vagina. This produced the squirting of urine in a jet. [*This description is that of a free-martin—a heifer, co-twin to a bull calf. They usually display hermaphroditism.—Tr. note.*]

The prairies of the Atakapas and of Opelousas, the true sources of provisions for New Orleans, provide the city the year round with fresh meat. This district also produces salt meat for maritime commerce. These two districts furnish to the colony a large part of its beef and milk produce. There can hardly be fewer than 200 thousand horned cattle. Oxen sell for about 15 piastres apiece and cows are almost as expensive. Cattle destined for the slaughter purchased in bulk on the spot sell for 6-10 piastres. The Atakapas and the Opelousas also raise horses of medium-size which are quite well formed, lively and robust. They sell from 23-60 piastres. If anyone would take the trouble to obtain good stock, which one could do by importing a few choice stallions, and would give to the mares and colts a little forage during the two winter months, then horse raising would become a considerable branch of commerce. It would be easy to produce horses worth several hundred piastres. It is true that Louisiana does obtain by contraband, horses from the internal Spanish provinces of neighboring Mexico but these horses, raised wild on the plains, are taken at an advanced age and are very difficult to break. Moreover, they often have defects and from lack of care are acclimatized with some difficulty. For these reasons, the horses of the countryside are preferable. They are called Creole, and are gentle and easy to break, and rarely have defects.

With these immense herds of cattle spread over the prairies of Opelousas and Atakapas, one would not believe that a pound of beef always sells from 2 to 4 *schellins* [escalins] (25 to 50 sous) and at that price is difficult to obtain. Such is the monumental idolence of the inhabitants. What is even more astonishing to the European is that in the dry season, especially in the winter, milk is a rare thing. The same inhabitants who have several hundred cows go three or four months without a cup of milk. It happens that I was crossing the Opelousas in the month of October when the heat is still intense, and I found myself greatly desiring this food and that almost everywhere there was none to be had. During the dry seasons the herds had already scattered and most of the inhabitants let them all go without bothing to keep near them a cow or two for their needs daily. One can see from this account how far the settlers are from obtaining all of the riches which greater industry could extract from one of the most fertile soils of the universe. At home man solicits nature, but here nature solicits man.

CHAPTER LXIII

Picture of this region since establishment of colony compared with the picture to be seen formerly. Observations on the prairie plants especially as regards the herds. Use of corn, different methods of preparing it. Its advantages over wheat, pumpkins or squash. The cultivation of cotton. Its manufacture. Caterpillars cause the culture to be abandoned. Observations on the natural history of caterpillars. These insects are not, properly speaking, a plague. They are only dangerous through the ignorance of men. The means of protection from them applied to the cultivation of cotton. The advantage of this culture compared to the production of hemp and flax.

Crossing the wide prairie, strewn with flowers, whose stems raise them to the height of the horse on which the traveler is riding, surprise follows surprise in this varied vegetation. One rides suddenly upon herds of cattle, who raise their haughty heads above the grass as one rapidly approaches. They at first seem to steadily regard him, attentively, as if stupified with admiration, but as one nears them they suddenly break and run, fleeing across the prairie in bounds. In the distance, the occasional houses scattered here and there along the brownish curtain of woods that border the windings of the rivers and bayous provide relief for this rich tableau of nature, so new to the European. The cannibals, with their horrible banquets, have disappeared from the land. No longer does one hear in the shadow of the night around their lugubrious fires their songs of ferocious joy, mixed with the doleful crys of the victims they are torturing. It has been hardly a half century that a man has been able to cross this laughing country in peace; that he has been able to cover them with herds of cows, horses and sheep and, to tend them himself under the beneficient laws of civilization. Say to us now, detractors of civilization, that Man is more noble in the state of savagery approaching close to nature; or whether he is not in that condition, a prey to hunger and to fear, only able to protect himself by crimes. Say also if nature is not more rich and more varied in those places where the industrious hand of man has fertilized it.

Near those houses where the herds pass most frequently, the prairies change. The plants are no longer the same. In these trampled places grow those species most used by the animals for food.

There, for instance, particularly flourishes a little clover; the couch-grass and several other grasses. Other plants, so common away from the house, disappear in these places. This observation, which I verified in so many places, proves again that each animal tends to favor the growth of those plants which are necessary to it in those places where it lives. The wild boar, who feeds upon acorns, favors their germination and their growth by digging the ground with his tusks. The bird who lives on the seeds of grapes dissemi-nates the wild grape vines by carrying the seeds afar. The gold-finch, who loves the seed of the thistle, lining its nest with thistle down, obtains this by breaking open its seed capsules and scattering its light and tiny seeds to the wind. Carnivorous animals, as I have shown elsewhere, also favor the propagation of their prey animals.

The use of corn is universal both among the poor and the rich. Corn is prepared here in an infinite number of ways. Usually it is ground with wooden mortars and pestles. The white corn is made into flour, and from this can be made a very good mush with either water of milk. The latter being thicker, is eaten with that type of soup called gumbo. Ordinary corn broken into small grains, like rice, is cooked almost to dryness in a kettle and is called *petit gru*. This nutritious food is quite common. Corn broken into larger grains and cooked with a larger quantity of water is called *sagamite*. It is believed that this last method is the healthiest, and it is especially refreshing. Fermented corn flour is boiled and is called *cassant*. This mush is made only with water, to which is added some sugar. Bread is also made of corn, as in Europe. The dough is placed on the fire as soon as it is kneaded. It may be baked in an oven, a dutch oven, or simply on a leaning board placed close to the fire. This bread is very tasty, especially when it is tender and hot, but it dries out quickly and then it is tough and disagreeable. For travel, a hard-tack is made of corn, but this is quite poor. If corn meal is mixed with wheat flour in small quan-tity, it does no harm to the quality of the bread. Finally, there is another type of corn meal, in which the corn is first roasted and during the roasting a little wood ash is added. When the corn and ashes are ground to flour in a mortar the result is called *cold* flour and is especially used as provision on long trips. It can be eaten simply moistened with cold water (and a little sugar if one wishes it). It is from this that it takes its name cold flour. It can be also boiled either with plain water or with a little meat stock and is much better. I have used it a great deal in my travels through the wilderness. This type of flour, being easier to digest, should be especially suitable to invalids and children. Corn is a valuable crop to use as the staff of life. It can be accommodated to all stomachs by a variety in preparation. I do not know why French travelers are the most ready to denigrate it. When it is green, Negroes, Creoles, and especially the English, eat the roasted ears, which they call dried corn. It is very tender, and the Creoles prepare it in the same way as garden peas. Besides this, corn serves as food for all the animals. It feeds and fattens all types of poultry, even pigeons, which wheat cannot do. It is also used to feed horses, cows, sheep and pigs. The dried corn plants (not the stem, but the leaves) also provide an excellent fodder for the cattle during the winter.

Corn has this advantage over wheat, that it produces more abundantly. One can obtain two harvests a year and do the harvesting in one's spare time. If time is pressing, one can, when the corn is ripe, content himself with breaking the stalk of the ear and letting it hang down. Hanging thus, protected by its shuck, the rain runs off without penetrating it, and the birds cannot get at the kernels. In their corn fields the inhabitants plant watermelons and other species of melon that they call French melons. But they plant especially an immense quantity of gourds or pumpkins. Their corn fields produce thousands of them. I have seen settlers harvest 8 to 10 thousand. These pumpkins do not have the insipid taste of those that are eaten in Paris, nor are they watery like those. They are substantial and tasty and especially very sweet. In cutting them, a sort of whitish transparent juice runs out which coagulates a moment after. Pumpkins are served on all tables, the Negroes like them very much, and horses will gorge themselves on them, and they cause the cows to give an excellent milk. This is a food stuff which will support both animals and men. Agreeable and healthy during the hot days, these pumpkins will keep out in the fields even after the frosts. But the industrious settlers always make sure to harvest and store a part of the best of them after the first light frost. The first frost adds to their sweet quality. They obtain this sweet flavor also early in the spring if they are sheltered and exposed to cool, dry air.

In the district of the Ouachita the inhabitants dry them in trenches dug in long rows, and by this means keep them all year round. I have seen the Indians cut them into strips and dry them like their meat, and they will also keep a long time this way. These same corn fields, besides giving abundant harvests of melons and pumpkins, produce in addition various kinds of beans, one among them especially abundant twining around the corn stalks.

Each settler encloses the portion of the prairie that he requires for his harvest near his house with palisades of cypress. He changes the place of enclosure according to his fancy, and, for that matter, the house as well, which he dismantles in the process. As he has no lack of land, he encloses usually more than he can cultivate and often enough he cultivates more than he can harvest. He has hardly finished the ground when harvest time has arrived. The lack of man power is so acute that rarely can a colonist retrieve all of his harvest. The cultivation of indigo has been abandoned because of the diseases of that plant, and it has been replaced in this country by cotton.

The cotton plant, a species of *Malvaceae*, succeeds generally better on lands lighter and less humid than those of Opelousas and Atakapas. Toward the mouth of the river the plant attains a height of six or seven feet, spreading a large number of strong branches, forming a large bush garnished with large leaves intermixed with beautiful white flowers. The capsules, which are derived from these flowers, contain the oval seeds enveloped by that fine and silky down which constitutes cotton. When the capsules dry, they open of themselves and the harvest is thus made easy. The roots of this plant spread out, so that in Louisiana, where there is plenty of land, they are spaced wide apart. One can saunter in these fields of cotton as among avenues of trees. One Negro can harvest at least 60 pounds of cotton a day, which, when the seed is removed, is reduced a third. This harvest begins in the middle of August and continues into December. Calculating this time at only a hundred days, a single Negro could thus harvest two thousand pounds of clean cotton. The price of this production under the Spanish government was from 15 to 20 sous a pound, but under the Americans this has risen to from 20 to 28 sous. One can see then that a single Negro can easily gain for his master, by his work alone, 2,000 pounds of cotton, and he is occupied in this work scarcely a third of the year. The other work involved in raising cotton amounts to very little. The ground is lightly plowed and sown in February and March. A little dressing and chopping to keep down the weeds are really the only care cotton requires, and this takes only a few days.

In order to rid the cotton of its seed, two horses are required to turn a mechanism composed of two cylinders covered with spikes which tear apart the cotton and separate it from its seed, which is too large to pass between the cylinders. From here the cotton goes to the press, where it is wrapped around with cloth and cord and formed into a bale, for in this way it occupies the least possible volume. This is the way we receive cotton in Europe. These bales are squeezed so tight that rain cannot penetrate them. Bales from wrecked boats, which are pulled out of the river, are found to be dampened only in the outermost inch. Some inhabitants have these machines themselves, others use those of their neighbors, ordinarily paying in kind at the rate of two sous per pound.

An arpent of ground produces from 250 to 300 pounds. The picking of cotton is not very arduous and may be done by old men and children, which is probably why its culture has spread among the Acadians under the Spanish government. The expenses of raising cotton are very low, but again, the difficulty of transportation and bureaucratic obstacles in the way of commerce have made for a low return on the crop.

The American government, whatever its numerous faults, at least has the good sense to allow the greatest freedom to commercial enterprises. This undoubtedly would have stimulated an extraordinary extension of the growth of cotton except for the appearance of a plague which caused consternation among the inhabitants and has forced them, as of now, to abandon this lucrative enterprise. Some have taken up indigo again, and others, sugar. This plague consists of caterpillars, which for the last two or three years have ravaged the harvests from one end of the colony to the other, except in the Ouachita and a few other isolated spots where they have not yet been seen. These caterpillars appear ordinarily on the cotton plants about the time of flowering. In two or three days they devour the leaves and the buds, covering the ground with debris. They go successively from field to field, doing fearful damage. One individual in the Atakapas, whose field was surrounded by a deep, wide ditch, observed them after having devastated his fields, crawling towards this ditch, accumulating in large masses and rolling down into the waters.

How unfortunate is Man, one might say, to see the reward of his sweat and labor snatched away in a few days by these insects, enemies of nature who everywhere torment and devastate. And you, who wish to believe that all parts of this universe are explicable by reason of utility to Man, or are even necessary to him, what then can be the necessity of these swarms of insects which are everywhere malign? Would not their non-existence be a benefit? Such is the language of him, who bent double with toil day and night, solicits of the earth its bounty, and he who at the foot of the altar prays fervently, as well as he who, audaciously fixing his eyes upon the vault of heaven, numbers its revolving spheres and calculates their masses. Yes, these insects who multiply almost instantaneously, covering your vinyards, your fields, and your forests to devour them, are the product of a beneficient providence! Without them the order of nature in the reproduction of beings would be destroyed and all would be lost.

Listen, audacious mortals, who in slandering nature blaspheme the God who is its author, and learn that your woes are due to your ignorance and lack of regard for the works of the eternal being! If I do not cover everything admirable in this majestic subject, at least I believe I shall be able to convince those who cherish the truth, and to offer them a universal means of preventing these disastrous ravages, particularly as applied to important crops like cotton.

Different species of caterpillars live on different species of vegetation. The juices which will nourish one are not at all suitable for others. The result of this is, that in wild regions, where the vegetation is almost always mixed, the caterpillars never produce a great damage. When they have eaten the leaves on a tree, finding no others like it in the neighborhood, they must necessarily perish. If a few of them are fortunate enough to reach another tree of the same species, their small number will insure that no great damage will be done. Thus in those places where the vegetation is wild, insects are scattered from the place where they have been born and their ravages are diminished consequently. Each species of plant is protected by isolation from other plants of its own species and by the proximity of plants which are unrelated.

But if it happens that a species of plant is introduced which spreads over a wide extent of land, so that many plants are contiguous, caterpillars born on a single plant will, after having ravaged it, pass on to the next plant, and so on to the next. The insects will grow in numbers from year to year until their ravages have exhausted these plants, finally destroying them partially and thus giving the opportunity for other plants to invade the area, grow and propagate in their turn. The earth, the air, and animals all require this prodigious diversity of plants, which is maintained thus through the office of caterpillars. They particularly act to preserve the weakest plants and those multiplying the most slowly, and I shall show elsewhere how caterpillars have proved useful even to the trees which they attack. The farmer, out of necessity or whim, disturbs this wise economy and diversity of vegetation. He wishes for forests consisting entirely of a few privileged species. In his orchards he puts each species together by itself. In order to teach him not to cover his fields with all the same species, nature has instructed him in spite of himself in the necessity for alternating and varying his plantings. In the colonies new land, more humid, more animated by heat has, year in and a year out, been uniformly covered with the same plants. This alteration from nature's plantings has produced extraordinary effects. Both the growers of indigo and cocoa have suffered from contagious maladies which suddenly wiped out their crops. Worms, reptiles, and ants have destroyed plantations of sugar cane, while the cotton plant, a spectacular, flowery and leafy plant, has become a special prey of caterpillars.* The more the culture of cotton has expanded, the more rapid has been the progress of caterpillars.

The first colonists who brought in the cotton plant, of course, went several years without seeing caterpillars on their plants. Either the butterlies, their eggs, or their nymphs had to be introduced, or perhaps some of the *Malvacaeae* native to the country harbored caterpillars like those which attack the cotton plant. But as soon as one butterfly or a few eggs began to multiply, the multiplication must have been progressive and constant. The eggs, laid in the cotton field, multiplied in number, and these increased numbers attacked the same field the next year. Thus from year to year, these caterpillars, having become butterflies, were carried in increasing numbers by the winds to neighboring fields, and, as soon as all the colonists in the same neighborhood began growing cotton, then the propagation of the caterpillars became general, and, once started, they became permanent pests.

The only thing that can happen to affect this cycle is the advent of rainy years. Rain at the time that the caterpillars are hatching diminishes their fertility, and then their ravages are less severe, but, as if in recompense, in the following years the weather favors their multiplication. Thus, once the caterpillars are established in a place in which plants suitable to them are cultivated, they will necessarily always be present.

Man, who by his skill can produce uniformity of vegetation over vast areas, could also prevent its destruction. The caterpillar of

---

*I designate the cotton plant in this way for a reason. I shall show that these showy and leafy plants are more destructive to neighboring vegetation and nourish especially fecund and voracious caterpillars.

the cotton plant is one of a numerous family. It is long, thin, and active, striped longitudinally with black and dull yellow.* It has 14 to 16 legs. It rolls the leaf into a little cone in which it produces a cocoon. The butterfly is a pale yellow, but I was not able to ascertain whether this butterfly was nocturnal.

In autumn most of the leaves of the cotton plant fall and are carried away by the wind. Around the enclosure of the cotton field is an uncultivated strip of land, 12 to 15 feet wide, in which tall grass is growing, and here most of the detached leaves of the cotton plant come to rest. Some of these leaves contain the caterpillars in cocoon, and others the eggs of the butterfly. One should, then, while the cotton field is being harvested, rake up and burn or, better still, burn it. If these butterflies are nocturnal, then at the time they appear, one should light fires at night in the fields, the dried leaves and cut off the tall grass surrounding the field for these moths will come after a man just carrying a torch.

Then the colonists should change continuously the place of their plantings of cotton. They should take a special care to isolate cotton fields from their neighbors' fields. They should try to shelter them from the winds during the time that the butterflies emerge, and it may be necessary to divide their plantations into large squares, each one surrounded by a large border planted in corn, for example. This sort of regulation should not be left to the colonists themselves. There should be ordinances to this effect with vigorous police action to punish those who do not obey.

But most important still, plantations should be visited daily at the time that caterpillars begin to hatch. The vigilant eye of the farmer is the best of all measures against this pest. The caterpillars hatch in little groups where a single butterfly has laid eggs in thousands. As hatched caterpillars grow up, they stimulate themselves to disperse more and more. I, myself, have carefully made observations on them. Although very small and hidden under the leaves, they are easy to find by looking for nibbled leaves. As soon as these fatal traces are discovered, the damaged leaves must be immediately removed and burned, and in the process it is better to cut too much than too little, for if too many caterpillars escape the whole harvest may be lost.

---

*The description of this caterpillar which I made with some care on the spot has been lost from among my papers. I am obliged therefore to give it from memory. If it is not exact in every character, it is at least correct in the essential points.

I advised one of the inhabitants of this expedient. He paid no attention to me. He did not even visit his fields until several days afterwards, when the damage was irreparable. A harvest that is worth 20 thousand francs to a single individual and which amounts to several millions for the colony; demanding so little labor; capable of being tended by women and children or people not habituated to hard work; is not such a harvest worth all of the reflections of the naturalist, all the vigilence of governments, and the solicitude of individuals? Is it not true, especially here, that consideration of the relationships between organisms, which allows us to discern an admirable order where before we had only seen disorder, will enlighten agricultural science?

Is cotton, whose use is becoming more and more common in Europe, a benefit to Europeans? Is its introduction advantageous or damaging in countries like France, which have an abundant production of hemp and flax? I shall address myself briefly to this subject.

Cotton is made up into cloth of all kinds. It can be made thick, as in blankets or flannel, and it can be made thin and transparent as in muslin. Between these extremities there are a great number of kinds; striped velveteen, plain, fully or partially striped, and variations without number; various kinds of quilting almost as durable; bombazine; fine cloths so varied in their design; coarser cloth; nankeens both of the Indies and of our manufacture; and strong cloths running down to muslin, which is dyed in colors so rich and so various for all ages, all tastes and all peoples.

These cotton cloths are used in our furnishings as well as in our clothes. They have an infinity of uses for which neither hemp nor linen is suitable, and they compare favorably with these two in those products where they are employed. The shirts of cotton, which are used in the colonies and are beginning to be used in Europe, last longer and are healthier than those of linen. They are warmer in winter and are more pervious to perspiration in the summer. Table cloths of cotton, as used in Louisiana, would also be suitable in Europe. The use of cotton is spreading daily in hat-making.

The increase in the demand for cotton is not due solely to the whims of fashion. The use of cotton is spreading among people who are not votives of that inconstant divinity. We elders, isolated inhabitants of far-off countries, are adopting its use with the same alacrity as the ladies, those creatures most changeable in their appearance. Everyone of all classes finds cotton appropriate, healthy, durable, and, consequently, economical.

These motives should carry great weight for the argument that cotton should be welcomed by the governments of the old world, even those who, with their scales in their hands, believe by virtue of their stringent (and always erroneous) calculations that they should admit only those products whose production is favorable to them. A good government, like a good father, would rather see his children clothed more properly, more comfortably, more sanitorily, and more economically, even if this costs him something. But even not considering this, the encouragement of the introduction of cotton would be advantageous also to the interest of European states, especially to that of France.

The growth, the harvest and the cleaning of cotton are much less expensive than the corresponding care of hemp or flax, which require great expanses of ground to be manured several times, worked, harrowed, etc., not to mention equipment; then other labors during the harvest, the retting, the scutching, and the ironing and finally the spinning of flax, which cannot easily be done by mechanical means.

An arpent of flax in Flanders produces, in an average year, a value of about 300 francs. The expenses come to 250 francs (not including taxes, the cost of spinning into thread, the manufacture of cloth, and its bleaching). It is easily ascertained, therefore, that an ell of cloth costs the proprietor 9/10 of its value and his net profit is only 10 percent.

In contrast to this, a single individual can harvest in a third of the year up to 2,000 pounds of cotton, which in a few more days it is possible to spin, clean, weave and put in condition for sale. The low cost of management of cotton will allow Europe to procure cotton at a lower price than linen and hemp. Europe, in making use of cotton, will sell even more of its hemp and linen cloth, or will see this land used for other productive labor. This will pay back the state with interest its outlay for the purchase of cotton. One must keep in mind the principle that the more that people make use of things that simplify labor, no matter what country they come from, the more they will augment their exports.*

---

*It is great stupidity to say that the books of the customs house are the books of statesmen. They are, rather, those of financiers, which is another thing altogether. These books are faulty even as indications of imports and exports, and become even more so as indicators of the balance of trade. The importation that they show as a burden to the state is really extremely advan-

But if, instead of buying cotton in our ports at from 30 to 36 sous a pound in specie, cotton were obtained from the colonies in exchange for goods of our manufacture, then, as I have proved in speaking of the Ouachita, it would be even cheaper, and the more cotton imported, the more of our goods would be exported. As the use of cotton becomes more extensive (and it is becoming more extensive from day to day than even that of sugar), it will soon be true that a colony whose principal crop is cotton will become more productive than a sugar colony. If, moreover, this cotton is cultivated by whites, working their own land, each of them will become consumers, so that cotton will produce a larger outlet for our manufactures than sugar, cultivated by miserable slaves. Cotton would thus contribute to the multiplication of a colonial population bound with ties of essential similarity in customs, inclinations, and interests to the mother country, from which it will derive, in addition to outlets for its produce, merchants, sailors, and warriors to serve it and protect it.†

---

tageous to it by an infinity of ramifications to the industry of the state to which they give rise. The ramifications, which escape the attentions of the casual observer because of their tenuousness and complexity, are like the fibers of plants, the principal channels of the economic vitality of the state.

What our compilers of statistics have not thought of yet, as they pursue their calculations within a framework as narrow as their own minds, is to calculate what these importations must add to the population. Then to ascertain what sort of population is thus increased, to weigh the worth of each of these individuals and to calculate the economic interaction between them and the other individuals in the state. That is what these masters of the books of records should do, and we shall concern ourselves with it no more.

Do you wish to assure that the balance of trade will always be in your favor? Then sustain the national character. Nurture it. Fortify its customs, and set free its own potentiality. It will fertilize and revitalize itself always. If, in certain circumstances it seems to lessen, it is only retreating to come forward again with new energy.

†Ships of the Anglo-Americans spread their sails on almost every sea. What do they carry? Goods of English manufacture. The United States would be at war with England, except that they cannot do without goods of English manufacture. Expensiveness of labor will prevent them, for centuries, from being able to establish any large-scale factories capable of competing with those of England. In spite of themselves, they are peddlers of English goods.

CHAPTER LXIV

*Two parties divide the Atakapas. The trial which gave rise
to this. Principal chiefs to the two parties. Their portraits.
An adventurer named Saint-Julien plays a principal role in
the affair. Murder of the wife of Saint-Julien in singular circumstances. Innocent parties are accused of the crime. Almost all the colony and the author are mislead on the subject. Researches of the author to discover the truth. The
dangers in this district, in the meantime, from the hates of
the two parties, who are ready to come to blows. Excess committed on the person of the sheriff. Idea and importance of
his functions. The governor comes to the district. His efforts
to stamp out these enmities. The political motives that determine these events. The author stumbles upon documents and
secret information of this affair. The reasoned exposition
of the circumstances of the murder. Who the murderer is.
Proofs. This affair still undecided at the author's departure.
Observations to which this gives rise. The spirit of party
tends to turn men's minds from the truth. Instruction in
morality the sole means of preventing this dangerous effect.
Proofs of this in what had happened in the Atakapas.*

The Atakapas, the most beautiful region in Louisiana, fortunate
land where Nature has done everything to make men happy; where
riches multiply with so little labor and expense; where the earth
holds back nothing from man, where everywhere man is unequal to
the earth; where there is so much need of industriousness; this
land, at its very inception, has already become a prey to fatal divisions. Already it is sullied by accumulated crimes, and at this very
moment crime raises its menacing head, continuing to outrage innocence and virtue. I pause in this narrative to set at rest a cal-
umny which has outstripped the truth, and to tear aside the hideous veil wherewith it conceals the truth. I felt honor bound to
fulfill this duty, the most holy of all, and I consider this task the
most glorious I have undertaken in this painful voyage. I had to
wrestle with my own preconceptions to give myself up to laborious
researches; to flounder along in shadowy uncertainty, and to brave
the resentments of hate. Reader, it is your duty as well to follow
me carefully in this recital. You will receive some benefit from
it no matter what may be your rank, your age, or your sex.

The first commandant, Fusillier, had for his successor in the

Atakapas another French officer named Desclouettes, who passed then into the service of Spain. This officer governed with justice and moderation. But one decisive act of his, though necessary, has had the most deplorable results since his death. Some herds of cattle which had become *marrones* (that is to say, who had no known masters) had obtained considerable size on these fertile prairies. The colonists used to hunt them, principally for their skins. These hunts, however, soon led to abuses, because among the wild cattle others were killed belonging to other colonists. This impelling reason caused the commandant to forbid the hunting of wild cattle. In spite of this interdiction (which was reiterated), the hunts continued. The commandant instituted a search, and he found at the home of several of the principal inhabitants piles of skins, easy to recognize as those of wild cattle because they were not marked as are those of the herds of each individual.

These prominent inhabitants were condemned to a few days in prison, the usual punishment for misdemeanors in the colony, especially under the Spanish regime. Time has not yet extinguished the resentment that this punishment aroused, however just it may have been, and I myself have heard several of the inhabitants still speaking of it with bitterness. The commandant Desclouettes, under whom a number of colonists established themselves here, often took upon himself the responsibility of surveying their concessions and setting their limits. After his death, two Acadian neighbors began to quarrel over their boundary. This was displaced by one of them. The other came to complain to the eldest son of the commandant established at the Atakapas. The younger Desclouettes thought it his duty to uphold the reputation of his father and to defend this individual. At this news the resentment of those who had been in prison rekindled itself with fury, and everyone took the part against Desclouettes. His opponents were, as I have said, the principal people of the district. They had become fathers of numerous families and had formed numerous alliances.

Everyone of any property in the district, sons, parents, allies, friends, without knowing the basis of the affair, formed a powerful league to combat Desclouettes.* They were more than merely

---

*I am able to affirm the general ignorance of the basis of this affair, because it was the chief persons of this league who had offered me hospitality. They were unable to explain the basis of the quarrel to me and had to submit that they did not know it.

property owners—they were those who make up the best society, who set the best tables, and who are most frequently seen entertaining each other, as well as those who welcome strangers with the greatest cordiality. It was, to speak properly, the party of the nobles, and those who affected their manners and customs.

Desclouettes' party, however, did not lack strength. M. Desclouettes was the commander of the militia of the district. He lived in a remote house in the district called *Côte-Gelée* and *Carencro* inhabited by Acadians who were entirely devoted to him, not so much because he was the commander of the militia, but because of his simple, affectionate manner. M. Desclouettes also had a numerous family, and another factor to be reckoned with was his mother, who, at an advanced age, was justly venerated in the district. Two of his sisters were suitably married, two brothers lived at his house, and three others were in the service of the king of Spain. The eldest, named Brognier-Desclouettes, had been promoted in rank, and had a considerable fortune, the fruit of some fortunate speculations. He was held in high regard by the chiefs of the Spanish government and, especially, he was in the high favor of the Marquis de Casa-Calvo. The priest of the Atakapas, a native of Bordeaux named Barière, through the duties of his ministry, was attached to the interest of the Acadians, who are very pious, and he had a very great influence on them. He found himself, therefore, allied to the party of Desclouettes.

The present commandant, M. Deblanc, of whom I had occasion to speak before, had been, while in Paris as a young man, a soldier of the guard. He retained the airs of these gentlemen still. He loved ostentation and titles. As a French gentleman, his real name, Leblanc, had appeared to him so bourgeois that he had distorted it into Deblanc. His royalist inclinations naturally inclined him to the party of nobles. Besides being sociable, liking to eat well, given to leisure and parties where he was very gay, he naturally took the side of those with whom he was so familiar. Easy going, easily persuaded, obliging, the best of fathers, he was incapable of the dark sentiments of hate, and still less was he able to retain them over long periods of time. But light-minded and weak, he was, without wishing it, susceptible to becoming an instrument of evil. How often are such men more dangerous than wicked people! Under these circumstances, when he came to be concerned in the affair of the elder Desclouettes, everything conspired to lead him into the opposition party and to keep him there.

But the individual who came to play the greatest role in this party, who brought it blood and tragedy, was Cadet Saint-Julien, an adventurer born in the environs of Bordeaux, who arrived in the colony as a sailor. After having wandered, as we shall see, in various places he came to the Atakapas, his oar in his hand. He settled here and married an Acadian girl.

This Cadet Saint-Julien knew how to read and write, more or less, and for the Acadians, who are profoundly ignorant, this is the *nec plus ultra* of all learning. They could conceive of nothing beyond that. With a great deal of boasting, audacity, and dissimulation, particularly intended to cloak the intentions of his insidious actions, Saint-Julien soon became the oracle of the neighboring families and their allies; and without the faintest knowledge of these affairs, he was delegated to uphold the families' interests against the Desclouettes party. This adventurer, who had arrived a short time ago as an inferior, became the agent, indeed, the soul, of the richest, and the most prominent and proud people of the district. He found himself, thus, necessarily allied with the commandant M. Deblanc, whom he learned how to flatter most adroitly. The judicial expenses of this affair originally came to no more than five or six hundred francs, but they have grown daily, and today they are up to sixty to eighty thousand francs. In the interval, one party or the other obtains provisional judgments, and when these are to be executed the opposite party opposes the execution by force. Thus the party spirit worsens from day to day.

This was the state of things at the arrival of the prefect M. Laussat, whom, as you recall, was in Louisiana a long time before he took possession of the colony, to give it up only two weeks later to the American government. M. Deblanc hastened to have himself introduced to M. Laussat, who welcomed him, the more so, because he wanted from this commander important information on the western regions of Louisiana and its boundaries, little known either to the French or the Spanish governments.

A short time after this first interview, M. Deblanc wrote to the Atakapas to obtain a census of the inhabitants. I should repeat, for this circumstance is very important, that M. Deblanc told me this himself. He met a commander of some post or other, who told him that he had received orders from the Spanish government to take a census. M. Deblanc concluded from this, that the same order must have arrived at the Atakapas. In consequence, he wrote, giving orders to have it done. The order was addressed to the syndic, M. Sorel, a rich miser of whom I have already spoken, and the principal execution was delegated to M. Saint-Julien. The Acadians of the Desclouettes party were loud in their outcry, wishing nothing to do with Saint-Julien, whom they believed to be guilty of grave misdemeanors, independent of the affair of the trial. M. Desclouettes took the position that the order for the census, in the absence of the commandant of the post, should have been addressed to him as commander of the militia, and it therefore should not be executed without an official order of the government, which neither Saint-Julien nor Sorel could produce. Saint-Julien in the course of this debate assumed the pose of a French patriot, and his statements rang with cries of liberty. The gist of his remarks was that everything connected with the Spanish regime should be abolished. The Spanish government, learning of the uproar caused by a census made without its authorization, named an interim commandant and ordered him to have Saint-Julien arrested and sent to New Orleans, in the meantime, forbidding M. Deblanc (who was in the city) to return home without a new order. It must be admitted, that the conduct of M. Deblanc, whatever may have been his motives, was extremely reprehensible. M. Deblanc, commandant under the Spanish government, which had loaded him with emoluments and from whom he had specifically received some magnificent land concessions, under the normal procedure of subordination, should have done nothing without the orders of his superiors. What he had been told by another commandant really cannot serve as an excuse. Besides, he was in New Orleans, and he could easily have assured himself whether orders for a census had really been given, but being weak, and influenced by an intriguer (the ring-leader of those whom I designated in Chapter 40), Deblanc attached himself to the administrators surrounding the prefect, which estranged him from the Spanish government. One of his reasons was that he did not like to meet the brothers of Desclouettes who were to be found there. In any case, the confiding of the execution of such an order to Saint-Julien, who was anathema to one of the parties on the post, was a grave blunder.

Saint-Julien was sent for several times by the interim commandant, but he evaded the order by feigning sickness. In the meantime, it was learned that his wife was murdered on the eighteenth of June 1803 in the most deplorable circumstances and that Saint-Julien had escaped death only by a sort of miracle. Toward nightfall, according to the story, his wife was in the room near one of the doors, occupied in spinning, with her back to the door. Another woman, who lived with them, was in an alcove in the same room. Both of them were singing at their spinning wheels. The husband, stretched out on the plank bed face down in a neighboring room, was listening to them. He was thus, in line with the door behind his wife, perhaps five feet behind her and on a line with the front door to the outside.

While Saint-Julien was listening attentively to the songs, which amused him, he heard a noise behind him, and turning his head, saw a man raising his gun to fire. He struck the gun with a sudden movement. The shot went off, and the bullet pierced his unfortunate wife's back, coming out of her breast and passing into the room beyond and burying itself in the window frame. Saint-Julien attempted to seize the gun of the murderer, who ran away. Saint-Julien ran after him and was pursuing him with a pick, that he had picked up as a weapon, when a second shot by a second man rang out, which, however, did not hit him. A third attacker appeared, and all three of them struck Saint-Julien to the ground with repeated blows of their gun butts, leaving him on the spot for dead. His brother-in-law and other individuals arriving some time afterwards found him stretched out in the courtyard covered with blood, and they carried him with much difficulty to his bed.

The news of this double attack spread rapidly among the inhabitants. Interest, compassion, curiosity brought together a great crowd of persons, regardless of party. This large crowd stayed for eight of ten days and ate up several oxen. Syndic Sorel, in the absence of the commandant, was informed of the affair in a manner that we shall see. The woman survived a week. Saint-Julien, in his statement, implicated his Acadian enemies, especially one named Carmouche and the elder Desclouettes. Several different versions of this incident were current in the city, but Saint-Julien's version prevailed and circumstances occurred to rekindle interest in it.

The Spanish government did not give up its attempt to arrest Saint-Julien. On the contrary, it issued most precise orders to this effect, and, finally, Saint-Julien, after having been interrogated by the interim commandant, was brought to New Orleans in chains and put in prison. This treatment, as well as the prohibition of M. Deblanc from leaving the city, appeared to the public to be the result of the murder. The two affairs were confused then and are confused now. Indignation became general. Apparently authority had been abused in the most flagrant manner. The unfortunate head of a family had been imprisoned to save the guilty persons worthy of the most extreme punishment. The party of Saint-Julien profited from this to heap opprobrium on the Desclouettes family.

The indifference of the Spanish government to public opinion, or rather the mysterious workings of its administration of justice, served to feed this belief . Saint-Julien, it is true, was interrogated closely by the judge auditor, but quite aside from secrecy, this judge's reputation for cupidity was so notorious that it is to be doubted that he could have changed the disposition of public opinion.

I arrived in New Orleans at this time to hear this confused recital of a strange catastrophe accompanied with a mixture of other circumstances and, as we shall see, I myself took part in the general indignation on Saint-Julien's behalf.

When the prefect took possession of the colony for several days, his first official act was to break the chains of Saint-Julien. So much was public sentiment in favor of this captive, that he believed it his duty not only to break these chains but to do so ceremoniously, and this was the reason for the proclamation which I reported earlier (Chapter 40). The clause in this proclamation stating that the 4,000 piastres bond which the prefect had imposed seemed to many to add to the persecutions of this innocent man.

Saint-Julien returned triumphant to his home. M. Deblanc took up once again his functions as the commandant of Atakapas, and one named Potier, a surveyor delegated by the prefect who took possession of the district, was such an enthusiastic partisan of the sentiments of the Saint-Julien party that 24 hours after he arrived he removed the curé Barière from the Presbytère where he had lived for 10 years. It did not even belong to the government, but had been established and paid for by several individuals. The curé had been accused by the Saint-Julien party of having heard the murdered woman declare the names of the murderers in the confessional and to have imposed upon her as penance an injunction to say nothing. This arbitrary act just missed having the most deplorable consequences. The curé of the Atakapas moved away a distance of 25 leagues from the church and, in a little while he was established as curé de facto. At whatever hour he was called upon by the pious Acadians, he came to them, braving all dangers. He accommodated himself to their simple way of life, bedding down, on the boards, when he had to, drinking water and eating coarse corn bread and salt meat. He became thus, their guide and friend, and they wanted no other priest and no other mass but his. In the eyes of the opposed party, on the other hand, it was an abomination to take part in this cult, led by an unfrocked priest.

Religious devotion thus became the focus of the discord. The two parties were soon ready to come to blows. Everyday the tumult mounted. The hour and day of combat had been fixed, and violence was avoided only when the American commandant, then in power, had the prudence to close the church.

The party of the nobles then had another pastor sent to them from the city, at great expense who, having had an opulent parish at San Domingo, had manners which suited them better.

I arrived in the meanwhile in the Atakapas and the impressions I had received in the city were strengthened. I found myself in the midst of the partisans of Saint Julien since those of the other party inhabited the more remote districts. The Desclouettes family, I knew only as a name of those proscribed in the most humiliating isolation. One day the curé Barière came to see me, I don't know why. I had conversed with him for quite a while when I became aware of his name. I experienced a revulsion which I could hardly repress, so strong had been the statements I had heard concerning him. When my botanical researches took me near his house, which was only about a league from mine, he came to assist me, and I dreaded even the sight of the house of the man whom I had been told used a most sacred religion to protect crime and oppress innocence. Numerous other stories were repeated to me about him which still further strengthened this painful sentiment of aversion.

Several months after my arrival in the Atakapas, I had decided to explore the region more widely. The first day after my departure, I stopped at sunset, having gone a few leagues, to ask hospitality. I was cordially recived, and passed an agreeable evening. The next day after breakfasting, in taking leave, I asked my host his name in order to write it in my journal. "Desclouettes, *cadet*," he answered. I admit that I was startled. I had always associated this name with criminal plots and murders and I suddenly found it coming up in connection with the amenities of hospitality, shown toward an unknown whose name he did not even know. "This Desclouettes," I said to myself, "does not seem to resemble his elder brother." I took my leave then, agitated in mind by various ideas. But a short distance from there, one of my horses, who had been badly packed, spilled his load and escaped across the prairie. He could not be caught, and I was obliged to return to M. Desclouettes and ask for help. M. Desclouettes soon had the horse recaptured, but he did not wish me to leave that day, telling me that it would take time to repair the harness of my pack horse, which he did himself. I did not leave until the next morning, and though we conversed freely I was given ample opportunity to speak of the Saint-Julien affair (indeed, he seemed to be inviting me to do so, in complaining of the disorders of the country) I did not dare to do so, so much was I persuaded that he would have been humiliated by it.

I wished to explore first of all, the settlement at Carencro and Côte-Gelée. M. Desclouettes directed me to various inhabitants where I should find a place to stay and, these were, although I did not know it, all partisans of his brother. I found them good people with simple manners. Everyone was occupied much as on our farms in France. On Sunday morning, I saw a great number of people all walking toward the same place. I inquired about this from one of those whom I met. "We are going," he said, "to hear the mass, M. Barière says mass every Sunday in that house which is large enough to contain everybody." I could not resist the temptation to see this religious meeting and so I was present at the mass. The altar was properly decorated. All of the communicants, showed attentive countenances very different from those I had seen at the parish church, where the new priest had replaced M. Barière. There I saw women coming from a great distance whipping up the sweating horses of their light coaches, arriving to display their sumptuous dresses. The men also arrived in haste in order to promenade indolently during the short mass, under the galleries of the church and, to chat of more profane matters, or to ogle the ladies. As soon as the mass was over, they all dashed off at full speed to the homes at which they were expected for dinner, dances, and games.

After this mass, these simple people, learning that I was a European newly arrived in the Atakapas, came to press me to accept invitations to dinner. When I had accepted one, and arrived there, I found 30 or 40 convivial souls, the Curé Barière among them. The crowd was so great that the first who had come got up to give their places to the women and children. During the meal, I heard the name of Carmouche, he whom Saint-Julien claimed as his principal attacker, and I found that I was dining in his house. I riveted my attention upon him. I have always believed, and I still believe, that any man who retains for a long period of time, deep and compelling sentiments, will show at least involuntarily traces of them on his face; and, if the soul nourished on great ideas, and generous sentiments finds the mark of happy hours imprinted on an open countenance, the scoundrel cannot entirely erase from his face the livid marks of crime. His somber look will disclose them to me even, through his feigned happiness.

All during dinner I studied Carmouche's face. I observed minutely the movements of his face to see if, in the expressions of affection, the truth would not betray itself. I observed with the same attention his accomplices, their wives, and their children. All of them seemed to me equally content and gay. I observed no brutality. Everywhere, I believe, I saw peace of soul. I saw none of the over heartiness which betokens a tortured conscience. The priest, Barière, who had been pictured to me as a somber hypocrite, was animated by an innocent gaiety.

I left this truly patriarchal repast full of contradictory ideas. I said to myself, "Are there really, under these hospitable roofs, only murderers and their accomplices? This peace, this semblance of happiness, these traits of virtue, would they be found here if the air were full of crime? And if among them, only a few are guilty, how would they be suffered to remain? Would they dare to raise their eyes and to take part in the general conversation, or in the general celebration, beneath the eyes of a stranger which did not leave them for an instant? But a crime has been committed. A young wife has been murdered in her own home, almost in the arms of her husband, and this husband who has shared her danger himself denounced the guilty party. What is the explanation?"

My journey took me about 200 leagues but I promised myself, that, upon my return I would make an attempt to clear up my doubts. I was absent four months. Some days after my return, I went to a place about a league away from my home to pay a visit to an inhabitant named Peytavin who had always especially welcomed strangers and, always had several staying at his house. He pressed me to say with him. During dinner, by chance the subject of M. Desclouettes came up. I made some circumspect remark on this unfortunate affair, which led M. Peytavin to tell me that the day of the murder M. Desclouettes along with several other people, had dined with him, and that he had been calm and gay, and that he did not leave Peytavin's until sunset. From there, he had gone about a quarter of a league to spend the night at his mother's house, near the church, and in the course of his goings and comings, M. Desclouettes had been seen by a great many people.

Even more remarkable, I learned that the murder had been committed at nightfall, six or seven leagues from M. Peytavin's house. Of the numerous partisans of Saint-Julien who had spoken to me of this business, not one had revealed this fact. I saw then how the spirit of partisanship darkened the minds even of those who are not criminals. When I mentioned this fact to them, their only answer was to attack the partiality of M. Peytavin, but this was a fact established by the testimony of a large number of other people.

I then examined myself the various accounts of the murder of Saint-Julien's wife. I cross-questioned those with whom I talked, and I found in their answers embarrasment and ignorance as well as variety, and I felt growing in my mind the conviction that the accused were not the authors of the crime. But who was, then? Could it have been Saint-Julien himself? Could he have murdered his wife in cold blood? Everywhere I was told that the two lived in perfect harmony, and aside from that, would not the fact that the parents and the father of the unfortunate woman had taken the part of their son-in-law and testified to his innocence? Must he not have been a husband above reproach?

The Desclouettes, at whose house I had received so much kindness, on the day of my departure were then in town and I wished to see them and to pay my respects to the mother of this unfortunate family. I found her with several of her children. Never have I seen a more kindly and more venerable countenance. Her hair, whitened by the years, heightened the pathos of her face, so sweet and frank, retaining a freshness rare at this age in the colony. Her manners had nothing of the indolent coldness of the Creoles, but showed the ease of manner and affability of the European who had passed her days in good society.

Her house was clean and was the best kept of any of the district. Her servants were well clothed and appeared happy, and showed that she must have been the best of mistresses (a rare thing among the women of the colonies. This is a matter to which I pay special attention in the houses which I visit.). While she shows affection for all her children she seems to show preference for her elder son, and misfortune has increased the bonds of tenderness between them. She must especially resent that her son is accused of a murder committed while he was dining peacefully with her. That same evening, he kissed her goodnight before going to bed, and the next morning was still there when news of the atrocity ran through the district. The legal processes in this affair, begun under the Spanish government, were stopped during the transitory regime of France, and drag on, becoming increasingly complex, under the jurisdiction of the Americans. The trivial questions of the manner of interrogating witnesses, and where they were to be interrogated, were the cause of interminable debates and delays. The numerous witnesses that were heard gave testimony influenced, all too clearly, by the party to which they belonged.

The first trial (that of the disputed boundary) dragged on with the same prolixity and multiplication of expense. A provisional judgment was again obtained in favor of the Desclouettes party. It provided the eviction of his adversaries from the house (which was on the disputed land). They paid no attention to it at all, and this simple refusal was enough to nullify the order. The sheriff of the county came to execute the writ, and he began to throw the furniture out of the house.

At this news all of the *chevaliers* of the district mounted their horses and galloped up in arms to prevent the dispossession. Members of the opposite party poured out to protect him. Both parties armed, and face to face, thirsted for vengeance. Louisianians, it must be admitted, are brave, and the slightest movement might have begun a frightful carnage, but the rare good sense of the sheriff prevented this. He harangued the warriors, declared he would not enforce the judgment if there were any opposition, even of a single person; that he would suspend his functions but would hold those who opposed him responsible for the consequences.

The sheriff thereupon retired, but the noble horsemen seized him, and as they knew from tradition that many times before them their illustrious ancestors had beaten their sheriffs, and wishing to be worthy of their noble race, they naturally beat this sheriff even more severely. Thereupon they bound him tightly and took him to the Honorable Nicols, first judge of the county. The latter, fearing the same treatment of his honorable shoulders, welcomed these noble knights courteously and found no illegal action.

However, he dispatched a courier to the city with news of this affair, and the *chevaliers* in their turn rushed there to recount their exploits. The other party complained bitterly. The governor listened to all this. The affair was becoming more and more serious and its consequences becoming more and more disturbing.

In the American laws, which are modeled on those of England, the sheriff is a political as well as a judicial figure and is really the arm of the executive power. Indeed, his functions have seemed to multiply in the United States. He seems to attain more power and greater stature here. He is especially responsible for maintaining public order, and he has the right to demand assistance of anyone when he requires it. Prisoners are in his special care, he supervises elections and watches over their honesty. It is he who compiles the jury lists for both civil and criminal affairs, and he summons jurymen, although he does not choose them to serve on juries. He is the depository of public monies and, in judicial sales, it is he who delivers to the acquirer his legal title. He is the actual executor of the law, and, if necessary, he is obliged himself to inflict the punishment ordered by the courts. In court, it is the custom for him to stand, not to show his inferiority, but to show the vigilance of the law. No modern institution seems to me more fortunately conceived for maintaining the vigor of political institutions, which are only maintained by the vigorous action of the law. Therefore the nomination of a sheriff is an important matter in the individual counties of the United States. Each party intrigues mightily to attain it, and those who attain the office carry it off in triumph congratulating themselves and celebrating the victory. The significance of the event just described will, then, be apparent, but these noble knights, less illustrious in feats of arms than those of the Round Table, are also all illiterate. Several of them could only make an X for a signature.

Governor Claiborne, after a rather long delay, announced that he would come and see things for himself. As a matter of fact, at the same time complaints were multiplying from all parties about Judge Nicols, and this also necessitated his presence, and after the announcement, he was not long in arriving at the Atakapas. He came rather in the capacity of a pacifier than that of the first magistrate come to find out the truth about a crime. Nobody seemed to have been better suited to fulfill these laudable aims. His manner was peaceful, his face and even his voice displayed his good intentions. If he expressed himself badly in French, he made up for it by his genial manners. His stay in Louisiana had caused him to lose the stiffness of the Americans without losing that noble simplicity so distinctive of officials of popular governments. He was a tall man, well built and about thirty-six years old, the time of life when one begins to attain that dignity so useful to persons in high positions.

M. Claiborne gave parties and attended them, hoping by this means to assuage the hatreds of the district by pleasure. In an atmosphere of good cheer at the table, toasts to mutual good health were drunk, and neighbor embraced neighbor with reciprocal promises of peace.

Madam Desclouettes, whom the governor had not failed especially to go and see, gave him a lovely party, to which the enemy party was invited, and several of them came. It was a remarkable spectacle to me to see mingled with this family those who for several years had covered them with opprobrium, and to see them seated at the table side by side with those they accused of a most cowardly murder. The former enjoyed their party, while the latter seemed disturbed by remorse. Love, that god whom no power can arrest, in the midst of this strange gathering, struck the heart of the governor with one of his potent darts. Indeed, the lady was one of rare beauty. She was the daughter of a rich inhabitant to be precise, the interim commandant, during the disgrace of M. Deblanc, who had directed the arrest of Saint-Julien, and had taken him to the city. He was, therefore, a partisan of Desclouettes. This event, presaging a marriage that must have taken place after my departure, swung the balance once more to the Desclouettes family.

On the day of the governor's departure a large number of members of both parties gathered together to bid him farewell. At the end of dinner when wine had placed everyone in a good humor, it was proposed as a guarantee for future peace that the events of the recent past should be absolutely forgotten. Tremendous applause greeted this proposal. Only Desclouettes remained silent. Then he said, "I had promised to maintain public order in this district, and I faithfully kept my promises. I have bent all my influence to this end. But how can I forget everything, when by doing so I shall achieve the ruin of a family I undertook to defend, and, when, in addition, I will leave unchallenged the accusation of murder to blast the reputation of innocent persons, indeed my own? I am not capable of such complete forgetfulness. I shall loyally defend my cause. Let my adversaries defend themselves too." A murmur of disapproval arose for this vigorous declaration, but for me it brought new conviction of the innocence of Desclouettes, and at this moment, with the two parties together face to face, I saw the difference in the tempers of their souls. Could M. Desclouettes, in effect, abandon a family in an affair where he was their chief support; where the expenses in the matter have already risen to more than 20 thousand écus; and should he allow the thick veil of mystery to prevail about a murder of which almost everyone in the colony suspected him to be at least the instigator?

It must be admitted that what the governor had done to heal the breach was illusory because he had never come to grips with the two matters which were involved. In truth, the true motives for the governor's visit were secret and not concerned with this trial. I discovered what they were, although I was not taken into his confidence. I shall digress momentarily to discuss this matter before returning to the matter of Saint-Julien.

The districts of Atakapas and Opelousas on the western edge of Louisiana are not clearly marked off from the Spanish provinces; an important situation in the present circumstances. In case of attack from the Spanish territory, the loss of this district would be a serious blow to the colony, especially to New Orleans, which it supplies with meat. It was, then, politically expedient not to alienate the inhabitants of this district from the American government; to attempt to secure the support of both parties but to allow them both to exist in order to encourage their rivalry in soliciting the help of the American government. By this means, they would act as an automatic check on each other. This plan was followed by the government with all imaginable art. First of all, the sheriff, whose conduct had been right and legal, was upon the arrvial of the governor sacrificed to the noble party. He was removed, while, if the law had been enforced, several of these noble families would have been prosecuted. Then Judge Nicols, though guilty of arbitrariness and venality, was retained because he was not a member of either party, and the demands for his removal were not so widespread. Wily, adroit, and knowing the district, he was useful to the government in observing what went on. This view of things required the sacrifice of the spotless lamb and the retention of the goat, loaded with iniquities.

Several months before the arrival of the governor, a captain of engineers in the American service, named Stille, came for the second time to the Atakapas. He enlisted the help of a Frenchman named Legrand to make a secret inspection of the internal provinces of Spain bordering on Louisiana. This Frenchman, learning of the dangers of such an enterprise (which at the least would make him liable to the condemnation to the mines), refused to go. I was at that time in the Atakapas, and I knew about it, having seen Captain Stille several times. He told me he was going to make a little trip to Opelousas, but I knew perfectly well what he meant. In spite of being abandoned by his guide Legrand, the captain disappeared for a couple of months from the Atakapas. When I saw him again, he told me simply that he had been to visit the region around Opelousas. Upon his arrival in New Orleans, Captain Stille was named by his government to a position paying more than 10 thousand francs, and it was only a short time after this mysterious voyage of Captain Stille that the governor came to the Atakapas and Opelousas. All that I had seen in the long voyage that I had made demonstrated to me that the American government would only yield to the will of the people whose instrument it is obliged to be. From the sea to the northern part of the colony, I met Americans everywhere pushing towards the Spanish colony, braving hunger and danger to do so. In the Atakapas, the Opelousas, on the Côte-Gelée, on Bayou Chicot, in the most inaccessible places, I found these people. The dark solitudes of the Bayou Aux Boeufs, the pine woods which stretch up to the rapids of the Red River, all of these regions are being settled from moment to moment by this hardy people. It is the same on the solitary banks of the river from Pointe Coupée. The wilderness which stretches from Lake Cataoulou [Catahoula] will soon be inhabited and the windings of the lake shore are already occupied by men subsisting on corn and salt meat, scorning the luxuries of life, and the shores of the Black River too will soon cease to be entirely wilderness.

Everywhere I stumbled upon camps of these families of travelers in the dense thickets almost in the manner of the Indians. At the Ouachita, in the short interval between my two trips, I had noticed astonishing changes. These wandering Americans had arrived from Natchez; some by water in frail pirogues; some boldly through the wild forests. "Why did you come here?" I asked several of them. "We came," they said, "to get to Mexico." That is the promised land that everyone sighs for. The immense prairie of Dahen called Mer Rouge has, since my departure, already acquired some considerable settlements. The inhabitants have cleared a route through the forest and now can reach the post in a day, while formerly it took three.

It was only a short while ago that a few Anglo-American individuals, striking by night from Bayou Sara near Pointe Coupée, almost succeeded in seizing the Spanish post at Baton Rouge. Before that, Nolins, starting from Natchez with a small group of Americans, penetrated deep into the Spanish provinces to seize some horses. At Natchez, he sustained a siege which might have been bloody if he had not been killed, and following this a multitude of other Americans came to Natchez to join him.

Already the American government had made an expedition to the Missouri and more recently another along the Ouachita. Seeing, therefore, everywhere the passion of the people for the invasion of Mexico, and the willingness of the government to concur in this, I could easily see the application of this policy in the conduct of the governor, and I could see that the contradictions of his behavior were only apparent.

The elder M. Desclouettes, whom I did not have the opportunity to know personally, except at those parties to which the presence of the governor had given rise, had invited me to come and see him, and had promised me to give me more information on the affair of Saint-Julien. I thereupon visited him a few days later I saw a father who tenderly loved his children and who was tenderly loved by them, who received continually indications of the regard in which he was held by his neighbors. His sensitive face clearly showed the marks of affliction. Only a few months ago he had lost his wife, and from my room at night I could hear his prolonged groans. 'I see clearly," I told him after studying the documents he had shown me, "that the only guilty person is Saint-Julien, a scoundrel covered with crimes, who after having besmirched himself again with the murder of his wife, audaciously accused the heads of innocent families whose conduct had always been above reproach. But how is it, that with so many means of making the truth known, and of giving the lie to this slanderer, that you have let this error be propogated throughout the colony? What pain you might have spared yourself. Think of how you could have shamed your enemies." "We have," he told me, "carefully hidden these proofs of innocence, even at the risk of appearing guilty, in order to trip up the criminal more surely at the trial. Surprised by the unexpected light thrown on this crime, he will not have the time to prepare new subterfuges in order to escape." There speaks the Creole, brought up in the conventions of Spanish criminal justice supposing the truth will be better served by the shadow of mystery than by the full light of public discussion. "But," I said to him, "do you not realize that the property of truth is to become more and more frightening to the guilty person in proportion as it approaches him; for it strips away part of his protective covering, and he can only cover part of his crimes by uncovering another? By this means, the entire truth can be dis-

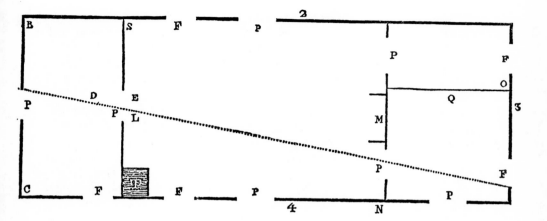

EXPLANATION

A. The supposed position of the murderer according to Saint-Julien's declaration.

A. F. Line indicating the route of the bullet.

B. C. Saint-Julien's room, about 8 feet wide.

D. Place where Saint-Julien was lying, his feet propped up on the door at A and his head behind his wife.

E. Position of Madam Saint-Julien according to her husband's deposition.

L. Position she would have to occupy in order to have been hit.

F. The windows of the house.

M. The fireplace of the room.

N. The place where Julien said he was attacked.

O. The office.

P. The door to the house.

Q. The room occupied by the Aubin woman.

S. The large room.

T. Table where the candle was placed.

    1. West   2. North   3. East   4. South

covered, for he becomes the victim of the artifices which he employs to escape." Independent of these authentic documents (of which I received from M. Desclouettes copies made in my presence), the interim commandant, who had made the first interrogation of Saint-Julien, who had conducted him to the city, and who had heard a large number of witnesses respected in both parties, gave me, on my departure to France, a very extensive memorandum touching on everything I have said heretofore. It is upon these sources that I shall rely in the following discussion.

According to Saint-Julien, he was spread out face-down on the bed in his room about five feet from his wife. His position, therefore, was in-between the two doors to this room, one leading outside, and the other opening into the room where his wife was seated. She had her back to him and was occupied at the spinning wheel. In an alcove in the room was another woman, also spinning, and there was present still another young person. It was nightfall and one lighted candle was placed in a corner of the room, so that Saint-Julien's room was in darkness. Saint-Julien had his two feet propped up on the door post of the outside door and was listening to the women singing when he saw the barrel of a gun appearing through the doorway about a foot from him. With a swift movement he seized the barrel and held it against the door post. The gun went off, the bullet went through his wife's body, came out of her breast, gouging the center post of the spinning wheel, and passing into the next room to lodge in the window frame.

Even this first part of Saint-Julien's deposition demonstrates its untruthfulness. Would a would-be murderer of Saint-Julien practically place the barrel of his gun in Saint-Julien's hands? Would not such an action expose him to needless danger in case the gun did not fire? Saint-Julien's position would give the murderer ample opportunity to attempt a shot from far away and to run away if the gun did not fire. Those whom Saint-Julian designated as his attackers are excellent hunters (as are most of the Creoles), and an excellent hunter who gets a good shot at a distance does not imprudently come closer to take up a more disadvantageous position.

Besides, Saint-Julien was in a dark place, facing the candle which lit the next room, and, under those circumstances, how could he have seen the barrel of the gun advancing toward him a foot away; that is to say, past his knees? How could he have seen so precisely the position and movements of the murderer? And when he pushed up the barrel with his hand and forced it against the door post, the bullet should have passed over his wife's head, and if the murderer were in the position described by Saint-Julien the bullet should have taken a more diagonal direction. It would have struck neither his wife nor the window frame, but would have lodged in the corner of the room. Are we then to suppose that the attacker waited to fire until his gun was no longer in a position to shoot his victim? Saint-Julien, continuing his narrative, said that the attacker had run away and that he had pursued him, picking up on the way a pick-ax with which to attack the murderer. But Saint-Julien had firearms in the very room where he had been attacked, only a few feet away. Why did he not take one of these? Why did he not see to his wife, try to give her first aid, or even die with her if necessary? Would he not that way be better able to defend himself against a new attack? On the contrary, he runs without arms after his atttacker whom he should have supposed to have had help. Then, he continued, he was fired on a second time, this time again by a practiced hunter. This was no more successful than the first shot, notwithstanding that this practiced hunter had plenty of time to take aim at Saint-Julien. Equally extraordinary, the third attacker did not fire at all. The three attackers fell upon him with their gun butts and struck him to the ground. But practiced hunters would hardly limit themselves to firing a single shot, nor would they come to commit a murder with a single firearm, and what does this beating with the gun butts of Saint-Julien amount to? We shall see.

First of all, what Saint-Julien did not say, but what was deposed by the woman and the young person who ran out of the back room, was that they had heard no sound of struggle at all and no cries, when, according to Saint-Julien, the scene just described took place just outside the room where these two persons were seated. What they did hear was the second gun shot, and after that Saint-Julien making a turn around the house. He came then to the casement of the window of the room in which they were and called out three times, "Manon." Receiving no response, they then heard him order his Negro to go and tell his brother-in-law that his sister had just been killed. Saint-Julien, then, had not been attacked by any murderers.

The same night when the priest came to confess Madam Saint-Julien, he asked four men to carry Saint-Julien into a neighboring room, but Saint-Julian got up from his bed by himself and walked to a room at the other end of the house by himself without any help.

Two surgeons, who it must be admitted were not very well trained, made separate examinations of Saint-Julien. One vaguely declared that he was covered with blows, the other said he found no trace of them except for a few scratches. Although his expectoration was tinged with blood, this appeared to come only from his gums.

The next day Saint-Julien wrote with his own hand a three-page petition to the Spanish government. This document, which I have examined with the most careful attention, hardly seemed to have been written by a man who only the night before was left for dead with blows of a gun butt. His ideas are dispassionately expressed and insidiously presented. They really accuse nobody, but seek to arouse suspicions, apparently motivated by his interest in the trial concerning the boundaries and his competition with the Desclouettes in the selling of beef herds in the city. A striking thing about this document is that Saint-Julien is concerned only with himself. A single sentence, the last, refers to his murdered wife.

After the murder two men found Saint-Julien stretched out in the courtyard, apparently unconscious, and took him up to carry him inside, but Saint-Julien, terrified by entering the house which he had soiled by a most frightful crime, forgot to feign unconsciousness. He braced his feet against the frame of the door, violently contracting his muscles, and the two men had to put him down outside the house and wait for the help of others to take him inside by force and put him on his bed. There, Saint-Julien manifested anew other signs of terror. All light had to be extinguished, and he could not even be approached, but he did not express a single word of interest in his wife, bathed in blood.

It is evident therefore that Saint-Julien was not assaulted or maltreated, and that no one wished to do him harm. He is guilty here, not of error, but of lying. But to lie in the manner of his wife's murder, when he alone was a witness to the crime and could give positive information about it, is to cover up the truth and to make oneself accomplice to the crime. Thus, even the proof that Saint-Julien is lying in his account of the murder necessitates that Saint-Julien be treated as guilty of the crime. His guilt is aggravated by a large number of other lies.

The yard around his house is guarded by ferocious dogs, and a stranger does not dare to enter there unescorted, but these redoubtable dogs said nothing at all to the attackers of Saint-Julien. They remained mute while Saint-Julien was seized by these same attackers, knocked to the ground and assaulted by them. Saint-Julien, faced with this unanswerable argument, answered that several days before he had seen several individuals throwing meat to them ,and it was then he knew that a plot against his life was being hatched. But pieces of meat thrown over the fence of the yard to ferocious dogs hardly suffices to tame them. If this had been so, would not he himself have recognized the men? Would he not have shown them the remains of the meat? But he did not mention it to anybody. Interrogated in the city on this same subject by a Spanish officer, he answered that his dogs had been charmed. Saint-Julien, strongminded, when on the arrival of the French prefect, he assumed the character of a French patriot, transformed himself into a credulous, superstitious person before the Spanish judge.

Carmouche, whom Saint-Julien named as the principal attacker, proved through the testimony of numerous witnesses that he was at home at the time of the attack. He ran up, attracted by the noise, as did his neighbors, and the next morning he conversed amicably with the unfortunate Madam Saint-Julien and the woman named Auboin who had been in the room at the time of the attack. Carmouche answered calmly all the questions put to him by the syndic Sorel while Saint-Julien was convulsed by agitation. Saint-Julien, who saw his alleged attacker and that of his wife, a few moments after the event, and who saw him again the next morning, did not hurl imprecations at him at that time nor address to him a single word of reproach.

Syndic Sorel, that miser of whom I have already spoken, had good reasons for treating Saint-Julien tactfully. He was about to sell him part of his herd at a very good price. Instead of taking the opportunity at the first instant of trouble to learn the truth by vigorous interrogation, the syndic became the vile accomplice of Saint-Julien. He occupied himself in collecting certificates of good conduct for Saint Julien; while his wife, that unhappy victim, was forgotten. She lived another week and died without having been questioned. At each step Saint-Julien thickened the veils that hid the truth. He alone was the sole author of this crime committed before his eyes, but we should ask ourselves what caused him to commit this atrocious crime, for even scoundrels are only scoundrels through specific motives. The inclination to crime is not natural to the heart of man, it is planted there accidentally like a disease.

A man named Auboin, the husband of the same women who was in the room at the time of the murder, lived at Saint-Julien's house as a hired hand. He formed with Madam Saint-Julien too great an intimacy. One day Saint-Julien surprised them in the office. Another time, returning inopportunely from the garden where he had been reading some papers, he surprised them again in the back room. Auboin jumped out of the window, but was seen by the husband. It was only a short time later that the murder occurred. Some days before that Saint-Julien had sent him away on a trip. Auboin has died since these events, but before his death he admitted under oath his affair with Madam Saint-Julien and Saint-Julien's jealousy of him. Several times before her death Madam Saint-Julien called for Auboin, whom her husband knew to be still away, and finally the unfortunate woman had to promise to erect a cross in the corner of the garden near a tuft of balsam. The cross was duly erected. It was doubtless an indication of other shadowy crimes repugnant to reveal. The family of this unfortunate woman, believing themselves disgraced by this guilty liaison, is all the more attached to the party of Saint-Julien. They imagined that this conduct would save their reputation. This is the strange motive that causes these weak and ignorant Acadians to take the part of the murderer of their daughter. A jealous husband, it is true, in the excess of his furor may be forgiven for striking down his unfaithful spouse, but to project the murder with malice aforethought, to coldly make the preparations, and to carry them out with a ferocious calmness, this is the lowest level to which a scoundrel can sink; and thanks again to nature, he arrives there slowly by degrees. Saint-Julien could not have committed this crime without having had experience with others. We will see how often, in fact, he had practiced the frightful trade of murder.

About July 1805, two years after the murder, Saint-Julien still supported by his powerful party and still outraging his humiliated enemies, dared to address to the criminal courts a complaint of the libels to his reputation circulated by Desclouettes and those of his party implicated in the crime of murder. Saint-Julien obtained a judgment of several thousand piastres in damages against them. The account of their defense will give an idea of the audacity of this scoundrel and the crimes he had already committed.

They accused him of the theft of 120 piastres from a worker named Saint-Pierre, who lived with him, and after the murder of his wife, to having approached him through a third party with a proposal to return the sum with interest if Saint-Pierre would not testify against him. They accused him of another theft, from Théodore Broussard and other individuals traveling with him. They include the declaration of a free mulatto named Masse, according to which Saint-Julien offered him 300 piastres, and then 500, if he would swear to having seen M. Desclouettes going toward Saint-Julien's house carrying a gun on the day of the murder. They accused him of having changed his name so often that it was impossible to follow his traces. Sometimes calling himself Louis Saint-Julien and other times calling himself d'Ernauville and most recently having remarried under the name of d'Armenonville.*

They declare further that a brother who revealed his name to be Barthélemi Castagne had declared to the entire family of Nezart called Charpentier, and the family of Bouleris, that Saint-Julien had left France in flight from a charge of murder, which obliged him to change his name. His brother further stated that, descending from the post of Vincennes on the Wabash, he had appeared with a barge loaded with liquor, guns, and ammunition, saying that he had found the crew slaughtered and that after having thrown the cadavers into the water he and his companions had unloaded the boat of what it contained and sunk it into the river. In addition, he was said to have boasted of having killed an Indian chief at the establishment of a man named Lopez, which act had caused Lopez's ruin. Since the murder, his brother-in-law, whose depositions could have shed more light on this affair, has died suddenly, but the fact which finally leaves no more room for doubt is that the Negro who was at his side in the courtyard in this scene, and who had been sent to announce to his brother-in-law that his sister had been killed, died a few days later of poisoning in most horrible agony. Saint-Julien took care that he would not be interrogated and, always audacious, charged his adversaries with the poisoning too.

This is the man, soiled with so many crimes (and indeed with many others which I was looking into upon my departure

---

*The new priest of the Atakapas has certified to me that these variations of the name are actually found in the registers. It is probable, going by the deposition of his brother cited below, that his true name is Castagne and that he comes from the region around Bordeaux. Those of my readers from that part of the country will do a public service by making known to the authorities the murder that he has committed there.

from the colony), who has menaced and outraged for several years families whose lives have always been above reproach. Perhaps at this very moment, as my readers read this, he is covering them with new ignominies. This man, without learning, without any other qualification except audacity and boasting, has come to be the leader, in the district, of those most distinguished by birth and education. This is the man whose partisans caused the prefect to issue his proclamation, a proclamation which he will surely regret. It is he, who feeding the fires of discord, has provoked the two parties to blows to inundate the country in blood and to cause mourning to families, and finally by the expenses he has piled up to bring about the irremedial ruin of several families. What could have been done to prevent these calamities from taking place? The facts of these crimes should have been spread abroad. Then the partisans of Saint-Julien would have blushed to march beneath his banner. They would have abandoned him and would have become his enemies. Hatreds which have become inveterate, which will be long in subsiding, would not exist to prepare the ground for new crimes and unhappiness in the future.

This tendency, which all men have, to be inflamed by party spirit, which makes them then capable of making the greatest sacrifices and running the greatest dangers, which shows itself in all peoples and in all societies, is always born of the need of men to associate with their equals. The more they extend these communications, the more their abilities enlarge and their forces grow. Violence and skill can from time to time slow down the effects of this need, but just as, when one stops the flow of sap in a healthy tree by tightly binding it, the trunk becomes covered with deformed swellings and a confusion of multiple stunted shoots makes the tree hideous and finally results in its death, in the same way there arises periodically among peoples periods of unquiet which presage revolutionary crises, so often fatal. The wise legislator, then, will not attempt to smother this indistructible need for communication, but to direct it towards useful objects. Nothing useful, good or lasting, but is not born of truth. The search for truth should be, above all, the aim of all society.

CHAPTER LXVII

Three states of man in America. Savage life, social state, and the condition of slaves. Negroes and colored people brought from Africa to America. How they are acclimated. Their houses, their clothes, their work, their food, their punishment. Treatment is better by Europeans than by Creoles or by women. Their intelligence limited by the effect of slavery. Vices that result from this.

Three states of man are to be found in America. All others are merely modifications or amalgams of these. These three states are, the savage life, the social state and the condition of slavery. In the first man wanders across the woods living by hunting and having as shelter only branches bent down and covered by a few leaves. This man enjoys complete liberty. He knows hardly any law except that of need. This type of life produces an almost uniform character. His needs always being the same, and restraints on his behavior being few, there is great uniformity in his occupations, his tastes and his behavior. His ideas and faculties are restricted. A great deal has been said about the change of character of the Indians through their relationship to Europeans. This change really amounts to very little. This is because, having always to hunt to exist, and being always in the deep shadow of the woods, these activities necessarily are those which most influence them, while behavior induced by their relationship with the Europeans being but momentary disappears in their uniform behavior, as waves produced by a passing wind on the flat surface of the water.

In the social state man no longer derives his existence solely from the hunt, but there are varied means of making a living according to one's education, location, talents, abilities, or means. There are, in the same way, as many types of behavior as there are means of existence and at the same time more relationship between them and more contact. Thus, it is necessary for everyone to adjust to the activities of other people, who must in turn put themselves out in favor of the activities of still others. In a social state, therefore, a portion of liberty is inevitably suppressed.*

---

*Although in our times we hear the word *liberty* spoken so often we do not hear enough explanation of its meaning. I define liberty as being the faculty of not being restrained in one's action through the desires of other people.

Liberty is reduced in order to enjoy the integration of activities necessary to the survival of individuals. The condition is like that of the proprietor of a large estate who not being able to obtain from it everything he needs for his existence, barters the greatest portion of his produce to obtain the necessities from others.

The social man in most of the colonies, and especially in these, participates more in the liberty of the savage condition but at the same time he enjoys fewer of the advantages of the social life.

In the condition of slavery, man has lost the possibility of attaining anything of his liberty. His talents, his industry, and his work do not belong to him, and his actions are all submitted to the will of another, and he must forget his own desires and place all his faculties at the disposition of this other, to receive from him the evil with the good, to support his caprices, his outrages, his punishments, and sometimes death. And even hope, that last companion of unhappiness, which when all is lost still softens our woes with fugitive illusions, is forbidden to the slave. What becomes then, in this state, of man, that being endowed above all else with the faculty of adapting himself? If, under the reign of liberty, these faculties acquire the greatest possible development, in the opposite state, that of slavery, one part of these faculties will not develop at all, and those that do will be repressed, feeble and vicious. Let us pause a moment to consider these strange effects and to see what the results of them are, even for these masters so quick to increase the immense distance which separates them from the slave. Philosophy, piety, politics, and even commerce, cannot be too much enlightened by this important subject. A comparison of the different manner of observation of different observers and the facts that they report should, through repetition, shed a salutory light, which little by little will confirm opinions, and will lead to the single end of reconciling the interests of the mother country, the colonies, the customs, reasons, and humanity.

Slaves in this colony are, as in others, the unfortunate Negroes exported from Africa. The chiefs of these people, always at war with one another, take prisoners from each other which they then trade to the Europeans. Often, also, parents, pressed by hunger or by necessity, sell their own children. Sometimes again Europeans who come to trade carry away these people in complete disdain of the rights of man.

Negroes imported directly into the colonies are called "raw Negroes." They do not know the language of the European, nor how to perform the work for which they are destined. In their own country they cultivate a little corn (and that hardly), and, above that, the live on wild fruits and the results of hunting and fishing. Almost all of them show some influence of Mohammedanism mixed with the ideas of their primitive beliefs. Their superstitions are inseparably mixed with despotism, for they all live under the suzeranity of absolute chiefs. They have idols or talismans which they venerate and consult, but they soon enough throw them away or burn them.

Like all people who lead the life of savagery, they are strangers to work or any sort of prolonged application, and like them, their passion for dancing is immoderate.

The slave ships are called *negriers* [*which we might translate by the old American term "blackbirders." — Tr. note.*]. They are crammed so full that sickness, bad air, and, worst of all, shame and grief, takes off a large number of slaves, which pretty well cancels the additional profit anticipated by the slavers. These, however, take pains to distract the slaves as much as possible during the voyage. They are brought up on deck every day to be exercised. They are encouraged to dance on the decks at night, an exercise so attractive to them that they seem almost to forget the loss of their freedom. It serves also to combat the deleterious effects of idleness and stagnant air. The women, decked with glass beads and bracelets, seem almost to have forgotten that they are no longer free, such is the power of finery upon that sex.

The women must be separated from the men, to prevent the ferocious quarrels that would otherwise break out, which indeed, in the excess of passion of the men, might endanger the crew of the ship. The Negroes, numbering up to eight or nine hundred, against thirty-odd crewmen, would be formidable adversaries, except for the arrangements made to restrain them and the constant vigilance of the crew. The Negroes are separated into different compartments in the hold and, sometimes, they are bound. A barrier prevents them from reaching the quarter-deck, where the officers and crew are stationed. Cannons, always loaded, are kept pointing toward the Negroes, and guns are always nearby. Only too often must these deadly arms be used, for the slaves plot and scheme even in their fetters.

If an uprising occurs below decks, the sailors fire into the slaves and continue their killing until the rest of the slaves, asking for mercy, surrender. If the uprising occurs on deck, the cannons, charged with grape, are turned on them. These victories, which are won as a matter of course if the crew is not surprised, are more costly to the victors than to the victims, for the latter regard death as a release, and believe that thereby, they will see their homelands again. The usual food of the Negroes during the trip, is rice, hardtack, and a little salt meat.

The Negroes are sold as soon as they arrive in the colony, the sick ones being bought up at reduced prices, by surgeons, who speculate on curing them. This is one of the c o m m o n means whereby surgeons make their fortunes in the colonies. The rest of the Negroes, purchased by the planters, are minutely examined. Here, modesty is no consideration at all. The Creole purchaser will examine a Negro in every part. If, in the process, the latter shows some sign of his virility, the purchaser expresses satisfaction at this guaranty of reproductive capacity. The females are equally meticulously examined. Such examinations become so familiar to these unfortunate creatures, that modesty is soon a stranger to them.

The new slaves are placed in with the work gangs of the buyer, but they usually are accorded somewhat different treatment from that of the old hands. They are only gradually introduced to work. They are made to wash often, to take strolls from time to time and, above all, they are made to dance. They are always mixed in with the older slaves as a minority, in order to encourage them to pick up the habits of the older ones. These attentions are not as a rule, dictated by any consideration of humanity. Economic necessity demands it. Only too often however, masters, either because they are poor and have no other slaves to employ in the breaking-in process, or because of their greed, require hard and constant work of these raw Negroes, and this soon weakens them, so that they die of disease, or even more often of depression. Often they encompass their own destruction. Some drown themselves, others draw out their tongues in such a way as to block the [An anatomical and physiological absurdity.—Tr. note.] respiratory passage. Others make use of poison, or run away to die of misery and hunger. Africans imported into Louisiana are even more exposed to disease than those in other colonies. The winter, with its sudden, biting cold is inimical to the Negroes, especially the old ones. It is particularly important therefore, to cover them and keep them warm. The stinginess of some of the inhabitants here, as I shall show, has cost them dearly.

The very high price of Negroes; four or five hundred piastres for a raw Negro and anywhere from a thousand to fourteen hundred for one with some training; threatens the fortunes of many people. If a man has only three or four Negroes and loses two, he is ruined. It takes a sizable amount of money to acquire even a moderate number of Negroes, and therefore, to establish a plantation, a considerable amount of capital is needed. This is the principal reason for the slow rate of growth of the colony.

The way in which Negro servants are treated, especially in the city, is more variable depending upon the character of their master. Those who are employed in agriculture on the plantations are treated more uniformly. They are housed not far from the master's house in a little house or cabin perhaps a dozen feet square. Each cabin is provided with a hearth on which to cook meals, for the masters do not concern themselves with the details of their food preparation. These houses are constructed of squared posts six or seven feet high planted in the ground about 2 or 2½ feet apart, the intervals between these posts being filled with Spanish moss.

These cabins are covered with long slabs of cypress called *pieux*. In a few days these simple buildings are complete. On most plantations where the masters take care of things, all the cabins are aligned and spaced regularly. It looks like a little village and is usually called a camp. The master's house at some distance apart dominating these humble cabins by its greater size and elevation brings to mind feudal times, when the haughty chateaux of the seigneurs looked out over the miserable huts of the serfs. There are even plantation houses with keeps, complete with muddy waters. The difference between those slaves and the slaves of today is, that their slavery is more abject, and their lot will only be alleviated by the passage of time and revolutions. Where, then, is this progress of the human spirit?

Not all the Negro cabins are constructed with the same care. That depends on the capacity, the indifference or imperiousness of the master. One finds them sometimes scattered in confusion around the principal house and instead of a tight mud wall, the walls may consist of only badly made slabs, leaned agaist the posts through which the winds and rains penetrate at will. It is not astonishing to learn that there are indifferent and lazy masters who are almost as badly housed.

At sunrise the Negroes must go into the fields which they call the wilderness. They are accompanied either by a Negro foreman or a white overseer, or most commonly, by the proprietor himself.

Some of the work consists of specific tasks, although other work is not susceptible to this. When a slave's assigned task is finished, any time remaining is his. They work much better under this arrangement, so it is to the interest of the master to establish it. If the Negroes are not working on their own tasks, the morning's work period runs till noon. Work is resumed at 2 o'clock and lasts until sunset. They should be free to work for themselves at this time but often this work itself is exhausting and painful, for they must tend their own cornfields, from which they feed themselves. The details of this work are exacting. At first the corn is dampened, and then it is ground up in great wooden mortars.

The various methods of preparing corn, together with the time required to cook it takes up a good deal of their time. The law requires the master to give each slave one barrel of corn on the ear, which is the equivalent of about 70 or 80 pounds. They also till the little garden which the master almost always provides for them. They cultivate there, according to the locality rice, corn, sweet potatoes, or pumpkins. The law requires them to have Sundays off, and if the master works them he must pay them at the rate of 4 *escalins* per day in winter or 5 in summer. They are usually permitted to raise chickens or pigs which, they may either eat or sell to procure other food or luxuries. The masters are required to give them as part of their clothing one woolen cape every two years. This cape, like those used by the inhabitants, is made from a woolen blanket which is coarse and longhaired provided with sleeves like a bathrobe, hanging down to the knees and having instead of a collar, a hood in the manner of the gowns of ancient monks. At the least breath of the north winter wind, they wrap themselves up, being extremely sensitive to the cold. Aside from that they dress in rags. The price of these capes comes to about 2½ piastres. Except for this cape the rest of the upkeep of the Negroes is at their own expense. This u p k e e p doesn't amount to much. During the summer, they go about almost naked. In the fields they wear only a tattered pair of pants, or more often a kind of breech-clout around the thighs as do the Indians. The women wear just as little, only a short tattered skirt. Ordinarily they are naked to the waist and such is the force of habit that the European, who is at first taken aback by this, comes little by little not to pay it any attention. The naked breast of the African is of a repugnant form. Even those of young girls are elongated and pendant, hanging like a sack almost to the waist. Among

punishment

whipping

few of these nations does the female form correspond to the European idea of beauty.

While they are at work the overseer, the master, or the foreman strides among them, his whip in his hand to lash the lazy ones, but those Negroes who are guilty of serious offenses are punished with 20, 25, 40, 50, or even 100 strokes of the whip. Here is the manner in which this cruel punishment is carried out. Four stakes are driven into the ground forming a rectangle. The culprit is stretched out naked between these stakes, face down. His hands and feet are tied to each of these stakes with strong cords so that his arms and legs are stretched out in the form of the cross of Saint Andrew which prevents the victim from moving at all. Then the flogger, who is ordinarily a Negro armed with a long coach whip, strikes the victim across the back and thighs. The crack of the whip can be heard afar as though an angry coachman were urging on his flagging horses. Blood flows, long welts criss-cross each other on the back of the victim, and strips of skin come away with the whip. None of this, in any way, softens the heart of the flogger, nor that of the master who urges him to strike harder.

The reader is disturbed, and so am I. My hand in its agitation refuses to depict this bloody scene; to tell how many times the sharp cries of agony came floating to me through the silent air; how many times I have shivered looking at the faces of those barbarous masters where I seem to see inscribed the number of victims sacrificed to their ferocity.

The women escape nothing of this rigorous punishment; even advanced pregnancy does not exempt them from it. In that case, before attaching them to the stakes, a hole is made in the ground where they estimate the belly will lie.

What is more remarkable is, that the Creole women are often much crueler than the men.

Their slow and soft demeanor, the meticulous tasks which they impose, are given in a manner of apathetic indolence, but if a slave does not obey promptly enough, if he is slow to interpret their gestures or their looks, in an instant they are armed with a formidable whip. No longer is this the arm which can hardly support a parasol, no longer is this the body that appears to be so feeble. Once she has ordered the punishment of one of these unfortunate slaves, she watches with a dry eye as she sees the victim attached to the four stakes. She counts the blows and if the arm of him who strikes begins to falter or if the blood does not run

— 239 —

fast enough, she raises her voice in menacing tones. The sensitivity of the women changes to furor. They require to see this horrible spectacle repeated at intervals. In order to revive themselves, they require to hear the sharp cries and to see again the flow of blood. Some of them in their frantic rage will pinch and bite the unfortunate victims.

These examples of inhumanity are seldom seen except among the Creoles. The Europeans usually retain traces of the sensitivity which the European upbringing has imprinted upon them even though the education of most of them has been slight, coming from the lower classes. But habit and stupid ignorance of the Creoles has fixed in them the idea that the Negro is only a property which they may dispose of at their pleasure like the meanest object. They do not consider that between them and their slaves they should maintain the eternal relationships of justice and humanity.

One should not be astonished to learn that the laws designed to protect the slaves are mostly disregarded by such masters. I have seen some make slaves pay for the miserable cape which is their due, or others not give them one at all, and I have seen masters not allow the slaves the Sundays which the law accords to them. I have seen barbarous masters keep their slaves in a revolting nudity during the winter, in a manner counter to their own interests, since they are weakening and shortening the lives of those upon whom their fortune depends. I have seen these Negroes obliged to hide their nudity with Spanish moss. I have seen masters prolong the working day several hours into the night after which the slaves before thinking of going to bed had to grind up and cook their corn and then, long before daybreak an implacable shrew, a whip in her hand, arouse them from their sleep. On this plantation more than 20 Negroes who should have doubled their numbers in 20 years were reduced to four or five.

The young Creoles, idolized by weak parents, make of the Negroes who surround them, the playthings of their whims. They whip as a pastime, slaves of their own age, as their fathers whip others out of ill humor. These young Creoles when they arrive at the age when impetuous passions do not brook contradiction, wish everything they order to be done, whether it is possible or not, and if it is not done they soothe their wounded pride by extended punishment of the Negroes. The gloomy melancholy of these unfortunate people, easily visible in their faces, the flight of some, the death of others, none of this makes any impression on their masters. They visit upon the Negroes remaining to them the vengeance they cannot exact of the others. These Creoles plunged thus in misery seem to be dead to remorse.

What especially distinguishes the Creole character from that of the European is that the latter punishes his slaves at the height of his anger, whereas the former will order 20 to 25 strokes of the whip without the slightest emotion. When the punishment is executed he observes it with equal coldness and he will double or triple this punishment with the same indifferent ferocity.

These Negroes continually under the hand of a master, who in truth have no property and can make no contracts, who cannot sue and have no rights of law or any of those activiities which in our country stimulates the intellectual faculty of our lower class citizens, these Negroes must necessarily have an extremely limited intelligence, and so it is, to a degree that a European finds it difficult to appreciate. I have seen some who were not able to count 5 or 6 pieces of money. It is rare to find any who can tell you their age, or even that of their children. They cannot tell you how long they have been away from their native land, or how long they have belonged to their masters. With so little idea of the past, they can hardly have any at all of the future, and the indifference of their minds is deplorable. They use up or spoil their own clothes without thinking that they will someday need them. They break or destroy everything they find in their hands with the same carelessness, even those objects which please them the most. Having no idea of thrift or economy in their own affairs, they certainly have none of their masters'. Thus, those who are used as domestic servants inside the houses, find this a disagreeable task. They cannot accustom themselves to a daily schedule, about which, man in the social state is so particular. Every day, one must repeat to them the order of the tasks which they do every day. The instructions must be repeated to them all the time, and the mistress of the house with a very large family, with a fair number of household details finds herself busy every moment of the day simply issuing orders to her servants. That which is especially drawn to their attention as important is no better executed than a matter of no moment, and those vases or furnishings cherished either out of expense or taste, are as likely to be broken or mutilated as any indifferent object, so little is their attention capable of discerning or recalling warnings about circumstances in which one must be particularly careful.

Happy Europeans, who are served with such celerity, whose orders are so scrupulously executed, whose intentions, to speak truly, are divined before being put into words, and who are thus left free for more important occupations, confiding with complete confidence lesser details to your subordinates. You would not enjoy these advantages except for the facts that the beings who serve you have an intelligence level closer to yours through education. Thus, when pride urges you to plunge into abjection those whom you command, and to establish your dominance over them, think of the price that you would pay! And you, rulers, of the world, what would become of your glory and your grandeur if it is built on despotism?

Even slaves who have been taught trades never attain perfection in them. They have no ideas of beauty, of utility, or of comfort to direct them and since they are not really interested, their intelligence is not really stimulated to perfect their ability. I have had occasion to employ them at several trades and I have always found their ability to be below the level of mediocrity even in this country. The object that they make over for me, has the same defect that it did before. However, it must be noted that among the Romans a large number of slaves did distinguish themselves in almost all professions. But the ability of slaves must always be inferior to those of free men and slaves today receive a very different education from those of former times. Those slaves did not live in nudity and misery. It is by the use of things that the intelligence grows. He who has nothing, has no means of instruction. Aside from that, the Romans lived in large cities where, apart from the bounty of their masters, the slaves had opportunity for income of their own, their *pecula,* which stimulated their interest and abilities. They therefore enjoyed the ownership of property and there existed the possibility that they could purchase themselves and become citizens. This prospect gave them the incentive to be industrious in perfecting themselves. In our colonies and, especially in Louisiana, the prospect is quite different. The lure of freedom is not offered to them. If they attain it they will remain in an abject condition, for their color will insure that they cannot rise above their station. The law here does not specifically grant to them a *pecula,* but if they take advantage of the hours of the day that are left to them and their Sundays to obtain money of their own it belongs legally to them. It must be admitted that in spite of the sordid interests of the majority of the masters, that property that a slave requires on his own, is almost universally respected, and infractions of this custom are rare. Public opinion and habit here take the place of legislation while many laws are continually trampled underfoot. H e r e is proof that the force of custom is greater than the force of law.

The different occupations of the slaves show considerable shading in their level of intelligence which demonstrates, in spite of the ignorant assertions of the colonists, that the incapacity of the Negro is the result of the brutalization of slavery.

note contrast
with Olmsted

CHAPTER LXVIII

Continuation of the preceding. The liberty of the slaves and their love life. Its effects. Impossibility of submitting them in this respect to the civil and religious laws. The appearance of the women; their balls. Their relationships between each other. Anecdotes in their favor. Multiplication of the colored people greater than that of the whites. The eventual result of this. Modern slaves compared with those of the ancients. Slavery degrades the master and the slave. Advantages of colonies that do without slaves. Whites capable of working in the tropical zone. Proof of this. System of indentured labor preferable to slavery for the masters and for the motherland. What has happened to the people who have established slavery. Our country can furnish colonies without diminishing its population. Means of re-establishing San Domingo.

There does remain to these people a very precious portion of their liberty, and its influence on them, and on the colonists themselves is very great. This remnant of their liberty is license in their love affairs, and in this, they are even more independent than their masters. The only limit to their choice, is their own taste. Religion and social conformity does not extend its power to them. They take up with each other, they leave each other, they return to each other to leave each other again, without being troubled by remorse or shame in their inconstancy. Love, soul of the universe, is truly their soul. As soon as they are old enough to notice it, they yield to it without effort, to remain forever in its toils. They speak of it constantly. It is the subject of their conversation. It helps them to sustain their labor and to forget their servitude. They smile with joy at the thought of a happy night, and the sentiments of love fire their imagination into song.

Upon this subject they make fertile improvisations. I once traveled for a month along the bayous and the river with a Negro. During all this time the subject of his songs was his mistress. He was composing for her a recitation of all his troubles and dangers. Sometimes he described his uneasiness at the thought of her infidelity. This Negro was an excellent navigator but he did not like to be interrupted in his lyrical composition. I had, however, seen so many poets even less inspired than he, even less reasonably stirred to anger by interruption that I indulged him in this.

The attention that a slave lavishes on his mistress, whom he treats as he would his wife, is extreme. The product of his savings, of his labor and of his little corner of ground is used to please her. He provides for all her needs and especially for her finery. It is the desire to please which softens all the social manners of man, which sometimes makes him capable of doing great things and has more than once been the spark which has produced a great man.

It is love, which reconciles these unfortunates to life, which causes them to rise above their labor and brings them from that stupidity which their degraded state continually forces upon them. A slave works better and is more industrious in order to make a better showing in the eyes of his mistress, and to see that she is better dressed and has more finery in their assemblies and dances. It must be admitted that it is for her also that he helps himself to his master's goods and makes those hazardous raiding excursions into the barnyard. The masters who are short-sighted groan about their losses, but it would probably be the worse for them if they did not take place.

Sometimes their mistresses live several leagues away. The fatigues of the day do not prevent them from going to stay the night with her to be back in time for work the next morning. It is no little astonishing that these men, enfeebled by difficulty and poor nutrition, are able to continue these noctural carouses. Misfortune indeed, for the masters or the neighbors who have horses in the charge of these gallants. They will work the horses harder than the masters work the slaves. It appears that the slave wishes to pass on to the horses the poor treatment he receives from his master. I myself lost an excellent horse to these amours.

In a house situated on the road communicating between Bayou Teche and Bayou Vermillion, where I used to stay occasionally, I used to hear the galloping of the horses of these lovers all night; coming and going.

It should be remarked that these slaves rarely take up with the women on their own plantation, in spite of the fact that their masters wish it. If they did so their amours would be monotonous, there would be fewer comings and goings, intrigues and interests. When this subject is one's sole interest, it must occupy much of one's time, and novelty is a necessity. It is for this reason also that inconstancy proceeds, promising them new subjects to occupy and to electrify their attention. A small number of slaves, whom I saw remain faithful to the same woman, and picking her from among their fellow slaves, usually consisted of the dullest and the most limited of the slaves, but the fact that their state of mind was closer to that of an animal, suited their masters better. The miser Sorel used to repeat endlessly that he feared nothing more than Negroes with spirit, and he bent his attention to insuring that they did not acquire any. He succeeded only too well.

In the social state, this kind of behavior would be stigmatized as destructive because it would imperil the social order. How, for instance, could one determine the paternity of children? Who would provide for their upkeep, their education, and their needs? A social order which wished to be founded legally on such license of behavior would be obliged to change its principles and to create new ones which would accord with these principles. But for the slave it would be unjust and impossible to subject him to manners which religion and laws prescribe in the state in which we live. How, for instance, could one tie together in holy matrimony these spouses, to make them swear to remain united when the masters of one or the other of them might separate them forever at any time? How would one produce and nurture in them the sentiments of paternity and maternity when their children do not really belong to them, when they cannot direct their education or provide for their needs nor hope to rely on them for sustenance in the infirmity of old age. Soon they will lose them, perhaps forever. If they are capable of real affection and tenderness, they will be still more unhappy and they will die of despair.

Slavery, being opposed to religion, necessarily tends to destroy it. If religion is to perish thus, it will be on the field of glory. Nevertheless, it is in her name; it was to bring God to these pagan souls; it was to light the torch of Christianity, that permission was obtained from the pious Louis XIII to seize Africans in their native land and to sell them to the highest bidder.

The masters encourage these transient unions which produced children the source of their fortunes and they encouraged the female slaves in their inordinate inconstancy. Often they are encouraged to use their free time in prostitution and to report back each day the amount they have taken. In town, especially, where the servants must behave with more circumspection, they are relieved of this burden, because they have liberty to make arrangements with generous lovers and the more the servants are indulged in this, the less they are required, to bother their masters with it. The lady of the house, who ordinarily has charge of the matter, grows accustomed to seeing lovers come and go to her Negro servant and she arranges to have them let in at night.

Our European ladies are less able to extend this indulgence to their servants. Their religion is less accommodating to this traffic in prostitution. But is not Heaven always concerned with accommodations? One may see these ladies surrounded by these unhappy women of whom they are, so to speak, the priestesses kneeling before the altar rail to receive the bread of souls, and even the priest is not exempt from this contamination. It is from the shock of these interests of customs and religions that arise the ferment which presages the dissolution of nations which is only suppressed to become more violent.

It is said that love unites the scepter and the bishop's staff. That is certainly true here. These sovereigns (for that is what they are since they exercise the right of life and death), then, more than once elevate one of their slaves to the rank of courtesan That does not prevent her from giving him rivals, who often enough is a miserable Negro who trembles at the master's glance. From these alliances spring the numbers of mulattoes, quadroons, *meti*, and *griffes*, etc., which give rise, as we shall see, to deplorable consequences.

Nothing is so extravagant as the finery of these women. Those who work in the fields all week naked to the waist, covered with a skirt of rags, on Sundays are transformed into great ladies. A dress with a long train, with wavy folds of a colorful calico or a richly embroidered muslin covered those charms only too scarred by beatings. Those bandanas of madras are adjusted to their wooly heads, white or gaily colored. Gloves hide their calloused hands and contrast with the jet blackness of their skin. Rose slippers sometimes shod their feet. Things are very different in the city. I have seen these ladies in San Domingo clothed in a dress embroidered with gold, although it is true she was clad in old shoes. In Louisiana, where the Acadian women are clothed so lightly, without the difference in skin one would mistake the mistress for the servant and the servant for the mistress. This finery is like the rose which keeps its freshness only for a morning. I had occasion to see, while I was in the Atakapas, one of their balls. The Negro slaves were present, clothed in taffeta sewn with spangles, and garlands of flowers festooned their heads which served to set off their dresses.

Such an upkeep as one may well imagine must be considerable, and those ladies whom the gallants are rich or fool enough to satisfy would dissipate the wealth gained by so much toil and labor. These amours make the slaves cherish their dances, the sole trace of the primitive customs of their ancestors. It is at night that they give themselves up to excesses. It is a time of illusions and a time of pleasures which are only that. This must be even more so for the slave who can only taste liberty in the shadows. Among the numerous plantations where the Negroes are tolerably well-treated, the ball begins on Saturday evening in one of their cabins, or rather under a wide-spreading tree, and as if they had to spend the whole week resting for it, everyone dances. Nothing is more joyful, daybreak overtakes them before they become fatigued. What a contradiction! The free men of color participate in these assemblages of slaves as the slaves are admitted to theirs. The pride of the whites who hold at so great a distance all those who have mixed blood obliges even those colored people who are closest to the whites to associate with these blacks. Thus, free or slave, black or mulatto, they seem to form a single family united in their abjection. Among themselves they display a touching affection. They never approach each other without displaying signs of affection and interest, without asking each other news of their relations, their friends, or their acquaintances. To the best of their ability they try to do each other as much good as they can. They are usually discreet, particularly in those matters that concern white people. When a slave is surprised in a misdemeanor it is rare that he implicates his accomplices. Even the most rigorous punishments do not obtain a confession from him. This mutual affection renders him capable of honorable traits. Those who have earned or found the means to obtain a portion of the sum necessary to buy their precious freedom will be able to borrow the remainder from among those of their color. In buying, they always favor merchants of their own color. I nave noticed especially in the city that while the funerals of white people are only attended by a few, those of colored people are attended by a crowd, and mulattoes, quadroons married to white people, do not disdain attending the funeral of a black.

While I was in New Orleans, an individual whose slave had run away promised a reward of 12 piastres to anyone who would return him. A Negro slave returned the run-away to his master. When he was offered the 12 piastres reward he answered, "The only reward that I ask is the pardon of him whom I have brought in." The master accepted the proposition and kept the money. To my way of thinking, this master had the soul of a slave and the Negro had the soul of a master. At Martinique I saw a Negro who, having earned enough to purchase his own freedom, prefer to remain a slave and purchase the freedom of his mother. Among the fugitives from San Domingo who came to Louisiana there were some whose slaves had followed them out of attachment for their masters. The reward of these too faithful servants was to be inhumanly sold.

These examples of magniminity and virtue are perhaps only exceptions, but they still show that this type of man carries within him a germ of goodness, and, if it does not come to fruition, that that is the fault of the condition to which he has been reduced and the behavior that has been shown him.

Population of this class of people of color is growing at a higher rate than that of the whites. It is growing from their own reproduction, their importation, and from their intercourses with the whites.

That which takes place through their own reproduction is larger proportionally than that of the whites, for among them, even among those who are free, the women never stand on matrimonial convention for having children. They begin at puberty. These children are raised with less coddling than those of the whites, are not subject to the diseases which take off a large number of white children, and even the children of slaves who are cared for by masters who have an economic interest in them usually survive better.

At the same time, the number of slaves imported is considerably larger than the number of Europeans who come to settle the colony, for in this country where almost all services are provided by colored people the principal method by which the Europeans make a fortune is by acquiring slaves, so that the more Europeans who arrive the greater is the necessity for importing slaves and the greater will be the means for them to acquire riches.

At the same time, in proportion as the inhabitants extend their plantation they will increase the number of slaves. Their children, in setting up their own plantations, will require still more slaves, which will require still a greater importation of slaves. It is in this type of property that most of the capital of the colony is tied up.

One may see, therefore, in the present condition of Louisiana how the need for slaves grows and why the price of slaves is higher here than in any of the other colonies, although Louisiana is not as rich as any of the other colonies. The co-habitation of whites with women of color more than anything else contributes to the multiplictaion of colored people at a higher rate than that of the whites. Travelers, Creoles, residents, everyone forms alliances with these colored women and many have children of them. This license extends also to the rural regions, where the Creoles prefer to live with these women rather than to give to a white woman the title of spouse.

Others only marry after having had a large number of colored children and some of these continue to co-habit with colored women after their marriage. If we compare them with the kept women of our great cities of Europe, we would see this difference, that those who have large numbers of children are proud of it. They do not lack the means of maintaining either their existence or their education, and they have no need to turn to crime. Thus, almost the whole male population contributes to multiply this type of colored person, whereas not a sole individual of color could contribute to the increase of the number of the whites. It is obvious, for all these reasons, that the number of colored people must grow at a much higher rate than that of the whites. What will be the future results of this? Simply that the colored people by reason of their number and power will one day be the master of the whites; perhaps one day exterminate them entirely. On the continent, the situation is very different from that in the islands. In an island, whatever may be the disproportion of the blacks over the whites, by external means the Negroes can be surrounded and prevented from providing themselves with artillery, munitions, and other instruments of external manufacture. Their retreat can be cut off, and they can be forced into their final retreats.

But on a continent, especially in Louisiana, when the population of colored people becomes numerous and powerful, if they revolt they will be defended by lakes, swamps, rivers and forest. They can advance or retreat, according to whether they are strong or weak. They can, favored by these regions so isolated, so vast and so fertile, defend their munitions and supplies. They can obtain new ones, even obtaining hidden harvests, and rely upon the numerous herds of wild animals. And what will be the lineage of the white people opposing them, necessarily degenerated through their richness, while that of the colored people, quite aside from their numbers, will not their lineage show the skill, the strength, the courage which makes for success in the arts, agriculture, navigation, and so forth?

Spartacus, who caused even the Romans, those masters of the universe, to tremble, had to contend with the best trained soldiers in the world, who rebounded after their defeats; but even so, what would have become of Rome if he had been able to place between himself and his enemies lakes, swamps, rivers, forests, and uninhabited regions?

These dangers and this passage of events are inevitable for Louisiana unless there is great change in the apathy of the inhabitants and in their opinions. This apathy is such that although they passionately love their children they give no thought to the need of protecting them from the dangers of idleness, from ruinous gambling and from disreputable unions, and they are still less disposed to turn their thoughts to what lies in the distant future for them. Accustomed to seeing the blacks as slaves, it does not occur to them that there could exist in nature another order of things . They laugh at, if they do not insult outright, those who attempt to draw their attention to the possibility of this disturbing future. How wise was Moses when, after having raised his people from slavery to the dignity of free men, he inspired in them so much solicitude for their descendants.* He glorified the fathering of numerous and powerful generations and thus transformed a people limited by slavery to one whose customs and laws would be favorable to a glorious future.

Opinion of the colonies, and especially in Louisiana, is that the colored people should never be given the rights of whites. This opinion is born of pride, an emotion which, always exclusive, isolates men from each other and weakens them. It is pride which lost San Domingo and turned it over to a tyrannical revolution, If the haughty colonists had not held themselves aloof from the mulattoes (who after all were their children), and if then these same colonists had not then even more foolishly divided themselves into rich and poor whites, and further yet, into non-resident whites versus residents who are coffee growers versus residents who are sugar growers, the most flourishing colony in the world would not have been changed into a frightful wilderness, and here in Louisiana, which has assimilated the fugitive debris of this superb colony, more ridiculous yet, the arrogant class, the wealthy sugar growers, have already scorned in a public meeting the modest inhabitants who grow corn. So one can see what the result will be. As in San Domingo, the whites regard black blood as having such an impure nature that the smallest portion will degrade white blood.

---

*The greatest symptom of degeneration in men is indifference to what will occur after them.

They suppose, in a policy equally absurd, that this abasement of the colored people is necessary for the continuance of slavery. The Creoles never cease to proclaim these boastful maxims. In vain, one points out to them that in former times the Spartans preserved their authority over their slaves for about 600 years, although these slaves were white and Greek like them, and that when they freed their slaves the slaves became citizens like them. It is in vain that one points out to them that another people called the Romans kept for even a longer time an even larger number of slaves who were as white as they were and, indeed, were also natives of Italy, and again when the slaves were freed they became citizens like their masters.

This belief in the necessity for a deep gulf between the two colors is certainly the greatest scourge of the colonies and to the growth of their trade with Europe. By restricting to such a small number the prerogative of citizens, the state exposes itself both to the dangers of internal revolutions, and, by its weakness, to invasions from without. The lives of the few, like their fortunes, have become precarious, a situation equally damaging to public morals, to abilities, and enlightenment. Since the primary criterion of one's position in society is the fact that one is white, one can do without being useful, virtuous or educated. One comes to believe himself above these qualities, because while they are to be found in the colored man, they do not raise him above the state of abjection. The latter then, tend to acquire, in addition to the vices of the whites, all of those associated with their own condition.

From the lack of the competitive spirit on all sides proceeds the indolence and the lack of progress in their agriculture, an art that requires so many multiple experiments and encouragements by example, and which differs from others in prospering only through competition. In producing less to exchange with European manufacturers, the colonists remain isolated and ignorant both of what is practical and useful, and still more of what is beautiful. Aside from conviviality, they scarcely care for anything but ephemeral luxuries. It is certainly otherwise with the slaves. With their increase, increases a race hostile to society. Those who order slaves about, wish the master's will to be the supreme law. Therefore, the master does not bother to explain the reasons for his orders, or the slave to use his reason during their execution. Slavery not only degrades the slave, it degrades the master. The less the mind is required to think, the more it loses the habit of thinking, and finally becomes incapable of it. At the same time, the master who always orders things done will lose the ability to do them for himself. His energy will be dissipated, and for want of activity he will not be able to acquire skill or practice. This degradation of the body will encourage the degradation of the intellect. The Asiatic, who lives under despotism, is inept and effeminate, because his inactive mind is never stimulated to action. These indolent Creole ladies, surrounded by their slaves, can hardly bend down to pick up a kerchief dropped from their indolent hands. They do not walk, they drag themselves along. In Louisiana a slave follows them to carry the train. Their languid conversation is pronounced in slow accents. Each syllable is prolonged as if the expiring voice were articulating its last sounds. Their manner of receiving people is cold and silent; one could believe that they have no soul. Novel objects, or unexpected events, do not stir their interest. They become animated only if crossed, or if their pride is offended. In most of the Creoles sensitivity appears to be related only to weakness or pride. They are thoroughly familiar with the cries of the slaves begging for mercy under the whip and with the sight of the bloody wounds and the long scars forever marking these whipped bodies. The Creole could not be expected to have that exquisite sensitivity which we associate with happiness and everything that is happy, and which makes us sympathize with those who suffer. The proof of this may be seen in the animals which surround them. The thinness of their dogs and their cats is frightening. I noticed, in Martinque as in Louisiana, that the Creole is astonished that a European takes any notice of such vile objects. They have no conception of how, in our cities, a bird, a dog, a cat, or any pet, will be doted upon with many caresses, or that savory coffee which we prepare would be less attractive if this faithful friend were not there every day to share it with us; nor could they imagine that our peasants, though living on black bread, will willingly share this with the family pet, stretched on the hearth, or the beasts in the stables. The well-to-do in Louisiana have their carriages drawn by thin, dirty, and unworthy horses. A generous master loves to feel the spirited impatience of a fine animal under his caressing hand. He takes pride in seeing a well-kept horse with attractive hangings. The Creole breaks his horses as a child kills flies. After a long run, he will tie up his worn out horse to the first place he comes to without regard to water or shade. Most of the time he pays no attention to this good and useful animal. Nor does it occur to any of the inhabitants in this country, so fertile in rare animals and curious birds, to solace the lonely hours by taming them. Flights of brightly colored parakeets pass continually over their heads, without their having any notion that this bird of rich colors can easily be tamed to human society. This indifference to the innocent pleasures of nature traces back to slavery, which dries up the soul. One hardly finds an interest in nature in those parts of America where slavery exists. In Canada, and in the northern states of America, customs are more humane, society is pleasanter, education is more widespread, work is more active, and industriousness better regarded. There is to be found the national character with all its energy, and this weakens progressively as one approaches the regions peopled with slaves. If, instead of this race of slaves, the implacable enemy of society, who would break their chains only to destroy it, for whom supreme happiness is exemption from work; if, instead of these races whose condition tends always to their degeneration, the colony had been settled by free white men, the colonies would have gained citizens who would have assured peace, both internal and external. Their more diligent labor would have rendered the colony proportionally much more productive. This would have made a larger market for European goods exported to the colonies and would have provided more goods from the colonies in exchange. San Domingo, for example, had a population of almost 500,000 slaves, 28 to 30 thousand free Negroes, and only 40,00 whites. and these last made up most of the market for European goods. The 500,000 slaves counted for practically nothing for this purpose. If these 600,000 colored people had been white, what an enormous difference in the market for French products in San Domingo and in the amount of produce exported to France.

I hear the argument repeated again and again that white people are not suitable for heavy work in hot climates, and it is for this reason that it is necessary to bring in blacks. I admit that whites are less resistant to the heat of the tropical zone than blacks, but it is false to say that the white people cannot acclimate themselves to work there. If that were true, it would be a crime to establish white people in a country where they would not be able to support themselves by agriculture. For the art of agriculture, which is the only source of nourishment for man, is a universal obligation of societies. In a complex society, if some do not work at agricultural pursuits, what they do work at supports those who do, who in their turn support the non-agricultural laborers. But if a type of man would establish itself in any country, to live at the expense of the agriculturist without doing anything for him, it would be an impious race, an enemy of those food plants who are the guardians of nature, and abhorred by her, would be struck down by a hoard of destructive vices. Like those plants transported to a site that is not suitable to them, these men would become degraded and eventually destroyed.

But these do not exist. Man has been endowed with faculties which make possible incredible modifications in his physical, as well as the moral constitution. The Negro, who is adopted particularly to inhabit the burning sands of Africa, gradually becomes accustomed to withstanding the freezing winters of the northern climates. The whites, at the same time, adapted to endure the colds of the glacial zones, in their turn can acclimate themselves to the rigors of the torrid zone. I traveled in January during a severe winter in northern Louisiana. Two badly clothed Negroes accompanied me who withstood the frosts, sleet and ice better than I did. In Saint Pierre at Martinique, I observed a Frenchman, a Parisian, who had been on the island about two years. He had landed with a troop of comedians. Originally, there were almost a hundred of them, but their intemperance hurried most of them into the tomb. This Frenchman became a blacksmith. Industrious and sober, he worked at his forge from morning to night in an airless hole, where the burning heat of the climate added to that of his forge. This blacksmith withstood the heat of the work better than the two strong Negroes who assisted him. He did much more work, and his work required him to be near the furnace more often than theirs. No work in the fields or in the sugar mills could possibly have been as difficult as this. This single example, which is not unique, proves that the white race can be accustomed to the heat of the tropics and can be used there even for the most difficult work.

Even in Europe, our foundries and ironworks especially, do not they require their workers to support a degree of heat higher than that of the atmosphere of the colonies? And these occupations, as well as others, are they not at the same time more difficult than that of the sugar mills, which seems to be the ultimate in work to the partisans of slavery?

In Louisiana, families originally from cold regions like Acadia and Germany, do their work in the countryside, usually without Negroes, and do it in summer weather just as hot, and sometimes more stifling, than that of the islands. They withstand this labor and are even less likely to sickness than those haughty gentlemen who, only at long intervals, expose themselves to the burning sun. The surgeons are more often called to the latter than to the former.

How did our colonies begin? They were started by filibusterers (a type of corsair or pirate) who came out of France to pillage and retreated into these island wildernesses where they joined hands with the *boucaniers*, or European hunters. Together they cultivated fruits, vegetables, annatto [*Bixa orellana, a tropical plant formerly the source of a dye used to color cheese and butter. —Tr. note.*], indigo, tobacco, cotton, and, finally, coffee and sugar cane. These founders of our colonies, simultaneously sailors, soldiers, hunters, and farmers on these uncleared and uninhabited lands, experienced dangers, labors and privations that an ordinary farmer would have not faced. Soon, their numbers being insufficient to maintain themselves, they sent for other Europeans to help them. These, not having the money to pay their passage, indentured themselves for three years to the captains of the ships who transported them, who sold the contracts to the passengers, to the inhabitants of the islands, where they became farm laborers. These indentured servants, who are known by the name of "36-month-men," labored at the arduous tasks of the plantations. At the end of their period of indenture, they obtained land grants, some animals and instruments, and became land owners in their turn. Old M. Labat recalled these "36-month" indentured servants and gave me the names of several at Martinique, the metropolis of our colony, who had become rich and prominent. Our colonies thus were rapidly populated and would have prospered except for the monopoly and despotism of the companies, and of the governors who vexed them with all sorts of taxations, and sometimes, out of various motives, transported them from one island to the other in order to despoil them and to destroy them. The English populated and made their colonies prosperous in the same way. The Irish, fleeing persecution, came in great numbers, especially to Barbados, which became in a short time a charming, rich, and bustling colony, where was found the pleasantness of European social manner and the arts of workmanship without useless luxury. How many crimes, how many calamities would not have taken place had this policy been continued in the establishment of colonies! San Domingo would still be an inexhaustible source of riches and of trade outlets for France, and much larger than it has ever been.

When the Portuguese, those incompetents, saw how little was their metropolitan population from which to draw on in order to populate their vast colonies, they hit upon the idea of transporting

African slaves. They were dazzled by the apparent advantages of this type of establishment. The colonists could see only the apparent advantage of acquiring, for a sum of money, men and families, subject to their will forever. Property and power have such attractions! Everyone wanted this type of property. No one had the wisdom or the experience to see what must have been the result. Indeed, no one concerned himself with the future of the colonies. The idea was to acquire wealth as rapidly as possible and to return to enjoy it in the mother country. Thus, arose those narrow views, so inimical to prosperity and to general peace. Even religion, whose glory had been the abolition of slavery in the most powerful states of Europe, served as a pretext for helping to rivet chains on the Africans. From that time on, indentured service was forgotten and neglected. A colonist considered himself poor if he did not own other men. One can also conjecture that the example of indentured servants as humble laborers might be dangerous to show to the black slaves, in whom it was necessary to fix firmly belief in the superiority of whites. The laws governing the indentured servants grew weaker and finally fell into disuse. Thus disappeared entirely from the colonies that class of people who could have populated America entirely with Europeans, whose customs, needs, and opinions would have multiplied and consolidated the ties between the mother country and the colonies.

What has become of the power of the Portuguese, those founders of slavery? What have the Spaniards gained from having placed so many people in chains? The supreme intelligence, by an order of things more miraculous than miracles, will cause those enterprises formed, counter to the order of nature, to turn upon those nations who have founded them; a dire prediction for those who persist in following their example.

Since the colonies were started originally by whites alone, and whites alone are capable of operating a flourishing agriculture; increasing its production, enlarging the outlet of trade for the homeland, and insuring peace for both the present and the future of the colonies; and since those colonies founded originally upon black slavery have returned to their founders only curses, and since we ourselves have already experienced so many calamities from slavery in the colonies, and since we see the future prospect of irreparable damage; it follows that France should prefer the system of indenture to that of slavery in her colonies.

It is to this system that the United States of America owes both her population and her agricultural prosperity. Ships continually arrive in her ports, even her most southern ones, loaded with Scotsmen, Irishmen, etc. The captains sell the contracts of these passengers to the inhabitants to pay their passage. The contracts run for about five years, and the laborers work at agriculture or other work for which they are suitable. The usual price is 24 piastres. These indentured servants, accustomed to work in Europe, are useful to their masters immediately, while one or two years of training are necessary to accustom the African Negro to work. For the price of one Negro, an inhabitant can procure 5 or 6 indentured servants, who in addition, sometimes have other skills. They are far easier to keep than the Africans, who are strangers to a regular and industrious life, and if the inhabitant loses one or two indentured servants he does not endanger his fortune as he would by losing one or two slaves. Immediately enjoying with his indentured servants, the fruit of their labors, he will quickly earn back what they cost him. This is certainly not true for the Negro. Indentured servants, treated kindly, will work faster, and the proprietor's business will be better done. The state will benefit even more from this arrangement, for during the time of the indenture of these men, they will acquire some money and thus will be more useful to manufacturers as potential markets than the pitiably naked Negro. At the expiration of their period of indenture, they will become new colonists and new land holders, spreading agriculture, augmenting the population, and increasing commercial intercourse.

This system of indentures which currently exists in the states of Maryland, Virginia, the Carolinas, and Georgia has still another advantage in that it reduces the excessively high price of Negroes. That is why they are cheap in those colonies.

It may be objected that this manner of populating our colonies might tend to remove necessary agricultural laborers from the homeland, for indentured servants drawn from the city, or from that class of men exhausted by misery and debauchery are hardly capable of maintaining themselves by laboring in the colonies. That much is true, but it is not true that the number of indentured servants drawn from the countryside will prove damaging to our agriculutral enterprises.

In France there are districts and villages where the population is not growing. The reason is that the low productivity of the land and other reasons prevent these places from maintaining a greater population, for the human species everywhere multiplies in proportion to the means of existence which exist, and if they are favorable the population should double at least every 20 years. It follows then, that in those places where the population is not reaching its normal size, and the surplus of that which the countryside can nourish, is disappearing through disease, misery, and emigration. Thus, those who leave these regions annually for the colonies will always be replaced in the families by a proportionate number of children. The population, therefore, will remain the same in spite of the emigration to the colonies. The emigration from Ireland and Scotland to this country has been considerable for a long time, especially since the American Revolution, and this has not diminished the population of Ireland and Scotland. In this respect, I might say, that emigration, far from being harmful, is actually favorable to England, because while she has still retained the same quantity of individuals in the British Isles, she has, by increasing the population of the United States, increased her commerce and her manufactures, for these emigrants continue to use English goods. And this commerce has increased all the more because these emigrants to the United States have become wealthy and the heads of families. The same will be true for France, if she populates with her own people, the colonies that belong to her. Of what use to commerce are miserable peasants who are clothed only in the smocks of coarse cloth which they have woven of their own hemp; who eat a poor bread which they have made themselves; and who languish for part of the year in inactivity because there is no work? If one balances their consumption with the product of their work, one can see that they contribute nothing to the state and are perhaps a burden on it; but transported to a colony, their labor will produce, annually, goods whose value on the spot will, without exaggeration, exceed 2,000 francs, to say nothing of the market for goods which their numerous families will bring into being.

And this order of things will not even be incompatible with the slavery of Negroes.

In those United States where slavery exists, indentured servants exist at the same time. By establishing these indentured servants little by little, and by encouraging the colonists to make use of them by subsidies, the colonists would come to rely upon them. They would see the advantages of using them over that of the use of slaves and slavery would be abolished without political crisis, and without violence to property. However wretched these establishments may be, however prejudicial is their existence to the general welfare, however deep their immorality, they have been formed under the protection of the laws, and the country has guaranteed them. If the country has erred, it should shoulder the blame for the mistake. The blame should not be shifted exclusively to individuals. It is the violation of this principle which, brutalizing the nation, destroys the love of the nation among her children and makes them unjust from having been so itself. How we should like to tear out the pages of the history describing our revolution, but rather, we should retain them for the instruction of future races.

If the above recommendation is followed at San Domingo, it may be recreated under better auspices than formerly. It would not be necessary to garrison it with troops whom death takes off as fast as the vessels can land them. Indentured servants, acclimatized gradually and accustomed to work, would be the best defense of this colony. What shall I say of the blood that has been spilled to exterminate the rest of the Negroes there? With the 20th part of this expense, one could re-establish a new San Domingo.

If an agreement were made with these Negroes ceding them the inland regions of the island, retaining under European control only the ports with the title of protector, France would retain exclusive rights to trading with them. France would enjoy thus all the advantages of their production that would be obtained in exchange for European goods. Without the expense of governing it, France would have, all at once, a lucrative colony. The Negro settlement would never be dangerous to the Europeans, because its inhabitants would have neither the intelligence, the activity nor resources of the French part. The last would grow and increase in size, both through its internal resources and with the help of the mother country. This population would add to its strength by assimilating the mixed bloods and giving to them the advantages of the whites. Intermarriage with them should be encouraged. Proud to be assimilated into the white population, they would become its most ardent defenders and most powerful support, because born to the climate, they are capable of resisting the rigors of the climate the thing especially desirable in time of war. [*The colony of Saint Dominique, or San Domingo; the western third of the island of Hispaniola, is the present-day Republic of Haiti. Acquired by the French in 1697, it had become the richest colony of France by 1789, the year of the outbreak of the French Revolution. The free mulattoes, inspired by the libertarian slogans of the Revolution, demanded equal rights with the whites. These were granted them by the National Convention in Paris, in 1791, but the edict was nullified by the opposition of the dominant whites. In August of that year, the black plantation slaves revolted. Efforts of the revolutionary government to restore peace were fruitless. By 1801, the Negroes, under their remarkable leader, Toussaint L'Ouverture, had driven out both the white and the mulattoes, and were masters of the island. Napoleon, however, determined to reconquer the island, and after the Treaty of Amiens freed his hands, sent out 25,000 troops under Le Clerc to do so. By an act of treachery, Le Clerc succeded in capturing L'Ouverture, and had him sent to France, where he died. The Negroes, however fought on, and this was the state of things at the time of Robin's narrative. Eventually, of course, England and France resumed the war with each other, Le Clerc's troops, cut off from France by British sea-power, succumbed to yellow fever, and the victorious Negroes founded the independent Republic of Haiti. Many of the white and mulatto fugitives settled in Louisiana.—Tr. note.]* Even supposing that the white party had slaves among them, they need not fear that the blacks will provide a haven for fugitive slaves. The blacks themselves will have slaves and they will return the slaves of the whites, in order that the whites will return theirs.

The colonists of San Domingo who survived the massacre of their loved ones, saw their wealth pillaged, and now drag out their days in indigence are hardly constrained to listen to the counsels of moderation. Embittered by these misfortunes, it would seem that their vengeance can only be satisfied by the torture of the blacks. A wise government, however, knows that it is better to retain than to destroy; that it is easier and safer to repair than to create. Just like the wise farmer who does not chop down the entire tree but instead prunes off only the excess branches to reduce the crown to the size which can be nourished by the root system, in a short while he sees a vigorous production of branches loaded with fruit. If instead, he had replanted the tree, it would have been his children who had harvested the fruit and not he himself.

CHAPTER LXX

The form of the government of Louisiana established by the Americans. Louisiana divided in two, then into counties. Depredations of the magistrates. American regime compared to the Spanish. Conflict of Anglo-American customs with those of the French. Various indications of the hatred of the Americans for the French. Unjust oaths requiring them to renounce the Emperor of the French and the King of Spain. Louisiana changes the relationship of the Americans with other nations. The methods of the Americans of learning trades; its effects on customs and political economy and especially on their navy. The remarkable administrations of the customs. New proofs of the salubrity of plants, the conservators of the human race. Effects of their destruction in the Atakapas. Maladies peculiar to this climate.

When the Americans took possession of Louisiana, they at first retained the Spanish forms of government. American commandants replaced in the various districts the Spanish commandant. These American commandants; young, ignorant drunkards; not knowing a word of French, or having the least notion of the customs of the people they were governing; often had resident in their districts, venerable heads of families who were former French and Spanish military officers. The haughtiest conquerer never treated the vanquished with less consideration. I saw the commandant in Ouachita dispensing justice in his fort, amidst the cacaphony of fiddles and the thick fumes of *tafia*. He reversed in the evening, judgments made in the morning. If one pary had no interpreter, the opposed party would plead for both. A woman came to complain of her husband. The commandant had him led in, in chains and thrown into prison, without a hearing. The young commandant of the Atakapas was, I believe, the only exception. He was sober, gentle, honest, and well brought up, and by diligent application, soon reached the point where he no longer needed an interpreter.

These commandants were succeeded by equally drunken judges*

---

*Drunkenness, which is indulged in by even the most highly placed Americans, is one of the principal causes of friction between them and the French. The Americans take as their usual drink, whiskey, tafia, and rum, whereas the French prefer wine. Salt meat and a shapeless biscuit are the principal food of the Americans, while the French insist upon fresh meat for their stews and more diversified leavened food for their bread stuffs.

who were perhaps much greater rascals into the bargain. These judges were surrounded by swarms of prosecutors and lawyers, who like swarms of locusts ravaged the colony. To give you an idea of this, one of them named Liwington [*I suspect the original is Livingston.—Tr. note.*] in New Orleans, in less than two years made three or four hundred thousand francs. A host of these people have enriched themselves, or at least have done very well for themselves, by these outrageous abuses.

Congress, scorning the treaty of cession out of hatred for the French, first divided Louisiana into Upper Louisiana and Lower Louisiana, making of them two separate governments. This division isolated and weakened the French and was the first step toward their total extinction from the colony. [*This is rubbish. Robin's figures show that the bulk of the French population was in Lower Louisiana. They were hardly much enfeebled by this eminently reasonable division.—Tr. note.*]

Next was organized a legislative body which would perhaps better be called a legislative commission. The code of laws produced by this body was most bizarre. What especially characterized it, was that it adopted English law in toto, even those of which the legislators did not even know the title. With the same impetuosity, they had forgotten to say when and how these laws would be put in force. *parishe*

They divided the colony into 12 counties, to-wit: Orleans, German coast, Acadia, Lafourche, Iberville, Point Coupee, Atakapas, Opelousas, Natchitoches, Rapides, Ouachita, and Concordia.

Some of these counties are more than a hundred leagues in extent and others are not more than fifteen. There are some in which the population is 10 times as large as in others. The divisions therefore take cognizance of neither population nor area. The sole point of this insane division seems to have been to deliver the unfortunate inhabitants to the rapacity of the lawyers. In this they certainly succeeded. Each county has its principal judge, its jus-

---

Anglo-Americans therefore, rarely enjoy eating with the French and still less the French with the Americans. Moreover, the different hours for mealtimes places an obstacle to communication between these peoples, apart from the difference in their language. In all parts of Louisiana, if a Frenchman finds himself neighbor to a Anglo-American, they have little to do with one another. If the American wishes to sell his house, it is rarely a Frenchman who buys it from him. The Spanish and the French, especially those with little education, have many fewer obstacles in language and in habits to overcome in intercommunication.

tices of the peace, its recorder, its sheriff, constables, treasurer, coroner, prosecutor and lawyers. I saw in the Atakapas, the three justices of the peace and the chief judge performing their functions in a spot so isolated that you could visit all of them without meeting a dozen people on the road. All of these people have a salary, prerogative, and above everything else, opportunity for graft. Under the mild regime of Spain, a single commandant (who if he was not French at the least knew the customs and the language) administered the district almost without expense, to the government. There were no sheriffs, prosecutors, etc. There were abuses, no doubt, these are to be found everywhere, but they occurred only here and there. The entire colony was not the prey to devestation. The lawyers did not awaken hatreds, or stimulate cupidity by going around the countryside encouraging suits, from which they were assured a share of the damages. These Americans have taken from Louisiana by this odious means in the short space of three years, more than Spain took out in forty.

The government of the United States itself, exploits Louisiana like a farm. It skims off in haste, by tariffs that bear no relationship, either to justice or politics. It seems to believe that this fertile country will escape it at any moment. [*It was a common belief at the time in Louisiana that the sale of the colony was not permanent and that Napoleon, at his leisure, intended to take it back.— Tr. note.*] How far, even this early in its career, has the United States estranged itself from the principles of equity and reason which are the basis of its Constitution and its laws! The dislike of everything that is French is to be seen everywhere. At the celebration of the independence of the United States, here in the middle of a French colony, not a word in the solemn discourses that I heard, referred to the memorable siege of Yorktown, where the French obtained independence for America. In proclamations declaring what citizens have the right to vote in public assemblies, not a word of the fact that all Frenchmen residing in Louisiana at the time of the cession are, by the terms of that treaty, citizens of the United States.

All those positions that Louisianians could fill much better than foreigners are given by an odious preference to the Americans. Those positions for which Louisianians are eligible are snatched from them by intrigues. The legislative body is composed of so many Americans that the others are simply their puppets. But what especially shows the hatred of the Americans for the French is the formula of the oath which they have prepared for the Louisianians. They were made to swear to be faithful to the Constitution of the United States, and to renounce the Emperor of the French and the King of Spain. It is conceiveable that during the torment of revolution, frenzy of feeling would produce such an outrageous oath, but that during a period of calm, in peactime, in the midst of cordial relations between nations, one could have imagined ordering such an immoral oath, as impolitic as it is hateful, is an example that perhaps no other people on earth could have given. To swear to support the Constitution of the United States? Nothing more reasonable. Those whom it protects should protect it in their turn, and this oath serves to include all the duties of a citizen. But to add to this an oath renouncing the Emperor of the French and the King of Spain, in the first place has no relationship to the obligations to the relationship to the Federal Constitution because the first part of the oath has covered all this and if the intent of the oath (as is only too clear) is to rupture those sweet affections and tender sentiments of recognition that sensitive Louisianians retain for their mother country, it is an act of abominable immorality. What? You make it my duty to be ungrateful toward my country! You admit by this that I may one day be so toward you. You forbid me to take pride in that heroism which astonishes the universe! And you wish that I shall be indifferent to my native land. Well, although I have promised to obey your Constitution and, to defend it and to give my life for it, my affections, my sentiments, remain my own. Human law cannot encompass them. You wish to conquer them? Very well then, let justice shine upon me. Do not treat me with reproach, but show to me the tender aspect of a mother. That which I will do through duty, I will also do for love.

Louisiana is a testing ground to test the morality, the politics and the economy of the Americans, and it must be admitted that, as of now the judgments are not in their favor. While the Anglo-Americans remained alone, isolated from other nations, their administrations and their commercial relations were simpler and easier. Their growth, like that of a vigorous well fertilized plant, was rapid. When they had extended their institutions to distant regions and came upon neighbors whose different manners and interests, and whose competition in a number of respects might be harmful to them, then, like the people of the Old World, their laws and politics, required modification. They became more complicated and more difficult to arrange, and if the bad beginnings in the possession of Louisiana are followed by other blunders, one can see that this possession will be a source of calamity for the Anglo-Americans, which will stop their growth even more quickly than they grew.

However, among their manners, as well as in their political organization, may be found traits that would do honor to the wisest nation. I shall cite two examples. A journeyman carpenter, who at New Orleans had come several times to my house on behalf of his master, bringing me various objects that he had made, ran into me again in the Atakapas. At this time he had acquired the important office of sheriff of the county. I expressed my astonishment at this sudden metamorphosis. "I come from New York state," he told me, "and the custom there is to teach all young men a trade no matter how high in the professions they later may rise. It was intended that I should become a merchant and I set sail for New Orleans with a considerable stock of goods, but my ship was wrecked during the passage and I lost everything. Therefore, when I had arrived in New Orleans, I had to work at the trade which I had learned and that was, that of a carpenter. I lived by this trade without having to humiliate myself by asking for help and I was even able to save a little bit. In the meantime, friends of my family recommended me to Governor Claiborne who recognized my abilities and finally conferred on me the distinguished and lucrative office of sheriff of the district."

This fortunate notion of a trade for every man works to the advantage of the state as well as the man.

If a country's wealth is measured by the total amount of the work, that is done in its economy, then it follows that he who has at his disposal several means of livelihood, especially a trade, produces more for a country, than he who knows only one profession. The first will never be unemployed, and his whole life will be filled with work. At the end of his career, his ability will have produced more for the state than he has cost the state. But the latter will experience gaps in his working period of months, years, or even a considerable part of his life, and especially will this be true of those who occupy administrative positions, and at the end of their career they will have cost the state more than they have produced for it. The custom, then, of teaching a trade to men of all professions tends to augment public good.

At the same time, the man who has a trade at his disposal can exist in time of need, without having to humiliate himself, to obtain the means of existence. Idleness will not have the chance to corrupt him into vicious and perverse actions.

What prevents Europeans from adopting these economic and efficient measures, is the common tendency to regard as lost from education that time employed in learning a low trade. This is a gross error. To my way of thinking, apprenticeship to a trade is one of the surest means of accelerating and perfecting education. It broadens the mind in a manner not otherwise possible. I pick for example one of the trades which deals with working in wood. Could one learn this trade without learning the practical notions of geometry and mechanics, without being introduced to the ideas of art, or knowledge of the various qualities of wood and their uses, or learning of different kinds of construction? While the body is exercised and strengthened, the mind develops through the uses of the many different instruments that are employed for sawing, hewing, polishing, piercing and assemblying. These notions will be absorbed, without broadening the uneducated man, but what development of the mind will not be acquired by him whom instruction has prepared in advance and will aid in the future? Whatever may be the career that he follows, he will see how his trade gives weight to his judgment, wings to his imagination, and enlarges his faculties at every instant. The farmer who is the center of everything in an agricultural country, will better understand what he needs to know and will better plan his plantings if he has learned a trade.

I should have not been astonished then, to notice that on board American ships, the officers, were simultaneously cabinet makers, carpenters, rope spinners, caulkers, and sailors, making use of the instruments of these trades with a dexterity which was all the more striking to me, because I did not understand several of them myself. With such men, the Americans will always have as many excellent naval officers as they need, but even with good officers, who are themselves good sailors, they will be a long time acquiring sufficient numbers of common seamen.

Under Spanish rule, there were a multitude of clerks and guards to prevent smuggling, notwithstanding which this took place openly. I arrived in New Orleans on an American ship, which was to then proceed up the river, but by order of the Spanish Intendant, no cargo was to be discharged at New Orleans. I found myself greatly inconvenienced by not having my baggage. Five hundred francs relieved me of this difficulty. My things were carried ashore in broad daylight. Under the American regime these squads of guards, these troops of clerks, have disappeared, and the whole cusoms house is run by not more than six persons. Nothwithstanding this, smuggling stopped abruptly, as if by a miracle. What adds to the marvel is, that the searches of the travelers baggage stopped at the same time. A ship arrives. It makes its declaration. This is received and written down, and the ship is unloaded without any further difficulty. The passengers present themselves to the customs, their trunks, sometimes filled with the most valuable goods. They make their declarations and carry off their trunks without even being made to open them. However if, after the baggage is carried away, the least discrepancy is found in the declaration all is lost. There is no mercy, the ship itself may be confiscated along with all the cargo for the slightest omission from the declaration. Among these Americans ordinarily so grasping, to whom interest is God, this particular type of fraud is rarely encountered. One loses cast for having even attempted it. In this respect American society is superior. How desirable it would be if they would give us otherwise examples!

The first inhabitants who established themselves in the Atakapas on those beautiful prairies to the west of Louisiana, found the region healthy everywhere. They placed their houses near, or among, the woods which stretch in strips along the rivers and obtained the benefit of a cooling shade for themselves and for their cattle. The waters of the bayou which wound around them never lost their limpidness or their purity. Contagious diseases were unknown then. I cannot repeat it too often. It is false that uninhabited places are dangerous to man, as is repeated in so many books and by so many academies. Too long, has nature been slandered thus, and we owe her a better attempt to know her. How indeed, would man have to complain, if in these wild and isolated regions, deprived of the help of the civilized arts, he had to combat in addition the unhealthiness of a malign nature. He would succumb, and thus would disappear those hordes of savage men living on the fruits of hunting in the wildernesses of the world. When civilized nations, soiled with vices and crimes destroy themselves leaving only unfortunate remnants, obliged to wander in the wilderness and to take up again the savage life, they too would perish in their turn and finally the last of the human race would disappear from the earth. That would be the destiny of man if nature were indeed so malign but no, the wisdom which presides over this universe has ordered things very differently.

These immense solitudes are reserves like a storehouse awaiting the coming of civilization to make use of them, to recreate new nations to replace those that corruption has destroyed and turned out in their turn into the wilderness.

The symptoms of contagion only appear in the places where civilization begins, in measure as careless man uncovers drowned lands, abandoning them to the action of the burning sun. This is what is happening today in the Atakapas, a region so healthy that stricken New Orleanians come there during their convalesence. The colonies are hastening to cut down those great trees near their settlements leaving near them uncovered stagnant water, which they neglect to drain off, and this will increase the unhealthiness of this district in proportion as the number of settlements increase. The evil is increasing, and during the first summer that I was there, many putrid fevers occurred there for the first time, because the summer, drier than ordinary, caused a higher degree of impregnation of the air by these swampy exhalations.

Intemperance has cut down several victims very suddenly and I noticed that these were particularly the strongest people with the ruddiest complexions which accords with what I have said earlier about yellow fever.

In the hot climate of Louisiana one sees fewer chronic illnesses, but acute maladies are much more varied and active. Putrid fevers are found there in a variety of forms, and to combat them, more vigorous remedies are needed than in our temperate climates. Sicknesses of the throat are very frequent and very dangerous, as are all illnesses resulting from a too excited blood. Young people are especially exposed and are especially its victims. [*Diphtheria, of course. Tr. note.*] Tetanus, that singular malady that suddenly stiffens the muscles of the front and back of the head and makes them so inflexible, that it is not possible to move them, as though the joints no longer existed; this malady only attacks the Creoles. A simple puncture by a thorn or splinter of wood can produce it. It is mortal, and almost incurable. It seems that the surest remedy, one derived from the Negroes, is to wash the victim in lye made from ashes.

The lockjaw, another type of tetanus, attacks and carries off a great number of infants in the first moments after birth, especially where labor has been difficult. Worms are common among the children. It is difficult to see how the intestine could contain so large a number or, how they could reappear so quickly.

Of all the chronic maladies, diarrhea is the commonest and lasts the longest. The stomach, worn out by intemperate eating and by violent tonics, is so relaxed that food passes through without being digested, but is merely in a state of putrefaction. These maladies, difficult to cure, most often end in death after several years of weakness. [*This is most probably a reference to amebiasis. The belief that various maladies was due to the putrefaction of the intestines is an ancient one in western medical lore. It can be traced back through the works of Hippocrates to the Egyptians.—Tr. note.*]

There are also in Louisiana examples of leprosy, as for instance, the Jew Carick in New Orleans.

INDEX

INDEX

CPSIA information can be obtained at www.ICGtesting.com
Printed in the USA
LVOW11s1403021015

456691LV00001B/34/P